The Necessity of Artifice

·Ideas in Architecture·

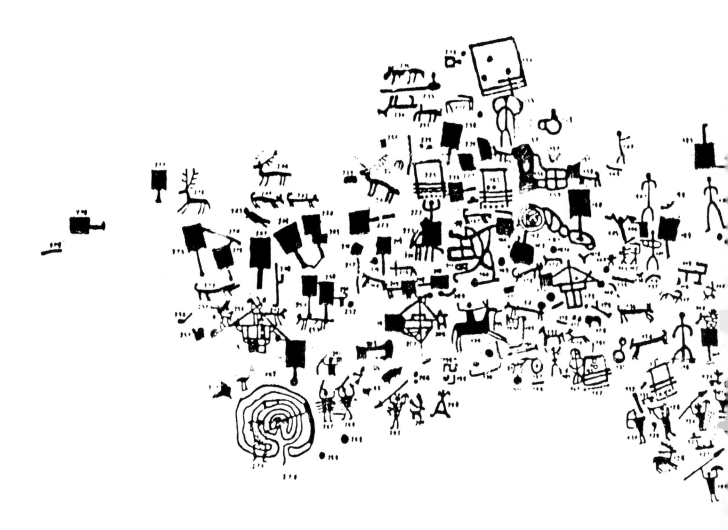

JOSEPH RYKWERT

The Necessity of Artifice

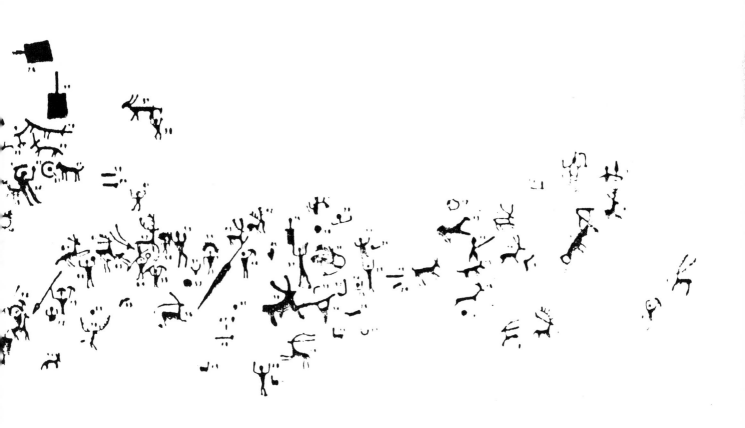

RIZZOLI
NEW YORK

To Marina and Sebastian

Front cover
HERBERT BAYER and PETER WEHR *Entrance Hall* Bauhaus Exhibition,
Kunstgebäude am Schlossplatz, Stuttgart 1968. (Author)

Front flap
JOSEPH RYKWERT with MARK LIVINGSTON and DAVID CASHMAN *Fish
Farm* Bay of Vela Luka, Island of Korčula, Yugoslavia. (Author)

Back cover
Temple of Olympian Zeus Athens. (Author)

Back flap
Author. (Photocraft, G. Cohn)

First published in the United States of America in 1982 by
Rizzoli International Publications, Inc.
712 Fifth Avenue/New York 10019

Originated and produced in Great Britain by Academy Editions London
Copyright © 1982 Joseph Rykwert *All rights reserved*

Library of Congress Catalog Card Number 81-51313
ISBN 0-8478-0402-X

Printed and bound in Great Britain

Contents

Foreword

These essays were written over a quarter of a century. As I was looking over them to make a selection, the remark of a French wit came to mind: 'I always say the same thing, but I never repeat myself'.

Outrageous as the claim seems, implying total assurance and a blind inability to learn from your own mistakes – or merely such hardcore conviction that experience will wash over it like so much water over a dyke – yet I envy the man who made it. I can't hope to emulate him in this book: every essay in it has been written in answer to some particular circumstance, whether it has been the unexpected encounter with some building which has aroused my enthusiasm or claimed my assent, or the opposite, some exhibition or polemic which aroused me to opposition. This collection has therefore deliberately excluded all descriptive essays and reviews, as well as purely circumstantial pieces.

Perhaps one thing I can claim to have in common with the French wag: what I have written in the past seems to me, even now, to have been an honest and considered response to the circumstances of the time. On re-reading, whatever infelicities jar, whatever enthusiasms or censures seem disproportionate, however much my thinking has developed since the time of the first essays, they still make up a sufficiently coherent body of opinion to require no further apology; and I hope that the diversity of subjects has forced them into such various forms that the coherence will not pall.

In writing these essays I have incurred many debts to friends and colleagues, too many for detailed mention, though it is fitting to recall the two most important: to Rudolf Wittkower and Sigfried Giedion, whose wayward pupil I count myself.

Joseph Rykwert

Meaning and Building

This is neither the first essay I wrote nor (in my opinion) the best. It has to stand first in this collection because it turned out to be something of a personal manifesto: a statement of the themes which were to occupy me for the next two decades and with which I have not yet done. It contains, incidentally, the nucleus of an essay on the sitting position which I worked out later (no. 3 in this collection) but which had formed the basis of a course of lectures that I gave in 1958 at the Hochschule für Gestaltung in Ulm.

Originally, this essay was commissioned by Eugen Gomringer for an anniversary issue of the Basler Nachrichten *commemorating the forty-fifth birthday of the Schweizer Werkbund, although I protested my lack of sympathy for the Werkbund and the policy of* Gute Form *which it pursued at the time. It gave me the opportunity, however, to set out my view of the current architectural situation as seen from the Ulm eyrie; this rather peculiar origin may account for certain timidities of expression – or what reads like timidity twenty years later.*

One thing will now seem an ingenuity rather than a timidity: my reference towards the end of the essay to a semantic study of environment. I had, at that point, no idea of a semiology as applied to architecture: this has since been done, on the Saussure'ian model by a number of people, with very doubtful gain. I had at that point in mind Charles Saunders Pierce's restatement of Locke's post-ulated science of signs (useful summary in James K. Feibleman, An Introduction to Pierce's Philosophy, *1960, pp 89 ff). Though, in all this, it is worth keeping in mind the Swiss master's under-publicised dictum: 'Il n'y a pas un seul terme en linguistique auquel j'attache un sens quelconque' in which spirit my remarks must be taken.*[1]

The circumstances of the publication were as I had foreseen: the Werkbund rejected the essay, which was then published as 'Meaning and Building' in Zodiac 6, 1957 *by Bruno Alfieri.*

'Toute oeuvre [d'art] qui n'est pas véhicule volontaire ou involontaire d'aveux est du luxe. Or le luxe est pire qu'immoral, il ennuie.' So Jean Cocteau in his *Essai de Critique Indirecte.*[2]

If Cocteau is right – as I believe he is – then surely every building, whole cities even, must carry declarations, confessions, avowals. I intend to consider here what the holding of such a notion might mean to a practising architect today. And that will involve me, inevitably, in speculations about first principles.

Which leaves me open to an objection at the outset; because many of my contemporaries, however patient they may be of *ad hoc* criticism even if it is directed against them, seem to think that speculation about architectural theory is worse than useless. Their argument would run something like this: The problems which the new industrial society raised for the architect a century and a half ago were first sharpened and later cleared by the invention of new materials and techniques. They have now all been solved in prototype at least. We can do no better than to multiply variations on the prototypes fast and in quantities. Quantity is our problem: we must perfect our planning methods, streamline site procedure, settle dimensional norms, learn to programme for computers and above all – prefabricate. First principles are all very well, but they have been settled for a good while yet. There is a modern idiom (the shameless even call it a style) and we will not go back on that. As for the ART in architecture, that is looked after by anything from ½% to 5% of the building costs being spent on paintings and sculptures. The products of this last guilt-offering, by the way, are called 'Integration of the Major Arts'.[3]

The attitude I have just described is familiar enough in Anglo-Saxon countries: it is the attitude of the technocrats and administrators of architecture, of zoners and curtain-wallers. It is very much the majority attitude.

But these very technocrats, if they are conscientious, are finding it increasingly difficult to give their undivided loyalty to the 'Functional City' and the 'Minimum Dwelling'. Even architects are beginning to realise that the people for whom they build are not physiological automata with brains attached, but complex beings moved by irrational urges. Anyone who claims to be on the side of reason but chooses to ignore this state of affairs, or deny it actively, is an idealist. The word 'rationalism' has for too long been associated with such an immoderate ideology, which seemed to rob humanity of all qualities except that of analytical thinking. This of course has now provoked an opposite ideology – based on an appeal to emotion which ignores the claims of reason. As one of Diderot's characters summed up: '...we don't really know what we do or want, so that we follow our fancy – which we call reason – or our reason – which is often nothing but a dangerous fancy, that sometimes turns out well, and sometimes badly...'[4]

And therefore some of my contemporaries (and I with them) would argue that the preoccupation of designers and architects with rational criteria has devalued their achieve-

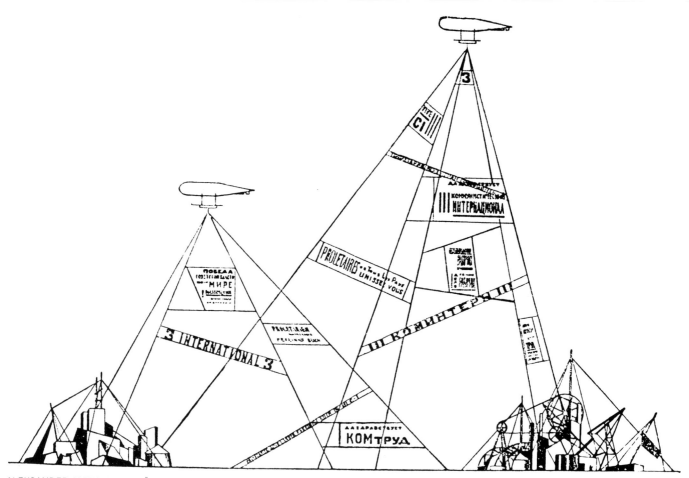

ALEKSANDER ALEKSANDROVIČ VESNIN Sets for Vsevelod Meyerhold's mass performance of *Strife and Victory* for the third Komintern congress, June 1921.

ments and cut them off from a mass public, so that now architecture cannot command public support or consent because it has lost the power of touching emotion. 'We do not have the ultimate power yet because the people is not behind us' Paul Klee said many years ago.[5]

To restate my theme: architects must acknowledge the emotional power of their work; this recognition depends on the methodical investigation of a content, even of a referential content in architecture. I believe this to be the most important and difficult problem which the architects of my generation will have to force next, and so I cannot offer more than a tentative programme. But as the problem has been in the air for some time in a rather nebulous form, what I have to say is open to several misinterpretations. That is why I should like to look at some of the ways in which the question has been set, and having been set, evaded.

Social Realism must come first. This return in the thirties to an eclecticism of the nineteenth-century type was the most thoroughgoing and also the most excusable evasion. For the artists who came in the wake of the Russian Revolution magnificently questioned everything in the name of reason: sets for mass demonstrations were suspended from captive balloons,[6] trees were dyed red and purple,[7] pages of newspapers back-projected onto the translucent fronts of editorial offices,[8] assembly halls revolved on their own axes,[9] and so on. The assault on the senses of a disorganised mass came too fast and was too violent.

The Mayakovsky generation had worked so intensively that when the reaction came it took the form of a complete about-turn led by the leftist-classicists, a minority group in the twenties. So the achievements of the Suprematists and Constructivists were never organised and entrenched –

Russian work of the twenties is like the creation of some prodigious *Wunderkind*. Now thirty years have passed and conditions changed so much that another policy about-turn has produced buildings in Russia which seem to differ little from the stuffier work done in the West in that mid-century technocratic style to which I have already referred. But the similarities are not limited to a stylistic levelling. If you compare the writings of some of the younger Italian architects with the apologies for 'leftist classicism',[10] you will see that the new regionalism there is only Social Realism stood on its head. The Russians were appealing to the manner of an enlightened despotism, to the classicism of Peter and Catherine the Great as a style of stability and intellectual comforts. 'The "isms" – the "leftist classicists" argued – had expressed the negative, destructive side of the Revolution, and the time had come to express its affirmative side, etc . . . ' So in Italy the appeal is to an anonymous, poor, unostentatious, popular manner of building, a popular style as against a polite bourgeois architecture – the cosmopolitan and rootless starkness which unaided reason had imposed.

Italy has also produced a brand of eclecticism which seems more closely related to Social Realism at times. I mean the influential and ably defended adaptation of Dutch and Italian fin de siècle architects' work: of Sommaruga, Kromhout, Berlage – and Art Nouveau more generally. Very specious and delicate arguments are put forward to justify this revival. It is even claimed that an artificially retarded society, such as that of modern Italy, must be housed in a style to fit its condition, that its shortcomings may become apparent through the irony of the treatment. It is just as well that such arguments are too thin and refined to have much appeal anywhere, besides applying to local conditions only.

LE CORBUSIER *Notre-Dame-du-Haut* Ronchamp 1954.

JORN UTZON *Sydney Opera House* 1957–74.

But in any case, eclecticism is much less of a danger nowadays than historical determinism. In its most insidious form, the determinist argument looks something like this: 'The modern style has arrived at a stage where monumental buildings provide us with problems which cannot be solved by appealing to functional criteria. The sense of overwhelming unity which such buildings conveyed in the past was often the result of a dome or vault covering. It is therefore clear that domes and vaults are the next problem of modern architecture.' This line of argument seems to lead to the sad situation where quite unworthy buildings are eloquently defended if they happen to be vaulted, particularly if the vault has a complex curvature. The reader need only think of the exaggerated praise which has been lavished on Jorn Utzon's winning competition design for the Opera House in Sydney. The praise focussed on the 'interlocking shell vaults... The white, sail-like forms of the shell vaults relate as naturally to the harbour [of Sydney] as to the sails of its yachts...' etc. (I quote from the Assessor's report on the competition). But of course sails have little to do with opera house roofs, and no amount of special pleading about holiday spirit and special occasion can still one's doubts as one looks at the section of the building, and sees the exterior has no bearing at all on the functions that go on inside it. It seems as if it were conceived entirely in a spirit of fancy, and had little to do with imagination[11] let alone method. Beyond the one blowsy overdramatisation it has few pleasures to offer. Allowing for all the differences, what I have said about Sydney Opera applies in equal measure to much of the work of Candela and Nervi,[12] to the 'white, bird-like' Idlewild Airport building for TWA by Eero Saarinen,[13] or to Hugh Stubbins' Assembly Hall in Berlin which, I am told, was intended to symbolise free speech, but is known to Berliners as 'the pregnant oyster'. But it does not apply to Le Corbusier's chapel at Ronchamp.

This exception cannot be justified at any length here, as I am not criticising, but theorising. I have made it to forestall any suggestion that I am a puritan who objects to all vaults, domes and curves of any kind in building. My case is quite different. To sum it up again, it is that admiration for vaults, even hyperbolic paraboloid ones, is not a substitute for reasoned principles.

To generalise this objection; I will go on to say that the use of the latest set of technological contraptions is no substitute for designing. What is more, technological advance is now so rapid that it demands a critical and discerning stand against the flood, not surrender. There is a kind of designer, however, who has been overwhelmed by it, inebriated. This consumer goods happy group used to be associated in Britain with 'Brutalism', though even that vague term has lost its temporary usefulness. I do not wish to say much about them here, except to point out how in Britain the acceptance of all the by-products of technology – American automobiles, tinned food advertisements, body-culture magazines, B-feature horror films, science fiction and all that – is allied with the confused protests of 'Angry-youngmannery'. In the literature of this protest there is a gamut of attitudes, from the callow, anti-social arrivisme of a novel like Kingsley Amis' *Lucky Jim* to the hysterical pseudo-mysticism of Colin Wilson's *The Outsider*. These literary attitudes are reflected in the lower reaches of 'Brutalism'[14] by their undiscriminating acceptance of motivational research as a basis for design, and their corresponding denial of any reasonable formal values. It is this last denial which reminds one so unpleasantly that behind the breezi-

ness there lurks a mystique of extreme individualism and immediate sensation.

I could go on cataloguing and criticising – but my purpose will be served if the reader will concede that the very existence of the various schools I have described, from social realist to brutalist, suggests that there is a general feeling that rationalism is not enough, that over and over again it has failed. But there are other designers who go on maintaining that strictly rational criteria are quite adequate, that the sense of separation between the designer and the public is entirely fabricated. Some even adopt a nobly despairing attitude, like that expressed by Sir Herbert Read when he suggested that in our materialist age 'art will survive as it did in the dark ages, in small circles, among the elite... universal boredom will lead to universal despair, and art will be renewed when life itself has been renewed...'[15]

This may be fine for those who can afford it, but will definitely not help most architects, of whatever persuasion, who must plan new towns and house millions without waiting until Utopia takes flesh. And if they are to build well, they must have faith in the value of their work and in the validity of their judgements. Which is why such noble and despairing attitudinising seems cynical and contemptible. Its implications in terms of building have been worked out in full tooled leather and gilt bronze detail by the less creditable followers of Mies van der Rohe, and I suspect that even the master himself is not free from it at times.

The rationalists who have made no concession, and who still believe that their position is foolproof, are much more deserving of admiration, even though they *will* maintain that the world of the mass public is quite irrelevant to their considerations, and the acceptance of their spare formal language for its own sake is merely a matter of education; the non-rational world must be kept outside the architect's calculation.

In recent years particularly this admirable attitude has led to all sorts of equivocations and misunderstandings. Because of the permissive nature of technical data, designers who claim to stick as closely to the bare functional requirements as is possible have produced results which are surprisingly like the work of more commercially minded *confrères* who claim only to provide streamlined casings for industrial products. Again, willful design solutions are increasingly difficult to justify on spurious technical grounds. What is even worse, speculators, administrators and technicians whom we architects have converted to such slogans as 'form follows function' or 'truth to materials' find now that they can dictate to us, because we have abdicated our responsibility as framers of man's environment.

We have given them weapons to produce buildings more quickly, more efficiently and more cheaply than before, without safeguarding those intangible values which even the most obdurate rationalist secretly holds dear.

I don't wish to make light of forms which follow functions, or even of truth to materials. Those slogans were most valuable once, and we must not discard them now; but an appeal limited to that order of disinfectant ideas forces the contemporary architect to falsify his position.

But before I go on to consider what such a position should be, I must insist on this reservation: an appeal against excessive rationalism should not be construed as an appeal against rational working methods. We must, of course, continue to work out problems at the rational level. There is, for instance, the vexed question of modular design; or the equally pressing matter of a physiological theory of colour;

MIES VAN DER ROHE and PHILIP JOHNSON (Associate Architects KAHN & JACOBS) *Seagram Building* 375 Park Avenue, New York City 1954–58. *Top left* View to the Lever Building (SOM) across the plaza: Seagram's hostility to its neighbours; *Top right* Main entrance: the duplicity of Seagram; *Bottom left* Four Seasons entrance: the forbidding corner edge; *Bottom right* Four Seasons entrance: Seagram hating its visitors.

or the conversion of the findings of Gestalt psychologists into terms of precept. All these are problems which will continue to exercise the best architects and influence their designs. But if we concentrate all our efforts at this rational level we shall go on evading the central issue which has now become so threateningly urgent.

To make my meaning plain I should like to consider the design of chairs. During the war the finding of an optimum sitting position had become one of the more important side-issues of aeronautical research.

Independently, some important experiments on sitting were carried out in Stockholm, under Bengt Ackerblom, whose findings were published in the form of a book[16] some ten years ago. Ackerblom certainly did recommend specific features in chairs, particularly in working chairs: a definite height, and two essential supports for the back. But his main result was more important than these summary data – and being intangible it was easy to overlook: that the human body cannot tolerate any one sitting position in comfort for more than a quarter of an hour at a time. Such permissive findings put the rationalist designer in an awkward situation:

Ackerblom's skeletal data cannot be coupled to a production process so as to result in any chair, either good or bad, without many decisions, independent of either factor, being taken first. Ackerblom was not the first to carry out this kind of research, nor were his findings totally unknown. But in spite of all the research and the publications, it was not the ergonomist's ideal chair which scored the great successes.

Even the most sophisticated and design-conscious public does not make its choice on rational grounds. So, after the war, the chair which had the most success among the customers of modern architecture, the chair which was most photographed in modern, architect-designed interiors is the so-called Hardoy chair. The prototype of this design was a folding chair made in England in the 1870s and used as an officer's chair by the Italian army in the 1920s. In the original form the chair had a wooden folding frame and a slung leather seat. When the frame was transposed into bent and welded metal rods all the advantages the chair had as a piece of light package furniture were lost without any compensating increase in comfort. But of course the metal and canvas model was very much cheaper and looked it. So

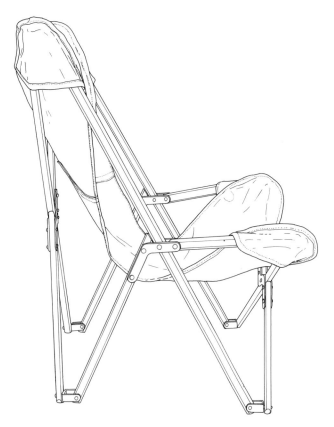

JOSEPH BEVERLY FENBY *Tripolina chair* 1877. The Tripolina chair was the basis for the undeservedly popular Hardoy chair.

ANTONIO BONET, JUAN KURCHAN and JORGE FERRARI HARDOY *Hardoy chair* 1938.

it is not only the relative discomfort which handicaps the chair, but its cheap materials. Its popularity, however, depended on considerations other than those of price and comfort. It may not be comfortable, some may object, but it *looks* so comfortable.[17] And the reason for this comforting appearance is that it unites the 'modernity' of an articulated construction with an archetypal chair form. The skeletal frame is compressive and has slung over it a womb-like canvas envelope which somehow manages to look tensile and elastic. So that while the articulated structure satisfies the demand for the kind of clarity associated with 'truth to materials', the general form of the chair satisfies an emotional need so completely that even after the inadequacies of the chair have become apparent, an owner often hesitates to reject it.

The association of womb and chair is neither arbitrary nor unexpected. A seated man demands of the chair he occupies not only adequate support and physical comfort, but also some feeling of enclosure, protection; and the assurance that he is not sitting on anything dangerous. Not every chair needs to satisfy all these requirements. But even a brief look at the history of chairs will show with what persistence the patterns of association reappear. So, for instance, the association of the chair with permanence means that it is connected with the most stable of all the elements, the earth; to mother earth in fact, the source of all authority. You will find that even in cultures where sitting is done without the mediation of chair or sofa, ceremonial and ritual seats will carry such associations. In Japan the Emperor addresses his ancestors seated on a waxed gypsum block which is let through the wooden floor into the ground and represents the earth.[18] In India the empty marble thrones on which epic heroes must sit down before they can assume their proper power is another variation on the theme.[19] As we go further west, examples multiply. The British coronation throne has a large stone let into the seat; the throne may bear the name of the country whose ruler occupies it. The ruler takes possession of his power when he ascends the throne, and so on. But the association may be taken further. The bishop's mark of authority is his cathedra, the professor's his chair, the judge's his seat, and so on. The armchair of the head of the family is only a commonplace reduction of the same thing.

Again the idea of possession, of ruling that on which you sit is emphasised when the lower half of the throne is carved with supporters in the shape of carrying slaves, as it often is in Asia Minor; in Africa a similar idea is sometimes represented by the ancestor-figures or totemic animals which carry the seat of a ruler's stool. Power in the sense of repression on the other hand, is shown in the clownish and even obscene figures which support the misericords in mediaeval cathedrals and abbeys.

Sitting and mother earth are associated in an even more elemental way. The Etruscans, for instance, frequently buried ashes in an urn set on a model chair; or even in an urn made in one piece to represent a woman sitting on a chair and holding or suckling a child.

Clearly this kind of figuration was a symbolic confiding of the dead person to the womb or the lap – the words are sometimes homonymous – of mother earth confident in her power to give them birth anew. If you look further back, to prehistory, you will find everywhere – from Peru to Scandinavia – peoples who buried their dead in a squatting position, the position of the child in the womb.

All these and many other ideas cluster round a simple object like the chair. But the chair is only one of many parts which compose our environment; and each one of them carries a proportionate charge of group memories and associations.

The designer's responsibility then, whether he knows it or

GUNNAR EKLOF Chair designed to a sitting position evolved by Bengt Ackerblom.

not, is to create order not only in terms of a sensible arrangement of physical function, but also out of the all-but-living objects which we use and inhabit.

Is this abstract discourse not pitching the argument too high? Now that discarding clothes, cars, houses as soon as they have passed from immediate fashion has become a moral duty in some places, is this not demanding too primitive an attitude to inanimate things? Surely – you may ask – we will no longer project in this way onto our environment, now it has become so impermanent?

I think we will. In any case, whether we finally arrive at an economy of total overproduction or not, certain realities will be with us for an indefinite time yet. Let me be quite commonplace. Consider a man returning from work. He should come to his house in the full knowledge that he is returning home. How is he to be assured in this knowledge? By a straightforward association, some will say. By having inhabited it long enough, bred his children in it, by being physically at ease there. If you have followed my argument, you will agree that all this will not be enough: what a man requires of his house is conviction that he is, in some sense, at the centre of the universe; that his home mediates between him and all the confusing and threatening world outside; that in some definite place the world is summed up for him in a place which is his, all his shelter and his castle.

So each one of the semi-detached houses which make up those wastes of suburbia round British cities will display somewhere a little piece of castellation, and the American equivalent will have odd token survivals from pioneer ranches. No wonder that they are not seduced by the anonymous apartment, however superior that may be. All the important economic considerations are often ignored – what sways people finally may really be that little piece of castellation or the fretwork on the gable.

Naturally this taking on of ornaments is not what I am

talking about. Nor is it some kind of 'symbolic' style to be cooked up by making a concession here, adding a bit of fancy work there. Am I, then, advocating the opening of our rational working methods to the designer to experience *participation mystique* in the things he is designing? Something of that, yes. But that can only happen at the strictly personal level – and this essay, as I have insisted before, is about principles and method. So I return to my main argument.

Take, then, the study of perception. Much work has been done by physiologists and neurologists to charter the workings of vision, and examine the configurations in which perception happens; some of it has already been applied directly to problems of design. You need only think of the study of the protective and articulating colouring of machinery in industrial plants. This kind of study has had a definitely mechanical bias until recently, when at last scientists have begun to consider the effect of feeling on perception. It all began some years ago when a coincidence suggested that the pattern of distortion in an experimental set-up called the Ames room was not the same for a husband and wife as for people with no strong emotional ties. It has since been tested in anxiety situations, particularly in the observation of mutilated people and in the relation between naval ratings and their superiors. But these investigations are still very elementary,[20] and their implications to designers not at all clear. What is obvious from this preliminary study, however, is that the ordinary 'mechanistic' perception tests are by themselves far too coarse instruments to apply to situations with heightened emotional possibilities. We have no idea, for instance, of how referential elements lodged in a field of *percepta* will affect physical sensation. To descend to the ridiculous at once, let me consider G.K. Chesterton's remark on seeing the lights of Times Square in New York that if he couldn't read he'd think himself in paradise.

There you have it. Looking at the mass of glaring advertisements, Chesterton forced his image-making faculty into a somersault: he abstracted all the content from sensations, and projected a new image onto them. But at a lower level, everyone is tempted to make an image when presented with a set of unrelated data. Present an unprejudiced spectator with a weak abstract painting, and he will immediately pour out a mass of associations, as he will make a programme for any piece of music. But what of strong abstract paintings? Even the best – think only of Arp – present their makers with all sorts of problems if figuration is to be avoided altogether. Only the greatest of them, Mondrian, overcame the fussy dodging of figuration by transcending it, by galvanising abstract patterns with such a powerful content that looking for abstracted resemblances in them, whether to Dutch tulip fields or to the street plan of Manhattan, can only be an irrelevant game. I am thinking particularly of the last few canvases, such as *Victory* and *Broadway Boogie-Woogie*, which I find more moving than even his best work of the mature period. He alone was able to electrify the formal experiments of neo-plasticism at the point of their greatest refinement to represent the release and the ebullience of the first post-war days. In these pictures abstraction has been left behind – they are images constructed out of autonomous and artificial elements. In these pictures figuration is not resemblance but analogy. Mondrian is the key. Here all the threads I have toyed with: psychology and anthropology, perception study and ergonomics, come together at last to be given a form. What that form shall be can only be worked out in time. But I believe that we have come to the end of a non-figurative architecture, and that we must now look to the scattered material which psychologists and anthropologists have been gathering. Not only myth and poetry, but the fantasies of psychopaths await our investigation. All the elements of our work: pavement, threshold, door, window, wall, roof, house, factory, school – all these have their poetry; and it is a poetry we must learn to draw from the programmes our clients hand us. Not to impose it by a cheap melodramatisation, but to spell it from the commonplace elements which we fit together.

It would be impardonable bungling and amateurishness to leave a matter of this importance to intuition – like leaving the functioning of the plan to luck. Intuition must be followed where method fails, of course – but the age demands, and demands rightly that we should acknowledge the unconscious element in man through our methods of work and make it a criterion of the workability of our buildings. If anyone objects that such an attitude is impractical, I would beg them to consider American advertising, a highly organised and still growing industry. An increasing proportion of the huge sum – large enough to float most European countries – which is devoted yearly to persuade Americans to spend more than they need, goes on to motivation research and its variants. Which means that it is being spent to harness the findings of psychologists to selling methods; translated into realistic terms, it is the deliberate sharpening of neurotic tendencies – anxiety and inferiority, loneliness fears, auto-eroticism, repression, infantilism and all the others – so that they may be assuaged or averted by some quite superfluous product which the advertiser offers. 'Luxe' – superfluity, gratuitousness – elevated into a moral value, as it is with us, becomes insufferably boring through attrition.

I am not here making a political judgement. We in Europe have not advanced in motivation research as far as the Americans, and I am sure that the psychological pressures in communist countries are equally sharp, perhaps even more invidious. But American advertising offers a useful instance, because the methods of the 'symbol-manipulators', as American advertising men call themselves, are almost the exact opposite of what I believe the architect's task to be: to make every building an integrating, reconciling and cleansing form.

Through a semantic study of environment we can discover the means of discoursing in our buildings. Only that way will we be able to appeal to the common man again.

People are only aware most obscurely of the forces working in them, forces which are fed on memory and association. But they feel rightly that those forces can only be propitiated and purged – which they must be constantly – through objects which carry 'aveux', carry some reference to which they may respond in the very moment of perception. If memory and association are starved visually by architects, then the result must be malaise and a rejection of the environment which they created. Heritage, and the silt up of individual experiences, memory and association make perception as an act of the whole person inevitable: 'there would be no present – and that means that there would be no tangible world with all its lushness and its inexhaustible riches, if perception did not, as Hegel says, contain a past in its present depth...'[21] Every moment of perception contains a whole personal and collective past, our body is the incarnation of that past; and with every moment of perception this past is reordered and revalued.

The Modern Movement in Italian Architecture

This is the edited version, prepared for The Listener, *June 21st 1956, of a broadcast prompted by the publication of Carlo Pagani's* Architettura Italiana d'Oggi *(Milan, 1955). It is the earliest essay I have included in this collection, and has the curiosity interest of being written at the time when La Martella (now partly depopulated) was barely occupied. I would be less severe today about Pietro Cascella's decorations of the church. On the other hand, Giancarlo de Carlo's approach has not, I think, suffered any radical change: he would probably stand by what he then said, as I would for my part. Although more than two decades have passed since its publication and perspectives have inevitably shifted, nevertheless a view of Italian architecture by an outsider ten years after the war, besides its curiosity, also has a rarity value.*

Modern Italian architecture has recently come in for a great deal of public notice. It seems fresh and crisp to us, and the assumption is often made that it is a sudden post-war growth. But if you consider this assumption you will see how improbable it really is – that Italian architects, however talented they may be, should in five years have caught up on almost half a century of European development. Carlo Pagani's book, *Italian Architecture Today*, might seem to encourage this misapprehension, since the hundred or so buildings which he presents in detail have all been built since the war. He has, however, added a summary but illustrated introduction giving a brief history of the Modern Movement in Italy. I should like to speak of two buildings which Pagani has shown in this introduction and which seem to me to point the contrast between what went on before and after the war in Italian architecture. The first is the Casa del Fascio in Como, north of Milan, designed by Giuseppe Terragni and completed in 1936. The second, completed last year, is a small village, La Martella near Matera in the south, planned by a group of architects of whom the most distinguished is Ludovico Quaroni.

The Casa del Fascio was the headquarters and rallying point for the local fascist party and its subsidiaries. It has long rectangular elevations on all four sides. Each of these is a double square divided into four storeys and seven vertical bays. The plan, as you may already have deduced, is a square, so that the building has a volume like four sugar-cubes laid touching each other. The edges of this volume are all sharply outlined and unbroken; but within the apparently rigid scheme the walls perform a precarious piece of juggling, particularly glaring where the panels within the

GIUSEPPE TERRAGNI *Casa del Fascio* Como 1932, main facade with superimposed (but unexecuted) photomontage by M. Nizzoli, and ground floor plan.

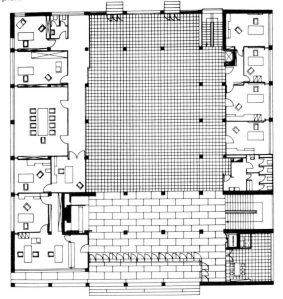

LUIGI AGATI, FREDERICO GORIO, PIERO LUGLI, LUDOVICO QUARONI, and MICHELE VALORI *Village of La Martella* near Matera 1952–53.

17

heavy concrete frame are cut into a complicated pattern of void and solid. The repetition of these screens sets up a syncopated and disturbing rhythm at variance with the apparent stability of the basic scheme of the building.

The disturbing effect was willed only in part – Terragni's primary intention was, in his own words, to 'include the complex of disparate elements in a unified structure and to reconcile them through the laws of harmony and proportion. Thus architectural order will reign on the political plane, to coincide with the new order conquered by fascism for corporative Italy.'

But in fact it was the hazardous interpretation of an ideology and the sense of inherent conflict between the elements that dictated the schematic plan and structure. The brutally schematic quality is the visual expression of the passionate nature of Terragni's appeal to reason. 'Rationalism' was the device he and his six companions chose as against the word 'modern' which they felt had been abused by their immediate predecessors. In 1926, when this small group, young men who had qualified that year, launched their first manifesto through the monthly *Rassegna d'Italia*, the fascist regime was firmly ensconced in power.

The post-war decade was to be dominated by opportunism embodied in a comfortable neo-classicism. The first sign of a different approach was a cautious but firm manifesto of the seven young architects, none of whom had as yet built anything. It proved to be the opening shot in a long campaign. They did not claim to create a new style, but believed that when the building fulfils its functions as closely as possible, a style will result simply by way of selection; and they go on to speak of the necessity of standardisation, of the belief in a formal abstemiousness, in anonymity. Such reasoning could not possibly appeal to the architects who had attained power in the post-war years. And in fact only one building dating from that period appeared in the first exhibition of rationalist architecture, organised in Rome in 1928.

The Fiat factory must not go on record simply as the first Italian building to be recognised abroad as belonging to the Modern Movement, but also because it served as a tangible justification at the most severely practical level of several revolutionary ideas championed by rationalist architects. They were realised in this building on a scale which these architects – and even their masters outside the country – had been able to employ only in theoretical projects. And, in fact, the designer of the factory was an engineer.

There is still something breathtaking about the speedway over the roof of that huge structure. A formal invention of this kind indicates a passionate curiosity towards the machine, an acceptance of it in terms of emotion and imagination. It is such an acceptance that the futurists had demanded, though on a pseudo-epic level. In reality this happened on the humble scale of light industry, of typewriters, motor scooters, and coachwork for motor cars. To the rationalist architects this acceptance was a godsend, since it meant that they had a quantity of lightly mechanised semi-craft workshops at their disposal. The standard of craftsmanship, the care in execution remained high, even if it is now declining, and industrial methods could be applied to small-quantity production: standardised window frames, for instance, or wall panelling. Such large elements may have a deadening effect on an otherwise excellent building when they have been shoddily designed, but may have to be used for reasons of economy.

An Italian architect can therefore afford to design the

GIACOMO MATTE TRUCCO *Fiat factory* Lingotto, Turin 1926–28, internal courtyard showing ramp and roof runway.

GIUSEPPE PAGANO *Universitá Bocconi* Milan 1936–42, exterior view and ground floor plan.

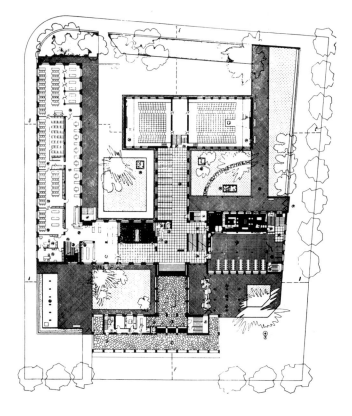

EDUARDO PERSICO (with G.C. Palanti and M. Nizzoli) *Entrance Hall* VI Triennale, Milan 1936. This was the most 'official' of Persico's commissions, the nearest he got to Novecento classicism.

EDUARDO PERSICO (with M. Nizzoli) *Parker Shop* Milan in 1951. The electric signs which were an integral part of the design were altered after the war. The shop, like the other Persico shop for Parker in Milan, has since been destroyed.

fittings and furniture for a single building. In this country it takes an enterprise of the scale of a county architect's office with a heavy building programme to get a manufacturer's agreement to produce, say, special wash-basins or door handles. The Casa del Fascio is an example of what degree of traditional fastidiousness it was possible to attain, while wholly accepting machine-made products. Terragni was insistent on making the whole building as nearly machine finished as possible; in spite of the rough treatment the building has been given over the last ten years, much of the finish has survived. What is less in evidence now is the equally fastidious attitude Terragni took to decoration. This was reduced to photography and lettering for the image and the message, and abstract compositions which were used to tie these extremely individuated elements into the architecture. The poetic qualities of the building are a result of this very stringency. Terragni had created the only memorable monument to fascism, one which still retains what there was of the universal in its appeal. The fascism for which he built it, however, was a chimera. It was a left-wing movement, irredentist, stern, uncompromising towards the bourgeoisie: what so many intellectuals who were seduced into it believed it to be. 'Even those who did not join the party', wrote the architect and critic Ernesto Rogers in 1946, 'made their contribution: exhibitions, buildings, magazines'. 'The best of us', he adds, 'were the most active in error: Terragni and Pagano; the first an instinctive artist, the second an intellectual gifted with great culture and acute critical sense . . . '

It was Giuseppe Pagano, himself a fine architect, who criticised the Casa del Fascio from within the Italian Modern Movement. His initial appreciation is qualified in these terms: 'The freedom of inspiration was fettered from the beginning by a very obvious solution of the planning problem which in turn is disguised in a desire to create an original work . . . If we accept this tendency towards a rhetoric of disquiet forms, we must be prepared for an era when function will become a pretext for conceits without our ever reaching a full knowledge of the formal and moral purity of the new architecture.'

I would like to draw your attention to the unexpected association of the terms 'moral' and 'formal'. They are crucial to the many and long architectural polemics which took place in Italy at that time. 'The "social" function of the architect', another brilliant critic, Eduardo Persico, had put it some years earlier, 'is resolved in his submission to the rules of his art, to its universal appeal'.

We are not accustomed to think of the social function of the artist in such terms. Rigour of form, so it seemed to these writers and architects, would, by empathy almost, bring about the rigour of behaviour, the ethical quality they desired. Their formal preoccupations were exacerbated by the hesitations of official patronage. At one period – between the opening of the second exhibition of rationalist architecture by Mussolini in 1931 and the building of Florence station in 1934 – the fascist party seemed to favour a swing to modernity. Yet the bulk of official patronage went to the opportunist architects who were perpetuating the post-futurist reaction. There was, however, one aspect of design for which these men had little aptitude or interest: exhibitions. It was with exhibitions therefore that the development of the new architecture in Italy became associated, particularly with the Triennale of Milan. At first the appeal was directly rhetorical; but if you look at some of the later exhibitions – the Italian aviation exhibition of 1934 or the Triennale of 1936, for instance – you will see how spare and taut the actual structure of the exhibitions became, and how the appeal to the spectator was reduced to the working out of a single formal idea, or a lyrical juxtaposition of straightforward documents, primarily photographs and texts.

Just before the 1936 Triennale, for which he had designed an extraordinarily lucid and modest entrance hall, Eduardo Persico, whom I quoted earlier, died at the age of thirty-five. Though he died of a heart attack, he is regarded as the first martyr of his generation of architects, since his illness was owing in large part to maltreatment during political imprisonment. With Pagano, whose condemnation of the Casa del Fascio I have quoted, he had edited *Casabella*, the most selective architectural periodical in the world. The openly anti-fascist Persico was able, in his devotion to architecture, to collaborate with the blackshirt Pagano. This architecture to which they were loyal beyond their political allegiance, and, sometimes at great personal risk, was an expression of social and ethical beliefs common to both, though each read different political implications into them. After Persico, its most perceptive theorist and critic, the architectural profession was to lose Pagano in a German concentration camp. Terragni, the most brilliant, broke down at the Russian front, was repatriated and died, also having repented publicly of his past political associations. With the liberation, the three leading personalities of the movement were gone.

These and the several other sacrifices which modern Italian architecture made through the resistance and concentration camps restored the honour of rationalism and gave avant-garde Italian architects, particularly those of the north where the sacrifices were heaviest, a new sense of solidarity. Nevertheless, immediately after the war, with the spate of new polemics, magazines, and plans, they soon became conscious that many ideas had lost validity, that rationalism was not enough. But the period had no strong orientation. Reconstruction was the most pressing problem and government action slow. The north, therefore, was where building started on a large scale. Since it was private patronage that initiated it, luxury building came first.

Pagani's book gives one a fair picture of this; roughly two-thirds of the buildings published in detail were built before 1950. And it was about 1950 that the concerted housing drive started. Nevertheless even the short period covered by the book shows an extraordinarily high common factor. The more famous buildings, such as the new railway station in Rome, have a consistency of formal treatment and abstemiousness of detail which owes much to the rationalist approach, and to the stringency of architectural polemics. Yet everywhere there is an increasing tendency to depart from strict geometry, and the apparent need to experiment with more complex, oblique or curved shapes.

This stylistic trait is again connected with ideas now widespread in Italy and associated with the word 'organic'. The word was first thrown into the arena of discussion by some Roman architects who were challenging the hegemony of Milan; soon the word 'organic' succeeded 'rational' as the approval term among architects. It was first used as a stylistic description; but the ideas which it suggested, and particularly the interest in the psychological function of architecture, have had a very strong influence on many projects connected with reconstruction in the south of

GIANCARLO DE CARLO Balcony access housing, Sesto San Giovanni 1952 and lower income housing, Quartiere Comasina, Milan 1953–55.

Church of La Martella interior with decorations by Pietro Cascella.

the country. This must be taken into account here even if only one scheme of those built so far has been of real importance: the village of La Martella. This is a resettlement of some of the inhabitants of the Sassi, the notorious caves where many peasant inhabitants of the nearby town of Matera had been living. The approach of the architects was not the usual one of simply housing the under-privileged. For these were people who had developed a way of life which had a dignity, a coherent pattern ennobling even the squalor of the poorest.

The result has been a grouping of semi-detached farm-houses divided from each other by outbuildings. They spread in short terraces from the core: the church with a spire at the centre, post office, shops, doctor's house and dispensary, school and communal bread-baking oven, and at one end of the centre an open fairground. It is all whitewashed walls, low-pitched tile roofs, and small shut-tered windows. No formal subtlety has been attempted; indeed there has been an austere renunciation of formal intention: 'If you consider this village in purely formal terms you may well be disappointed and you will certainly miss the point', wrote one of its architects. The point may in fact seem rather laboured to a visitor from this country: it amounts to survey before plan; a familiar slogan. But here the accent is different. Our planners do not have to deal with a way of life as tenaciously atavistic, as ancient, and as dignified.

It is not only the southern farmer who has been accorded this very proper respect in Italy. One of the most interesting younger Milanese architects, Giancarlo de Carlo, after build-ing a block of flats to a carefully reasoned programme at Sesto San Giovanni, the industrial suburb of Milan, returned there one Sunday and spent all day in a café facing it, watching the way in which people were using the amenities he had provided: 'I suffered all the violence they generated

in attacking the building to make it their home. The secluded balconies facing the south were covered with laundry out to dry and the people were all on the access galleries facing the north. They had put out stools and chairs to watch and take part in the spectacle of each other and of the street. The very narrowness of the galleries excited the children who were running their bicycle races along them...It was then I understood how mistaken my approach had been, in spite of its apparently rational basis. Orientation matters, and so does a view of the landscape and light and privacy; but what matters most is to be able to see each other, to be together. It is communication which counts most.'

Where the rationalists used their asceticism as a formal sermon, the approach of these younger architects is almost one of the psychologist, a minimising of all formal intention so as to give a total accommodation – physical, moral, and psychological – to the inhabitants. Architecture, however, is an art, and those who practise it are in duty bound to use the terms of a formal language. The refusal therefore on the part of the designers of La Martella to consider the formal problem with which they were faced squarely must be condemned as a shirking of responsibility. To quote Persico again: 'The social function of the architect is resolved in his submission to the rules of his art'. But the approach of the planners of La Martella, and of the younger architects such as de Carlo, is still new and will be faced with many unresolved problems. The decorations of the church at La Martella are one instance of this: folksy wood carving, artfully patterned tiles have an air of archness, of falsity, which suggests that something has gone wrong – especially if you think back to the rigour and appeal of the decorations of Terragni's Casa del Fascio. Nevertheless, it is true that the achievements of rationalism are being ploughed back into the soil of Italy. As to what the upshot of this process will be I cannot now hazard a guess.

The Sitting Position – A Question of Method

For an issue of the Italian magazine Edilizia Moderna 86 *specifically concerned with the relation between the study of history and the teaching of design, I decided to present again the material about sitting first collected for my Ulm lectures of 1958, and summarised in one section of 'Meaning and Building' (no. 1 in this collection) a decade earlier. It seemed to me that a comparison of the material from different periods and cultures would allow me to focus accurately on the relative importance of human comfort, methods of production and of cultural association as parameters – both conscious and unconscious – of the design process. The last factor seemed to me consistently, even insistently repressed by many teachers and theorists; I was therefore concerned to show how its repression in some ways strenghened its controlling power.*

Everybody's first action is to get up. When the child stretches its legs inside the womb it enters on the shocking experience of birth; in the womb we all spend the beginning of our existence in a sitting or crouching position. Every time we get up, therefore, we repeat – more or less consciously, more or less significantly – that original shocking experience; and every time we sit down we retreat into it.

All over the world nowadays people perform the action of sitting down and getting up with the aid of such commonplace objects as chairs, sofas, stools and so on. A great deal of attention is devoted to their exact shape since – notionally at any rate – the user demands comfort of such objects and the aim of all designers engaged in producing them is comfort. But comfort is a complex notion, which varies from person to person, and from social group to social group; varies for the individual throughout his life and more important goes through very violent changes independent of our physical constitution but directly connected to the inconstant pattern of convention. The dependence of comfort on social convention is one of the factors which trips up writers on ergonomics when they attempt to define comfort and prescribe the conditions under which it can be obtained. Two writers recently attempted to refine the static results provided by anthropometry into a more accurate description of sitting in comfort by suggesting that comfort is the product of the greatest possible relaxation of the largest number of muscles.[1] It is quite clear, however, from the briefest study of the positions described as comfortable that the situation is relatively independent of the measurements and materials which they use to attain comfort. So for instance in Yoga the primary aim of the different meditation positions is to achieve the greatest relaxation of the Yogi's muscles so that he becomes unaware of his body. This is usually achieved without any mechanical aids or supports, but through internal bodily balance and the control of breath.

Clearly the achievement of this kind of comfort is limited to a small minority – and for relatively short periods of time at that. The many will find it in postures from sitting on the ground with legs fully extended and back unsupported (a position adopted frequently in Asia and Polynesia, particularly by women) to standing upright on one leg with the other one thrust into the crutch (a position favoured for rest by certain tribes in Central Africa). The continuing, elaborate research on human measurement and the publication of such data as if they were of vital importance indicates a sharpened awareness in the mind of the observer of the mechanical complexities involved in the sitting position, also of his inability to appreciate the meaning of the term comfort as it relates to the whole personality rather than any real difficulty in obtaining satisfactory measurements. Anthropometric measurement is not a new technique in any case. A rude form of it interested the Egyptians in relation to canonic proportion; stories about classical artists who attained perfect beauty in the human figure through an aggregate of measurements taken from various subjects admired for their beauty already implied the difficulties which are met by the practitioners of anthropometric ergonomics. The inclusion of the human figure in square and circle by Vitruvius suggests a further attack on the problem at a higher level, that of reducing the measurements to a total function which would fit all cases. A millennium and a half later Dürer, in his *Von Menschlicher Proportion*,[2] measured a number of human subjects: fat men, thin men, tall men, small men, women of all sizes, babies, dwarfs and so on – but he was unable to reduce the measurements to a formulated canon. The lesson to be learnt from Dürer and his successors is that the variety of human physique cannot with advantage be reduced to a single systematic statement.

In considering objects for human use however, the designer cannot cater for the whole range of these varieties but must seek the type. Even in the days when patrons commissioned the artisan directly, such objects as chairs and tables were not intended for the patron himself but for any number of users. So that in the past, much as now, it was the average for which the designer had to cater; he could not hope to mould the object to the individual.

The great period of furniture design in Western Europe,

Grimaldi, near Menton, Grotte des Enfants. Two negroid skeletons of the Aurignacian period buried in a foetal position.

F. Leducq weeping with exhaustion during the Tour de France of 1930.

when there was any number of great individual cabinet makers – Chippendale, Sheraton, Jacob, Oeben – and the first manuals on furniture design appeared, was also a period in which the human posture was investigated scientifically. The first to do this, perhaps, was Nicholas Andry who, in his *Orthopédie*,[3] pointed to the relationship of the postures habitually taken in work and leisure to postural defects; he also noted basic anthropometric facts needed for the design of work and leisure chairs. It is interesting that at least one recent publication specifies a good chair height as being between 8 inches and 12 inches, which is hardly any indication at all, while Andry had already got it more closely to between 9 inches and 11 inches, the usual chair height adopted by cabinet makers and joiners in his day; a lumbar support strictly recommended by Ackerblom in his *Sitting Posture*[4] is already mentioned as being desirable by Andry. The only notable difference between the two is Ackerblom's suggestion that the seat should be a little lower and slope backwards; but even this last recommendation has now been put in doubt by more recent writers. In spite of our very sophisticated measuring techniques and highly specialised approach to the problem we cannot reduce these indications to a formulation tighter than had been available to the eighteenth-century cabinet maker. We have only one advantage over him: our superior technical achievement allows us adjustable elements in furniture; these, however, are only used in working furniture by people who occupy the same seat habitually. They have never been adapted (in spite of the attempts of some designers) to leisure furniture. The considerations which guide a designer, therefore, are not refined anthropometric data but the much coarser considerations of material and fabrication, as well as the persistence of certain traditional shapes from which little departure is made.

The dream of certain Utopian designers who thought that the time would come when the anthropometric and technical data would simply be fed into a computer to be processed into a complete specification for a chair is turning out to be chimera. Given a set of data of the kind I mentioned, the computer could – in theory – produce an infinite number of specifications; which means that it is pointless to feed this kind of information into a computer at all. What a computer can do for a designer is to produce a rapid check of a given specification in terms of cost in relation to material and manufacturing process. The mechanised analytical proposition, therefore, does not narrow down the designer's field of decision appreciably; particularly since a specification must be made before it can be checked and, for the sort of purpose that is being considered here, the specification is the design. The computer, therefore, operates on the design once it has been formulated. This situation is not likely to alter in the foreseeable future.

Although I am considering the chair as a useful instance, what I say about chairs is equally true for any other object which needs to be designed. In spite, then, of the promise which the 'functionalist' theoreticians of the last generation made, the functional solution of problems will not lead to an ideal situation where the arbitrary aesthetic choices will be relegated to a marginal exercise. On the contrary, it appears that the ergonomic study will be entirely permissive and that within the norms that it recommends – which will not depart much from those we already use – no surprising conclusions will be forced on us. It is inevitable, of course, that this should be so, since the subjects of ergonomic enquiry are

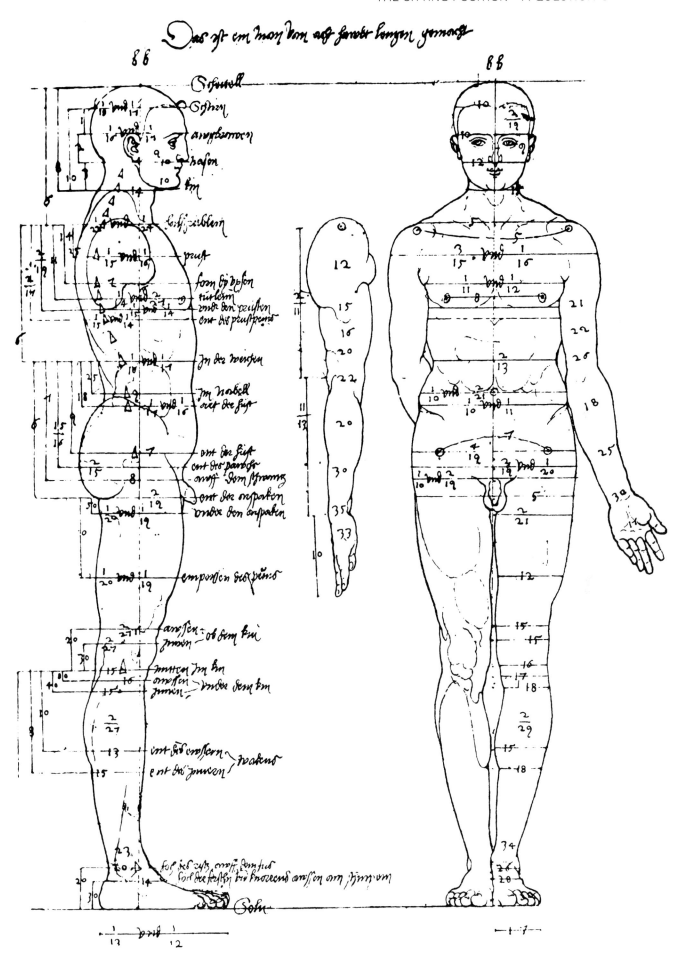

ALBRECHT DÜRER Manly proportions, preparatory auto-trace for engraving in *Vier Bücher von Menschlicher Proportion* (Albertina, Vienna).

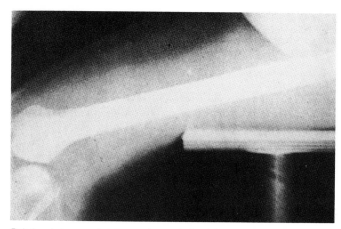

Relation between skeleton and muscle in sitting position after Dr Bengt Ackerblom.

ANTONIO BONET, JUAN KURCHAN and JORGE FERRARI HARDOY *Hardoy chair*, 1938.

BENGT ACKERBLOM and GUNNAR EKLOF Chairs designed to a sitting position recommended by Ackerblom, 1954.

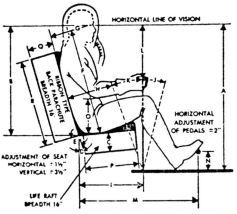

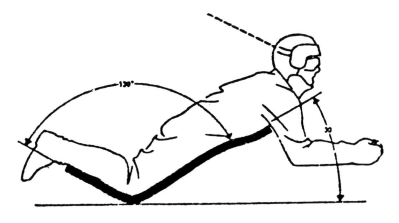

Seated and horizontal positions of pilots of combat aircraft.

entirely conditioned – we all are – by the norms of comfort which our environment prescribes. Ergonomic study based on a statistical sample must inevitably sanction the norm. It is highly unlikely to suggest, for instance, that the cross-legged sitting position (known as the 'tailor' position) should replace our way of sitting on chairs with the legs hanging down. Or even that the standing position is inherently more comfortable than the sitting one. Many functionalist designers have thought of avoiding the problem through turning to intangible factors which they label 'invention' or 'intuition' and leave the final choice which the designer must make to these unquantifiable operations. When the designer comes to exercise his craft, therefore, he is left without the support of a method in spite of the elaborate operations by which his decision has been hedged about. The whole ergonomic discipline can only narrow the field of action for the designer; rational discourse about his specific formal procedure is excluded.

I have already observed that little help is forthcoming from the study of materials and manufacture. They again can only provide the designer with points of reference for each individual job. Of the large number of new chairs which appear on the market most are still made of timber and leather; a few of metal and cloth or leather. Among the most popular of post-war models – particularly so with the design-conscious public – has been the Hardoy chair, a cheaper but more rigid descendant of the old folding wood and leather chair which was devised in England in the 1870s and adopted for the Italian army as a camp chair in the twenties. Anyone familiar with ergonomic literature, or just willing to think sensibly about posture in relation to furniture, will know the hazards which someone using the chair must meet. And yet this discomfort does not appear to have deterred prospective buyers. The chair as it is now marketed consists of a rigid metal rod frame so bent that it provides four vertical hooks or points for a canvas seat slung between them. This means, of course, that the seat, which is loosely suspended, will mould itself to the thighs and buttocks, and that support will not be concentrated, as is thought desirable, on the ischial tuberosities; also that there will be no lumbar support so that the spinal erectors will never be completely relaxed. The hard edge of the canvas must always press on the under side of the thighs and cause considerable discomfort. What is worse, the fixed form framework and its high protuberances make any changes of position very cumbersome. The popularity of the chair – it continues to be a standard production line in several countries – clearly indicates that the buyers who choose the chair cannot do so on rational grounds. We must therefore assume that the buyers of the Hardoy chairs, like many other customers for design goods, are guided in their choice by promptings quite different from the dictates of reason. The very fact that they do so should be a matter of interest and not of regret to the designer: nothing human should be alien to him.

I have already pointed out that any statistical enquiry, particularly if it is unsupported by sufficiently detailed anatomical information, could only lead to the sanctioning of prevailing norms; the difficulties which attend an anatomical enquiry into such a matter as the sitting position were alluded to many years ago in that fundamental essay of Marcel Mauss on the techniques of the body.[5] It is curious that, although the linguistic and the social anthropologist have a vast area of comparative material on which they can operate, in such matters as techniques of the body, interest is concentrated on extreme situations: Yoga, Polynesian and Bushman tribes, workers in highly stressed situations such as aircraft gunners, etc. But in fact the material available includes the whole range of historical documentation from all civilisations, particularly as it is recorded in memoirs, folk tales, works of fiction and above all (from the designer's point of view) in works of art. A beginning has been made by certain social anthropologists: Gordon W. Hewes, for instance, has made a preliminary attempt to sort out the thousand or so comfortable human postures which have been adopted in various societies.[6] But neither he, nor as far as I know anyone else, has made an attempt to relate these positions to the emotional charge which they must carry or to relate them to the various forms of seat with which they are connected. The seat in particular is a more complex object than is usually realised.

In the West, and I mean from Asia Minor to the Pacific, it has for instance always been associated with authority: so a professor is only properly appointed when he has ascended his chair or *cathedra*; the central church of a diocese bears the name of cathedral because it is the place where the bishop has his seat or *cathedra*. Papal pronouncements which are to carry the full weight of his authority are in fact delivered *ex-cathedra* from his throne and the seat of the first bishop of Rome, St Peter, is enshrined in Bernini's enormous bronze reliquary in the west end of St Peter's, which is known as the altar of the chair.

The Western church even celebrates a special feast-day of this great relic on January 18th; as well as another one of St Peter's throne at Antioch on February 22nd. Judges and magistrates give judgment also from their seat or bench and in English the collective noun describing magistrates is a 'bench' of magistrates.

King Sesostris I (XIIth Dynasty) seated on his throne. The sides of the throne represent the gods of lower and upper Egypt tying the two kingdoms into one with a knot.

'Throne' stool supported by an ancestor figure, Manyema tribe, Zaire. The Baluba and other tribes make similar throne stools, and variants recur throughout West Africa. Chiefs are sometimes buried seated on such stools.

Seated Buddha on the Lion Throne.

The adoration of the Buddha from the Stupa at Amaravati, second century A.D. The Buddha's presence is indicated by the empty seat and other symbols.

Christ and the Apostles, dome of the Arian Baptistry, Ravenna. Christ is represented by the empty throne surmounted by a jewelled cross.

To continue with English examples, the coronation throne of the British Sovereign is a large mediaeval construction supported by four lions on the corners and containing a shelf underneath. On this shelf rests a large piece of stone from Scotland known as the Stone of Scone which King Edward I carried off from Scotland. It was on this piece of stone that the Scottish kings were crowned in mediaeval times and the stone, rather than any other emblem, represents the authority of the British king. Edward I and his successors on being crowned sitting on this stone could claim to be kings of Scotland. The Stone of Scone is variously reputed to be the pillow stone of St Columba, one of the Irish saints, or the pillow of Jacob on which he dreamed the famous dream at Beth-el.[7] To sit on a holy stone or otherwise touch it so as to obtain communication with unseen powers is an action which is familiar not only from scripture and the legends of saints and martyrs but which also seems to be a permanent feature of Indo-European folklore. But the fascination of the holy stone, and the way in which the stone is a concentration of earth, has been studied at length by certain historians of religion[8] who have also remarked on the extraordinary way in which the sitting position has come to be associated with authority. This is so in civilisations where sitting on the ground is customary, amongst the Ashanti for instance, and certain other West African peoples. But power of the great chief resides in the stool on which he is enthroned and the stool itself is one of the relics of the nation. In a country where no seats were employed except under Western influence the sitting position is still associated both with authority and with the ground. In the Seiryo-den of Kyoto Imperial Palace the Emperor sealed his authority by pouring

out a libation to his imperial ancestors into a large piece of gypsum which was let into the timber floor so as to allow him direct contact with the soil: the stone block stood for the soil of Japan.

Sitting, authority and the earth are closely associated. The emperor or king, professor or bishop, sitting on their thrones, are therefore sitting on what they rule. The more despotic or repressive the rule of authority the more distorted and misshapen the supporters of the seat will appear: which accounts for the violent grotesques which support so many misericords in mediaeval cathedrals; or the wildly gesticulating papier mâché seats of nineteenth-century France and England.

The seat puts a distance between the bulk of the body and the ground and it seems that in that vital space gather the mysterious creatures which inhabit our more frightening dreams. It is under the bed that we always look for the burglar; women frequently raise the skirts of a chair to see if there are any of those imaginary mice which nibble on their ankles. These anxious gestures betray fears which often direct and may distort our ways of thinking.

Symbolism, said J. J. Bachofen (overstating his case) begins in the tomb. Symbolism springs from the way the three fundamental experiences of man, birth, copulation and death, stress his description of the outside world. Inevitably the sitting position can be associated with the position of the child in the womb. During the early ages of mankind most peoples buried their dead in that position, so that by returning them to the womb of that mother from which all things are born their dead might be born again to a renewed life. Every chair is, therefore, in some sense a comment on

29

our conception of authority and/or our conception of birth and rebirth. This is true both for the designer and for the purchaser.

The Hardoy chair is an obvious instance for examination. Its success, as I have already said, must be based on considerations which have little or nothing to do with ergonomic choice. On the other hand it would help very little if we were to enquire from purchasers or owners of the chair why they were moved to buy it in the first place, since we must assume that here considerations of a symbolic nature, which are in conflict with ergonomic – or as some would say 'functional' or even 'rational' ones, must be unconscious. In the context of what has already been said, one aspect of the chair at least is obvious. A concave sack, despite the physical discomfort it inflicts on the user of the chair, is very much a womb and offers, if not the physical protection, at least the material semblance of the protecting womb. In an age where the relationship with one's mother is so much discussed (one need only open a psychological text book of any school to see how true that is) a chair of this nature was bound to have a success, particularly among the intellectual public, where this question poses special difficulties. It is also this section of the public which is particularly distrustful of any imposed authority whether political or religious and prefers authority reduced to a minimal structure like the cage supports of the Hardoy chair.

The Hardoy chair, moreover, divides flexible from rigid elements with great clarity, which implies that a statement is also being made about the essential structure of the object. On examination this turns out to be a pseudostatement; since it is only one about the articulation of the materials and not about differentiated functions: the hamfisted joining of the cloth bag to the metal frame is a curious indication of intellectual imprecision.

My account is necessarily *post facto*: my elaborate analysis of an agreeable if arbitrary shape will seem gratuitous to some, absurdly over-literary to others. The enormous success of the Hardoy chair, however, both in terms of sale and prestige, is such a sharp contrast to its operational failure that it requires a rational explanation; particularly so, as it exemplifies the situation (I might even say the failure) of modern design about which enough has not yet been said. This situation arises out of the unarticulated need which most designers and many members of the public feel for shapes whose vitality would have that suggestion of modernity which fashion requires and the change in visual language dictates; but with it also the charge of meaning weighty enough to fill out the visual discourse. This can only happen when the charge is compounded of emotional and intellectual elements. In fact, such a mixture will occur

Top
Capitoné papier-maché stool, French c. 1850.

Centre
Caricature of Martin Gropius' spring chair, from Kladderdatsch, c. 1850, captioned: 'You receive a visitor and ask him to sit down. The newcomer admires the resilience of the chair but can't believe that it contains 24 springs. That is when you quickly cut the upholstery and the visitor redeems his unbelief in a swift and not altogether disagreeable movement.' After S. Giedion, *Mechanisation Takes Command*.

Bottom
THOMAS SHERATON *The Chamber Horse*. From the appendix to the *Cabinet Makers' and Upholsterers' Drawing Book*, 1791–94. The boards, separated by the longest springs Sheraton could obtain, provide an elastic enough stool for indoor imitation riding. After S. Giedion, *Mechanisation Takes Command*.

inevitably whether the designer is aware of it or not; a designer who ignores this, and attempts to work as if the objects he is producing are not emotionally charged statements, will find that the charge may backfire on him as has happened in the case of the Hardoy Tripolina.

Memory is to a person what history is to a group. As memory conditions perception and is in turn modified by it, so the history of design and of architecture contains everything that has been designed or built and is continually modified by new work. There is no humanity without memory and there is no architecture without historical reference. In a critical situation such as ours where collective memory is continually being denied and its relevance to the contemporary situation questioned, we approach (collectively) the malaise of the psychologist's patient who represses his past in order to justify his irrational behaviour in the present. It is obvious that in such a situation a chronological account of the patient's past would have relatively little value, particularly if it is obtained from the patient himself. What needs to be examined is the twisted or hidden memory of an experience which will illuminate the current malaise. This must, therefore, be the nature of any historical study which would attempt to relate memory to present experience history to current design. Such redirection of historical study will take time. Its most conspicuous example is Giedion's *Mechanisation Takes Command*, but one or two other writers are beginning to follow suit. However, in *Mechanisation Takes Command* Giedion had not quite (to my mind) drawn the final conclusions which appear by implication in his more recent *The Eternal Present*. Of *Mechanisation Takes Command* one might make the criticism which Claude Lévi-Strauss made of Marcel Mauss' attempt to produce a social theory of symbolism. What Mauss did not realise, and Lévi-Strauss did, was that the attempt was bound to fail because society itself was a symbol.[9]

The great lesson which designers have to learn from Freud is that even the extremes of wilfulness are the products of some form of motivation: and motivation can always be discussed in rational terms. As the psychiatrists have extended the area of responsible moral decision through exposing the pseudo-motives with which we rationalise our approval and disapproval, so they have also expanded the area in which rational discourse about design problems becomes necessary through making us aware of the strong emotional charge which symbolic forms carry. It is no excuse to think that only certain areas (as, for instance, the fronts of public buildings) can be carriers of symbols. The whole of environment, from the moment we name it and think of it as such, is a tissue of symbolic forms: the whole of environment is symbol. To understand how the situation can be managed we are forced to look to the past; no contemporary guide can offer any real help here. This burdens the historian with a task to which he is not altogether used: that of acting as a psychoanalyst to society.

Historiography, particularly as it applies to the history of art, will have to be radically modified if the historian is to perform this kind of function. The grand classification of styles which handbooks teach us will become the immaterial skeleton. But iconology by itself will not provide an adequate substitute: the history of environment must take account of the total persons moving in a social and temporal context. The value of individual works of art or even of overall iconological themes must be studied by reference to the general form of discourse to which they belong: the way

in which their makers wanted to address their fellows, to communicate within the given context; also perhaps how this kind of communication can be transformed as the context changes; which suggests that the grand perspectives and the metaphysical speculations of a Riegl or a Wölfflin will decrease in relevance, and the sort of work which will turn out to be relevant will sometimes appear more like the moralising of the sixteenth-century rhetorician than the pseudo-objectivities of our contemporaries. A knowledge of history on this showing can no longer be treated as a cultural ornament or extra-curricular pastime: nor even as a useful substitute for theoretical thinking: it is clearly a central part of the designer's equipment and of his method.

The Corinthian Order

In response to a naive question from an intelligent student, who could not think why the Greeks, who devised two orders of architecture based on male and female beauty (Doric and Ionic respectively) also needed a third one, I had to think afresh. The matter did require a certain amount of philological interpretation; yet the problem seemed to impose a statement of principle. My answer was in fact published in Domus 426, May 1965 by way of an introduction to the work of two architects for whom I have a particularly close sympathy: Aldo van Eyck and Gino Valle. The great Virgilian scholar, W. F. Jackson-Knight, had died a few months previously, and this article was therefore dedicated to his memory.

All architects used to learn 'the orders' by rote. They were told that there were five of them, and if they bothered to use the better handbooks, they were given some idea of where these 'orders' came from and when. But nobody ever seemed to have worried about why these orders originated, and what their differences were intended to convey.

I should like to re-consider one of the orders here. I shall consider it as an architectural figuration, as an expressive theme, not as an abstract formal device. Nor will I be interested here in references or apparatus. I hope therefore that the reader will forgive me what may sometimes seem to him arrogant assertions. I make them in the interest of providing him with a self-contained statement.

To speak, then, of classical architecture I have to speak first of stem and stone, of tree and altar. A holy tree and a holy stone together in one place are the most primitive kind of shrine we know of, a miniature universe: the growing-and-dying joined with the permanent-and-incorruptible. The men of antiquity could see shrines anywhere. A god might choose anything at all through which to reveal himself. Also everything which was made was holy, because the making of anything was invented by a god or a hero; and therefore any making was an imitation of some first divine action. Each house built was by this token a new world made. To make this clear to themselves as well as to the onlooker many peoples still mark the building of a house – as the ancients always did – with ritual words and gestures which imitate the divine creation of the world.

In the houses of ancient peoples there were very few

columns and these columns were always very important; particularly as they imagined that the world was supported on columns. Sometimes they thought of it as standing on four columns like an animal's body or a table; at others, that there was only one column, a growing one, on which the sky hung like a star-embroidered cloth on a tree and whose roots were fed by the ocean underneath the earth. The ancients sometimes thought that the world turned round such a growing column. Many of the oldest or most primitive columns are reminders about that world pillar; in all probability such earliest columns were wooden. But in time the tree became stone. Stone was already holy in its own different way, so this transformation was not a one-way process; the tree gave to the stone something of its growing, evanescent beauty; the stone gave the tree some of its density and stability.

For more than two thousand years architecture has been dominated by the way in which the Greeks fixed the relation between the different parts of a stone column; also between the column and the beam it carried. The Greeks knew three such canons and the Romans added two more. Apart from the surviving monuments the source for our knowledge of the orders are the writings of the Augustan architect Vitruvius. He was not interested in the Roman interpolations, having over-much respect for the Greeks, perhaps; and so concentrated his attention on the three Greek orders: Doric, Ionic, Corinthian.

Vitruvius' book has been studied with attention by architects since the time of Charlemagne, when it was acknowledged as the only treatise of importance on architecture to have survived from antiquity. Later, in the fifteenth century, these precepts were closely compared with surviving monuments to arrive at a clear idea of ancient methods of building, of the orders in particular, so that architects might imitate them as closely as possible while adapting them to suit the needs of the time. In the end the men of succeeding ages dictated ever-new requirements with such urgency that the orders became a dressing in which the erupting forms were disguised. In the end it was not the methods of the ancients which architects wanted to emulate, but their formulae they wanted to copy. So the orders became a numerical recipe for a correct, dehydrated ornament. The first vernal enthusiasm which led Renaissance architects to look for hidden meanings in Vitruvius' description of the orders sounded like irrelevant fairy-tale twaddle to the reasonable men of the eighteenth century.

'Callimachus drawing the acanthus plant' from R. Fréart de Chambray's *Parallèle des ordres antiques et modernes* Paris 1651.

We are now free to look at the orders afresh since we no longer need them for daily use as ornament. The recipe is worthless but the intention of the ancients and the enduring power of their formulae are very puzzling. Vitruvius himself did not find it altogether easy to explain the origin of the orders and the nature of their differences. Of the Doric and Ionic he says 'in inventing the two kinds of column they [the ancient Greeks] took bare manly beauty quite unornamented as a model for the one, feminine beauty for the other' and so he goes on to the Corinthian 'it has the appearance of maidenly slenderness'. At once aware of the unsatisfactory dissymmetry – two female columns to one male – he offers something of an apology in his detailed account of the origin of the Corinthian order.

Vitruvius begins by suggesting that the 'maidenly' Corinthian was mothered by the 'matronly' Ionic. This has the ring of truth; the two orders share many common characteristics as against the Doric, also the first Corinthian appears four or five hundred years after the first primitive Ionic order. Vitruvius goes on to give an account of the legendary origin of the Corinthian capital: 'a freeborn Corinthian girl, just old enough to think of marriage', he says, 'fell ill and died. After the funeral her nurse gathered into a basket the pots and cups which the girl had liked most when she was alive, carried them to the monument and put the basket on top of it. She covered the basket with a tile so that the things might survive that much longer than if they had just been put out in the open air. By chance she had placed the basket right over an acanthus root which, being pressed down by the weight, put out rather stunted leaves and shoots next spring. The shoots clung to the sides of the basket as they grew and – since they were pressed down by the weight of the tile – were forced into curves and volutes at the corners. Callimachus, who for the elegance and refinement of his carvings in marble was called ''catatechnos'' by the Athenians, passed by the monument just then and noticed the basket and the tender leaves. Pleased with the whole thing and the novel shape, he made some columns for the Corinthians based on this model and fixed the canon of their proportion.' In this curious tale the fictitious elements all fall into a pattern: the girl, the death, the grave offering, the monument, the acanthus, spring, re-birth. Acanthus is the clue. It is not surprising to find it here. The Greeks used many different plants in funerals and commemorations of the dead: marjoram was spread on the bier, cypress boughs nailed to the door of the house of mourning, at which a laurel branch was placed in a bowl of water for lustral sprinkling. Hawthorn leaves were chewed by mourners on the anniversaries of death and on the days when the dead were commemorated. Acanthus leaves were placed at the foot and the head of monuments.

Two varieties of acanthus are known in Greece, acanthus spinosus, (a spiny plant, a small artichoke or cardom) and acanthus mollis. Both have large floppy leaves and straight stalks such as Callimachus must have seen. Like dandelion or lettuce, acanthus oozes white juice when you break the stem and like them, is associated with motherhood and fertility. Like dandelion, too, it will grow even if seeded on

Left
'The Ionic order and its model' and 'The Corinthian order and its model' from John Shute's *The First and Chief Groundes of Architecture* London 1563.

Opposite
'The Corinthian column and its origins' from Claude Perrault's *Les dix livres d'architecture de Vitruve* Paris 1673.

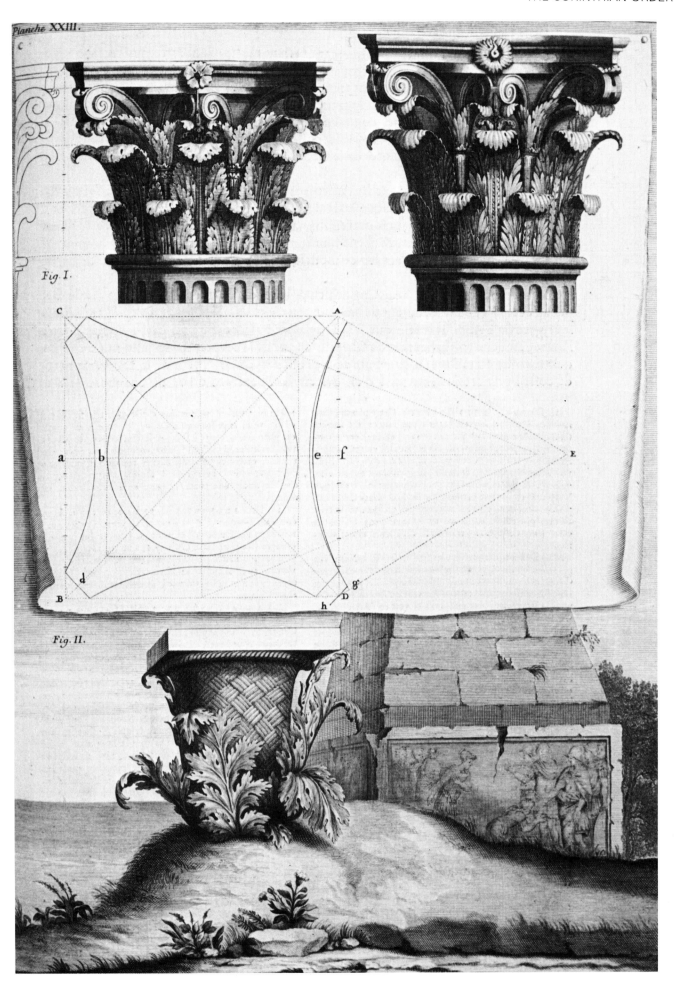

Acanthus spinosus and acanthus mollis.

the stoniest ground and is therefore associated with endurance and the power to renew itself.

The biggest acanthus in art is a great stone one at Delphi. This was a column made up of five limestone drums, altogether about nine metres high, which stood on a podium just before the main entrance of the temple of Apollo at Delphi. The foot and the capital of it survive at the Delphi museum; it had a great acanthus plant as the base and a curiously vegetable shaft, though not clearly an acanthus one. At the top were three diademed, lightly clad women, dancing. They were linked back to back and between them the thick stem of the acanthus grew on to support the cauldron of a bronze tripod whose three feet came down on the acanthus leaves on which the ladies danced. The tripod itself was only 2.5 metres high; only a few steps away there was a bigger and earlier one, a six metre snake tripod; a trophy of the battle of Platea. In any case the approaches to the temple and the treasures were full of votive tripods and at the centre of the cult, at the alleged tomb of Dionysius, at the navel of the earth, stood the golden tripod on which the sibyl sat when the god possessed her and she prophesied.

Apollo is only the god of the sun and the day, he is a playboy of the muses to us; we forget his dark and cruel side; also that at Delphi he reigned alternately with Dionysius according to the seasons. The ladies on the acanthus column belonged to Dionysius, not to Apollo. They are Thyades, priestesses of the dying and resurrected god. Dionysius incarnate in animal or a man was torn apart and buried; from his remains new life sprouted in the acanthus. The name, Thyades, means earth-beaters: who danced at night in winter on Parnassus, and the thumping of their feet awoke Dionysius Lyknos, the new-born spring baby Dionysius cradled in a basket.

Acanthus and Thyades, with a hint of spring; a death too, a ritual death, and perhaps re-birth. The Delphic incident would remain a hint only if the link were isolated, but the Greeks used the acanthus freely in association with their dead. The most common document of this custom are the white-figure lekythoi which crowd the reserve rooms of all important museums in large numbers. They are smallish pots, anything between 10 cm to 1 metre high; tall in proportion with a thin neck, they served for dispensing a thin trickle of expensive oil to pour over the corpse or the monument. On the white unbaked ground which covers most of the body of the pot are represented – drawn rather roughly – various subjects, mostly connected with funeral customs. A common one is a monument, sometimes with the dead person sitting before it or being laid under it. The monument is practically always shown bound by taenia, woollen bands which were often dyed purple and which mourners put over the body after it had been laid out. At the funeral these same bands were tied in knots round the stela. They had a quasi-magical function; they secured the dead person from evil influences; they also ensured the mourners that the spirit of the dead person would not easily return from the grave to pester them. In many, perhaps most of the drawings, a ring of acanthus leaves appears to be stuck in the taenia tied round the top of the stela, or perhaps planted

Right
Acanthus column, Delphi, before 389 B.C. (reconstruction). The largest surviving acanthus in art, which probably stood on an inscribed dedication base to the north east of the temple of Apollo at Delphi.

Far right
Acanthus column, Delphi, details of the Thyades on the capital and of the foot of the monument.

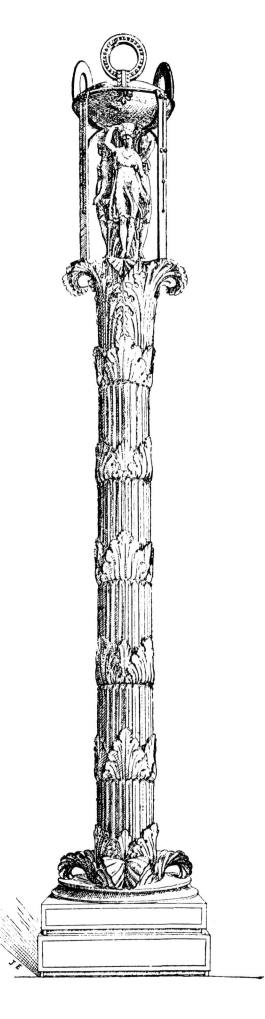

Large white-ground lekythos. Pedimented stele, bound with taenia, has a palmette on the pediment and plants on either side. The stele stands in front of a funeral mound and on steps with small lekythoi and wreaths. On one side of the stele is a young man with spears (dead man? chief mourner?). On the other side is a young woman bearing a wreathed basket.

White-ground lekythos. Two mourners carrying baskets of pottery and taenia on either side of a monument which is crowned with a large acanthus(?) plant. The person in a grieving attitude, seated on the step of the monument, is either a 'professional' mourner or the dead person.

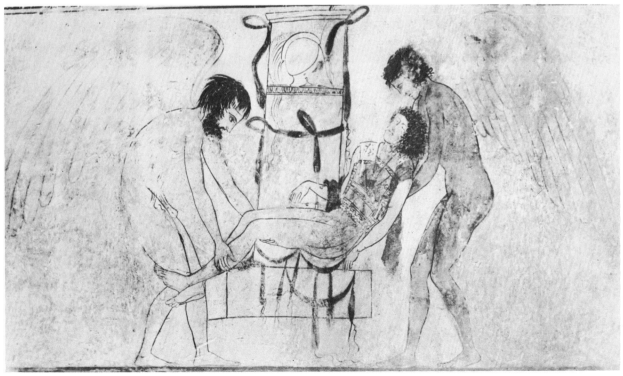

White-ground lekythos. Two mourners at a funeral mound at which lekythoi and other vases, as well as a lyre and a wreath, are set. The mound is crowned by a monument-column bound by taenia and wreaths. The lyre-player may be the dead man.

White-ground lekythos. Death and Sleep lay the dead warrior at his tomb, which is bound by taenia.

Monument of Lysicrates Athens, after 334 B.C.

Bronze archaic lebes on three deity-supported stand of white marble.

in a pot or a basket on top of the monument; sometimes there is an additional bunch of acanthus leaves at the bottom of the column.

The drawing of the leaves is rough and thickish as against the tight conventionalised indication of the palmette finial, so common on Attic gravestones that historians of pottery have always assumed that the acanthus leaves and the palmette are made of different materials. Bronze has often been suggested because many instances of bronze acanthus leaves have been recorded: the most famous perhaps are those which decorated the bronze chariot on which Alexander the Great's embalmed body was taken from Babylon to Alexandria; but more generally there were many other recorded Corinthian columns even as late as the portico of Cn. Octavius in Rome, where the capital of the Corinthian order was formed by attaching bronze leaves to the stone. The green patina of the bronze seemed important since it replaced the live acanthus tied to a wooden shaft. That is what the original Corinthian order must have been made of; and the Greeks wrapped their dead in green shrouds.

On many lekythoi you may see, too, a woman servant

carrying a flat basket like that winnowing basket in which Dionysius Lyknos was cradled, containing ribbons and pots to be put on the tomb. So all the elements in my Vitruvian text have come together and may now be seen to have a more natural and purposeful connection than appears at first reading. Unlike the rather charming fictitious reconstructions of this event by seventeenth-century writers on architecture, my explanation can claim to be satisfactory in that it takes in every element in Vitruvius' melancholy story, though I must turn again to a feature I have introduced, the tripod which I have shown you standing on top of the acanthus column at Delphi.

Not only the Delphic acanthus, but several early Corinthian orders are associated with tripods. The choragic Monument of Lysicrates is the obvious example. This little circular building was really a pretentious stand for the tripod which Lysicrates' choir won in the Dionysiac festival of 334 B.C. It was eighteen metres high and was one of many such monuments of different shapes and sizes that lined the street known as the Street of Tripods which led to the theatre and sanctuary of Dionysius. Above the theatre two further trophy stands survive, Corinthian columns of Roman date. Tripods had the same functions in Greece as the great silver cups which horsemen and football teams win at their various games nowadays. They were competition prizes, particularly in those associated with Dionysius. You may remember that I mentioned the many tripods dedicated at Delphi. Since Mycenean times and probably earlier, the tripod was a prestige object used in exchanges between princes or as an item of display. But tripods were also holy objects; at Delphi the sibyl sat on one so as to be possessed by the god with whose voice she spoke. The tripod started its career as a cauldron, a stewpot on three legs for standing it over a cooking flame; but it acquired meanings which transcended this function. In saga and epic (particularly in those of Indo-European people) there are many stories about inexhaustible cauldrons; cauldrons which represent the miraculous and generous womb of mother earth from which we all come, and to which we must all return; but we return to the womb so as to be born again. Many myths tell the story of a god or hero who short-cut this process by being dismembered, and stewed in a cauldron or tripod to be rejuvenated: Medea specialised in this operation. It may well be that the myth had its origin, as some anthropologists have suggested, in the custom of boiling the dead, to separate the bones from the flesh, current amongst some primitive peoples. The bones were saved for a 'secondary' burial, possibly within the family house or enclosure.

Acanthus and tripod, both of them carrying the message of re-birth, belong together there as did the tripod and maenads, the wildly dancing attendants of the god who died and was reborn. Many of the tripod stands in the Athenian Street of Tripods must have represented a maenad on each of their three faces.

There are few buildings before the end of the fifth century using the Corinthian order; apart from those I mentioned there is the temple of Apollo at Bassae built between 450 and 425, which only has one – the earliest Corinthian column – in the sanctuary. This column was produced within the lifetime of Callimachus of Athens; Callimachus was also credited with perfecting marble drilling and it may well be that he was the first to transform the existing natural or bronze forms into stone. Scopas built the temple of Athena Alea at Tegea about a century later, where there is an external Doric order and an internal Corinthian one; the same combination occurs in tholoi: the Delphic one built about 375 by Theodore of Phocea (perhaps in honour of the hero Phylakes) and the finest of them, by Polykleitus the Younger, the tholos of Asklepius at Epidauros. In these temples the sky god was often paired with the power of the underworld; as at Tegea, Athena with the serpent-king Aleus, or at Epidauros, Apollo with Asklepius. This pairing of orders became a device which fourth-century architects used increasingly: Doric and Corinthian, as at the temple of Zeus at Nemea, or that of the Mother of the Gods at Olympia, or a little later near the end of the fourth century, at Olympia again, the heroon-tholos of the Macedonian kings which combined a bastard Ionic with Corinthian. In the third and second centuries the Greek loss of energy and the orientalisation of many hellenistic princes means that the canonic authority of the order loses a little of its force until it is revived in a new form by the Romans.

I still have to explain why I think the Corinthian order appeared at the moment it did. At the break of the fifth and fourth centuries religious feeling in Greece suffered a transformation. The self-effacement of the individual and the ordered piety of classical Greece had been corroded by attic realism and stoic rationalisation. This provoked a reaction: a pathetic desire for personal salvation, for the comfort of individual survival, prompted a revival of interest in various mystery religions and in such archaic cults as that of Pythagoras. At this time the Ionic order, which with its matronly identity had signified all the world of ideas related to the mother goddess – fertility, death, immortality – gave birth to the order of the maiden, the column of Kore. Persephone, daughter of Demeter and Queen of the Under-world, was the virgin of Greek religion; it is only proper that the order of architecture which was devised to carry the message of personal survival should be maidenly in honour of her. The much later popularity of this column with the Romans responded not only to their taste for elaborate forms but also to their religious preoccupations, and the yet later popularity of the column with Christian builders may have been an echo of this connection.

* * *

If the tone of this article has been bald and assertive, the reader must pardon the unacademic approach to an eminently academic subject. Unacademic because – and here the reader may feel he is owed an apology for being misled – this is not an article about ancient, but about modern architecture. Architects, with all their talk of structure and function, have blinded historians of art to the real nature of the subject they were discussing; and architects once more must look at the buildings of the past and search for the true motives which inspired their predecessors.

The Corinthian order is admirably suited to such a reading. It appeared at a moment of particularly acute self-consciousness, was abundantly documented; a moment of painful transition, when a certain archaic immediacy re-emerged to strip the surface from hellenic sophistication.

So the disruptive influence of orientalising spiritual individualism engendered the Corinthian order, where previously the Doric and the Ionic signified the total polarity of Greek religion: as between Gea and Zeus, between Apollo and Dionysius. The orders were never mutually exclusive, always complimentary.

To understand the orders aright, it seems to me you must think of them as linguistic elements – not of a precise, clipped kind, but as distilled, poetic allusions, having the force of proverbs, or familiar quotations. As the Corinthian order represented the complex of Kore: the underworld, death, resurrection, spring; so the Ionic stood for the world of Demeter, of the mother goddess: fertility, the earth, plants and animals, and also death and resurrection; and the Doric, the world of Zeus and Apollo, of the order dictated by the sky: justice and law, cosmic immutability, fate, and prophecy. All I have done here, therefore, is to read the overwhelming statement which seems to me inherent in these elements of the architectural vocabulary of the ancients, elements which have had a dominant influence on all later building. And I hope to have established that the origin of these elements is not in formal fancy, but that it was a necessary, willed product of the feelings and ideas of the people who devised and used them. That is also the secret of their enduring power. Some of my readers may think that statements of this kind are outside the scope of modern architecture. I think they are not. And since I believe that modern architecture has not yet reached the maturity of a linguistic discipline, I have proposed this interpretation of an ancient commonplace as a lesson and a corrective.

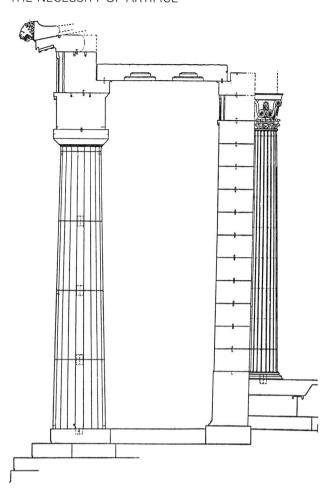

Tholos at Delphi, section.

Opposite
Temple of the Olympian Zeus Athens, after 175 B.C. This great Corinthian temple, designed by Cossutius and dedicated to the greatest of the gods of the sky, was a shrine over that chasm leading into the underworld where the waters of the flood were swallowed. It was founded – according to legend – by Deucalion (the Greek Noah) and contained his tomb, as well as shrines of Kronos, Rhea and Ge.

Tholos in temenos of Athena Polias, Delphi.

The Dark Side of the Bauhaus

This, as it seemed to me, unexceptionable contribution to the history of the Bauhaus provoked the fury of a number of Bauhäusler, who felt that I was trying to denigrate the holy house. In fact my intention – in showing its diversity and richness, and the awareness on the part of some of its masters of the deeper issues touched – had been rather to underline its importance beyond the clichés of the handbooks.

An edited version of this broadcast marking the occasion of the Bauhaus exhibition was published in The Listener, *October 3rd 1968 and a full text in Italian in* Controspazio, *April/May 1970.*

The apologists and the historians of the Bauhaus have always presented it as the shrine of reason in an unreasonable, confused world. I wish to show that this picture is a distortion of what was thought or done. And I propose to suggest that the Bauhaus remains interesting and relevant because it had an irrational, strong dark side.

The rational side of the Bauhaus has particularly strong local roots. The Bauhaus started in Weimar, the 'German Athens' and the birthplace of the German republican constitution – so that even if it only produced about a thousand graduates in its fourteen years of existence, it cannot be treated as the art school of just another small provincial town.

The tag 'German Athens' was Goethe's legacy to Weimar. He lived there most of his adult life, for a time as president of the ducal chamber. Other poets lived there at about the same time – Schiller, Herder, Wieland. Liszt spent some time in the town. Finally Nietzsche retired there; and when he died in 1900 he left his papers and his library in Weimar. When Henry van de Velde, who was one of the founding fathers of Art Nouveau, was summoned to Weimar from his native Brussels to be the Grand Duke's artistic adviser, one of his first tasks was to design the Nietzsche library and archive, which was turned into a kind of philosophical academy. But van de Velde's principal achievement was the foundation of the Grand Ducal School of Arts and Crafts, as an institution quite apart from the old Academy of Fine Arts.

When the First World War broke out, van de Velde, who was a Belgian, found himself in a difficult situation, and cast about for a successor. Finally, in the confused weeks between the fall of the imperial government and the constitution of the new republic, Walter Gropius was appointed. It is with his ideas, as well as those of three other artists, that I propose to concern myself: Kandinsky, Itten and van Doesburg. If I don't say much about Klee it isn't because I don't admire him – he is to my mind by far the greatest artist connected with the Bauhaus (perhaps the greatest artist of his time) – but I choose to discuss those artists who provide a conveniently schematic panorama of attitudes to compare.

Gropius, when he was made head of the Bauhaus (or the Weimar School of Arts and Crafts, as it was called before he effected its graft on the Academy of Fine Arts) was already a well-known figure. He had designed two factories – one of them for the Werkbund exhibition of 1914 – and a number of lesser buildings. As an active member of the Werkbund, which is the ancestor of all design and industry associations, he had given his attention to problems of architecture and industry and had taken a particular interest in the education of designers. He had spent several years working for Peter Behrens who had an enormous influence on his way of thinking, as well as on his taste and style.

Behrens belonged to another generation. He had come to architecture late, having earned his fame as a painter and illustrator. His first building, a house for himself, went up in 1901, and from then his practice grew rapidly. In 1907 he was handed one of the most remarkable commissions of his time: he became the visual dictator of A.E.G., the largest electrical manufacturing company in Europe, which was in rapid expansion at the time. Behrens designed or supervised everything that went on in the firm, from trade catalogue to factory building, from the first electric water-kettles to

WALTER GROPIUS *Model factory* Werkbund Exhibition 1914.

workers' housing. His office was by then sufficiently famous to have attracted, besides Gropius, Mies van der Rohe and Le Corbusier.

Although the A.E.G. commission was more or less unique there was plenty of other work handled by Behrens. *He* was moreover not at all unique. A whole generation of excellent artist-designers, such as Bruno Paul, Hans Poelzig and the brothers Taut, all worked in the spirit which already then was associated with the word *Sachlichkeit*. *Sachlichkeit* is a notoriously difficult word to translate. *Sache* means thing, and the word therefore taken literally means 'thingness' or rather 'thinginess'; it is usually translated as matter-of-fact, realistic, sober, objective. It had been given currency as a slogan in matters of art and design early in this century.

Sobriety is an excellent criterion, though there is nothing new about it. Since Vitruvius practically all writers on architecture have advocated it in their different ways. The sobriety of Behrens' generation was abstemious about particular things, however.

Gropius, who about 1910 was setting out on an independent career, sums it up in a memorandum prepared for Emil Rathenau, the chairman of A.E.G. The memorandum outlines a proposal for an industrialised building undertaking, a factory making prefabricated parts of buildings. It begins in the time-honoured way by explaining what is wrong with architecture at the time – both in terms of taste and in terms of solidity and comfort. The reasons Gropius advances for this state of affairs are the conflict between the contractor whose main interest is to pare his costs, and the architect who wants to raise the cost so as to raise his fee correspondingly. The client's ideal, he says, is the artist, who cares for the quality of the work only, even at his own expense.

But the artist-craftsman would stand no chance against even a partially industrialised building industry. The answer is to mass-produce and to rationalise. Then the architect may be able to devote his attention to the smallest detail without worrying about his fee, while the client will be guaranteed a minimal standard of quality in building elements. This rational and economic solution raises another problem, however: the elements have to be designed in the style suitable for the time. Such a style will arise through harmony resulting from the rhythms of repetition, through a unity of such forms as are acknowledged to be universally good. And Gropius goes on to give a significant list of historical examples where standardisation had excellent

results: Dutch brick houses, French apartment houses in the eighteenth century, German building around 1800 and finally the English terrace house where the mere search for economy brought about a stylistic unity almost as a by-product.

All the examples are of sober, middle-class building; all would have been approved by the architects of Behrens' generation. Gropius' taste was entirely conventional in this sense, even if his consciousness of the pressing industrial problem was relatively novel.

His detailed proposals are not relevant for me now. But I shall come back to a later text of Gropius and point to a shift of emphasis in his thinking: a shift which his contact with certain ideas in the Bauhaus must have operated.

These were ideas current more among painters and sculptors than architects. At the time of which I speak, the decade before the First World War, German art was dominated by such Post-Impressionist painters as Max Liebermann, a friend of Behrens. But vital younger artists were already vocal and demanding of public attention. Prominent among them were two groups – one the Expressionist Die Brücke, who had moved to Berlin in about 1910. Their ideology combined Nietzsche and the primitivism of the South Sea Islands. In Munich another group, Der Blaue Reiter, came together round the dominating figure of the Russian Wassily Kandinsky. It was in every way a more important group, and included Franz Marc, August Macke, Alexei Jawlensky, and above all Paul Klee.

Kandinsky's intellectual springboard was Theosophy, which at the beginning of the century had a wide and excited following. The word Theosophy means, generally, speculation about the nature of the world with the aid of some direct revelation as against philosophy which has to do without such props. More specifically it appears in the title of a society which was founded in 1875 by Helena Petrovna Blavatsky, a Russian lady who claimed to have been initiated in Tibet and who produced psychical phenomena under the alleged guidance of Mahatmas, universal sages possessed of universal secrets which they communicated to her. Whatever the authenticity of these revelations, Madame Blavatsky was acknowledged by 1891 as the head of a great international organisation. Concisely put, this society had three aims: the universal brotherhood of man; the study of comparative religion to find their common elements; and the investigation of what was then called 'the hidden power latent in man' by which was meant some of the things that now go by the name of para-psychology.

All this is worth rehearsing here because of the society's great influence on the arts in northern Europe, particularly in Germany and Holland. In Germany a branch of the society was founded before the turn of the century, and in 1902 Rudolf Steiner, who until then was chiefly known for his studies of Goethe, became its secretary. Steiner was to claim private revelation himself. The nature of these revelations appears to have been influenced by his Goethe studies; but in any case, they were so particular that in 1913 Steiner came into conflict with the international leaders of the society. He then founded his own group, the Anthroposophical Society, with headquarters in Dornach, in Switzerland. Its buildings are one of the most remarkable monuments of German Expressionism. Steiner's followers still practise a modified version of the master's style, as being the only one consonant with divine revelation. Before that time, early in the century, Steiner had not exalted his taste into an immutable canon. But he was already a famous

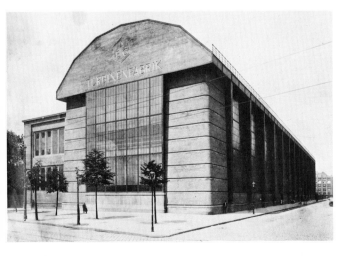

PETER BEHRENS *A.E.G. Turbine Factory* Berlin 1908–09.

RUDOLF STEINER *Goetheanum* Dornach. The first wooden building of 1913 which was burned down in 1922 and the second concrete building of 1923. Steiner died in 1925 before the completion of the second building.

writer and lecturer. Kandinsky read some of Steiner's books and heard some of his lectures, and was – clearly – very impressed. There is no doubt that the strong revival of interest in Goethe's theory of colour, for instance, is due largely to this contact between Kandinsky and Steiner.

The fundamental doctrine, which Steiner claimed to have found through – or rather in – Goethe, was that the artist does *not* (as Hegel thought) make a sensory phenomenon out of an idea; but on the contrary, he shapes the sensory phenomenon *into* an idea. The artist's work does not open the doors for the spirit to enter everyday life; on the contrary, he raises the everyday to the spiritual plane, he releases the spiritual content of physical reality.

For these abstruse reasonings Steiner claimed the status of a Copernican discovery. Certainly, there is no doubt that Kandinsky found it highly convincing, that he believed it as the only valid explanation of his activity. It followed (to him) that he must search for the immutable laws of artistic creation, which would correspond to the laws of nature. Such laws, Kandinsky thought, were dictated by an inner necessity. This interior necessity operates through three spiritual elements: firstly, the element of the artist's personality; secondly, the stylistic constraints determined by the society in which the artist operates; thirdly – and in conflict with the other two – the element of eternal and pure artistry.

To Kandinsky, and to his friends of the Blaue Reiter, the laws of art, like the laws of nature, seemed not only immutable but universally applicable to all the arts. In particular music and the visual arts corresponded very closely. Again, this is not a new idea, but one which has been endemic to esoteric thinking since the Pythagorean school. Kandinsky had been confirmed in his conviction about this unity by a quasi-mystical experience when he was moved to see music during a performance of *Lohengrin*, and on the contrary to have heard the colours while examining a painting by Monet. He had intended to write an opera on the subject, which got no further than a ballet suite, called *Der Gelbe Klang*, the Yellow Sound.

Even in his time Kandinsky was not isolated. The Symbolists in France had similar ideas; Debussy and even Satie subscribed to them. And Scriabin, the musician who was perhaps closest to Kandinsky's way of thinking, published a colour exegesis of his tone-poem *Prometheus*. Behind all these is the figure of Richard Wagner with his conviction that his music-drama could only be properly experienced as a total work of art: *Gesamtkunstwerk* is the German word for this idea. Wagner's demands engulfed not only the music, the words, the sets and costumes, but the movements of actors and dancers and the architecture of the very building; all had to be woven into a similar pattern of rhythm, of intention, of design. These ideas were familiar through Wagner's work and writings, as well as through apologists: one of whom, Edouard Schuré, devoted the two final chapters of his Wagner monograph to these ideas.

Schuré was one of the principal apostles of a general occult movement, not necessarily associated with organised Theosophy. For that matter none of the Blaue Reiter artists ever made much of the membership of any such official group. But with Schuré, with Steiner, and with most of the theosophists, they believed that a new spiritual epoch was about to begin in the world, and that the preparatory time of regeneration had already started. Kandinsky thought that the dematerialising of the arts was firm evidence of this tendency: in his first book, *On the Spiritual in Art*, he expressly names Matisse's freeing of colour and Picasso's

decomposition of the solid form as pointers in this direction. Since the beginning of the new era was expected soon, those who received the esoteric doctrine did not need to keep it secret any longer. In fact, it was their duty to hasten the beginning of the new epoch by teaching and proselytising – all of which was consonant with Kandinsky's highly didactic temperament. It is hardly surprising therefore to find that he attached an enormous importance to teaching. When he returned from Russia (to which he had gone for the duration of the war) he was soon summoned to the Bauhaus, of which he quickly became the assistant director, remaining in this position until it was wound up by the Nazis in 1933.

At first sight there would seem to be little in common between the rational, Behrens-guided attitudes of Gropius, and the ultra-cosmopolitan Theosophy of Kandinsky. The link was established by a third person, Johannes Itten. The circumstances of the meeting between Itten and Gropius are themselves interesting...

In 1910 (as Alma Mahler has told the whole world in her autobiography) Gropius fell in love with her while on a summer holiday in Austria. Mahler was still alive, and it came to nothing. After Mahler's death, Alma went off with Kokoschka, and only when *that* story finished did she try to find Gropius again. By then he, like Kokoschka, was at the front. But in 1915 Gropius and Alma Mahler married: it was a short-lived marriage, with Gropius at the front most of the time, but spending his leaves in Vienna; and during these he came into contact with Alma Mahler's highly varied and brilliant circle. Many of its members had interests like Kandinsky; though linguistic philosophy and psycho-analysis were the two intellectually demanding things happening in Vienna at the time. Kokoschka and Loos were both connected with Alma Mahler; and she regarded Arnold Schönberg as her husband's heir. Schönberg had exhibited with the Blaue Reiter when he had painted; as had Johannes Itten. The meeting with this Swiss painter was to prove the most influential for the Bauhaus.

Itten had begun teaching art in Stuttgart but went to Vienna in 1916 to start an independent school. Gropius must have been very impressed with Itten's results, because he invited him to the Bauhaus as part of the original staff, to draw up an initiatory course for new entrants. This elementary course turned out to give an impetus to the whole of Bauhaus teaching. Moreover, Itten came with a group of some fourteen students of his from Vienna, who formed a kind of nucleus for propagating his ideas.

Itten's teaching was highly structured. It was explicitly intended to rid the student of his previously acquired schemata, and to force him into thinking problems through in a coherent fashion. But not only to think, also to experience them with the whole of his person. The course began with free associative drawing, tightened to the tonal analysis of planes, with reference to the old masters in particular. Then came the study of materials: precise representation made the student acutely aware of the structure of what he represented. More complex formal studies introduced the analysis of the work of the old masters: both in terms of mathematical proportion, and also in terms of rhythm, and the way the two are combined with tonal values to give a picture the meaning the artist had intended. This last exercise was sometimes done by simplifying the tonal pattern of the painting into calligraphed forms, so that the meaning of the elements in the picture was condensed into a text which communicated by its own form as well as

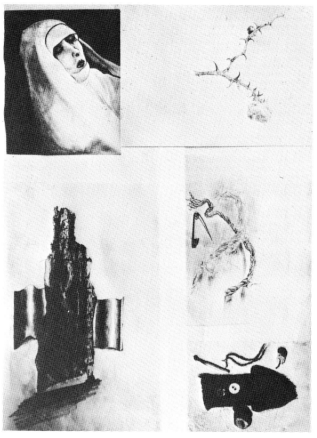

evoking the original work of art as a rhythmic and tonal unity. From these exercises the student proceeded to the practice of free rhythm – a gymnastic resulting in drawn exercises – and the theory of colour.

Let me assure you that all this has very little to do with the various play-therapies which in this country and in America pass for an elementary design course. For Itten the exercises were not an isolated pedagogic experiment. He thought of the Bauhaus as a way of life. Hence the elaborate pseudo-rituals, so insufferable to some of his contemporaries, with which he surrounded it – the examination by a hierophant co-pupil whose intuition was regarded as absolute; the design of special costumes for the students, which Itten himself also wore; the introduction of a highly seasoned, supposedly Mazdean health-diet in the Bauhaus canteen, of which Alma Mahler complained on one of her Weimar visits to Gropius – you could smell a Bauhäusler round the corner, she said, because they reeked so of garlic. These absurdities were to some extent eliminated from the Bauhaus when Itten left in 1923 and the foundation course was remodelled by one of Itten's pupils, Joseph Albers, and a newcomer, the Hungarian artist, Laszlo Moholy-Nagy, though the remodelling made it that much more like play-therapy, and it lost some of the high charge and bite that Itten gave it.

Moholy appeared in Weimar at the invitation of Theo van Doesburg. Although van Doesburg never taught at the Bauhaus himself, he went to Weimar because of the Bauhaus. He was – as his assumed name implies – a Dutchman (his real name was Kramer) and he was an abstract painter and a Dadaist poet; all under different names. But the essential thing to my theme was his foundation of the de Stijl group with Piet Mondrian.

Again I must introduce Theosophy. Although van Doesburg's connection with Theosophy is sketchy, Mondrian joined it before 1900, and went on keeping a photograph of Madame Blavatsky in his studio for many years. There is no doubt that Mondrian and van Doesburg had a great deal in common with Kandinsky, although van Doesburg appears less interested in esoteric teaching than either of them. The ideas of the spiritual life were probably first mediated to him by Kandinsky, whose book *On the Spiritual in Art* van Doesburg read when it appeared; and later through Mondrian, with whom he had so much in common. But in his own aphorisms his attitude was more dogmatic, as well as more directly Hegelian than Mondrian.

'All the arts have an equivalent content. Only the mode and the means of expression are different.' And again: 'Aesthetic experience is expressed in relationships'; almost as a corollary, another aphorism: 'The objective, natural appearance of the thing, sensorily experienced, will be destroyed – the more radically *in* the experience, the

Top
Exercise in rendering the characteristic qualities of various materials, from Johannes Itten's preliminary course. In the top left hand corner is a charcoal drawing after Grünewald.

Centre
CHARLOTTE VICTORIA *Volume and space study in glass and calico* from Moholy-Nagy's preliminary course.

Bottom
Studies in the three dimensional use of paper from Joseph Albers' preliminary course, c.1927. Different paper foldings, a multiplicity of possibilities for different designs with, and despite, economical utilisation of the given material.

stronger this experience.' Again, directly following from this: 'In aesthetic experience individual difference becomes organic indifference.' Behind van Doesburg's teaching there is the conviction that the accidental, the individual, breeds confusion and disharmony. The universal, the constant, leads to harmony. This was a belief shared with Mondrian, to whom all that was individual was inherently tragic, and who sought, first through the experience of Cubism, then through the successive reduction of his expressive means, to attain a law of universal polarity. Behind this search are ideas which owe more to Hegel than to Goethe; and perhaps even more to the quasi-scientific neo-Platonism of the Dutch philosopher Schoenemakers, whose friendship with Mondrian produced the whole vocabulary of Dutch abstract art.

All this comes into focus with van Doesburg's arrival in Weimar in 1921. Van Doesburg was not asked to teach at the Bauhaus, but he held public classes, not altogether with the blessing of the Bauhaus hierarchy.

He disapproved, of course, of the intensely 'material' and 'individual' nature of Itten's foundation course. In his view everything had to be pared to minima: studies of old masters were in this sense completely useless; the development of collage encouraged concentration on the accidental, the contingent. Moreover, the insistence on physical emotional involvement in the process grated on van Doesburg's modernity, as it would have on Mondrian's. Kandinsky may have practised Yoga; all this business about breathing exercises while drawing, the diet, the costumes – made up the very environment in which, as he said, he had spread 'the poison of the de Stijl doctrine'.

And yet, in another way, the ideas of Kandinsky and Gropius by-passed those of Itten when they came into contact with van Doesburg's. The idea, for instance, that by breaking down the physical structure of material, modern processes of production denaturalise matter, and therefore make it more nearly 'spiritual' must have been very sympathetic to Gropius, as well as to Kandinsky. As against the curious 'naturism' of Itten, the followers of de Stijl insisted that the metropolitan environment is the only one for the artist. The metropolis (says Mondrian) is nearer to the artist than nature, because in the city what is natural has already been stiffened up, and given order by the human spirit – again this may have appealed to Gropius, but I doubt if Itten, or even Klee, would have found it very congenial. The irony of the situation was that although van Doesburg, being too dogmatic for Gropius and his friends, found no perch in the Bauhaus, Itten too was forced to leave Weimar.

From this turmoil there arose a curious synthesis. The 'elementarism', as van Doesburg called it, of the three principal plane forms – square, circle, triangle – and of the three primary colours, is absorbed by Kandinsky. The famous Bauhaus exercise, in which the uninformed were given a sheet with the three forms and three coloured pencils – red, yellow and blue – and asked to fill each form with the appropriate colour dates from this period, and is a reduction of the many ideas to which I have alluded.

It is sometimes quoted as an instance of extreme rationalism. But there is nothing particularly rational about it: on the contrary, it is the product of a highly developed esoteric doctrine, according to which the inner laws of nature are becoming increasingly apparent to the general.

When a thorough-going rationalist like Hannes Meyer, who succeeded Gropius as the director of the Bauhaus in 1929, tried to eradicate the esoteric heritage of the Blaue Reiter and Itten's pedagogic experiments, he was instantly got rid of. Meyer, the rationalist, was in fact the odd man out, for the Bauhaus certainly cultivated a mutual awareness in its members. Van Doesburg's attitude to the machine may well have persuaded artists like Kandinsky and Klee that standardisation in building and industrial design were quasi-spiritual disciplines. While Gropius grew impatient of his self-imposed sobriety, writing for the English public in 1955 he speaks of Modern architecture as a movement that 'must be purged from within if its original aims are to be saved from the materialism and the false slogans inspired by plagiarism and misconception'. Catch phrases like 'functionalism' or 'Die Neue Sachlichkeit', says Gropius, or 'fitness' for 'purpose' have deflected appreciation from the new architecture . . . The aesthetic satisfaction of the human soul is just as important as the material . . . What is far more important than structural economy and functional emphasis is the intellectual achievement which made it possible.

I should perhaps say here that the German word *geistig* can be translated into English as either 'spiritual' or 'intellectual': and I wonder if 'spiritual' is not what Gropius meant here. In any case, he has as it were inverted his attitude. The aims whose fulfilment seemed self-justified in 1910 become, by 1955, the means to a spiritual and intellectual liberation.

I hope that I will not risk paradox if I now accuse the Bauhaus masters – not of an excessive rationalism – but rather of not stating the religious, or quasi-religious postulates for what they were doing; or at any rate of not stating them explicitly. Only Itten and Klee have a clean record in this respect: and they were the two Bauhaus masters who realised most clearly the danger of van Doesburg's excessive devotion to modernity; to interpreting every technological advance as a spiritual leap forward.

The Bauhäusler were only remotely aware of the great issue of alienation of the conditions imposed on the industrial worker in a society which accepted productivity as the ultimate criterion of values. They had of course heard of Marx, but Ruskin and Morris were mainly writers on art as far as they were concerned, and Brecht does not seem to have interested them – not collectively, at any rate.

Itten seems to me the central figure of the Bauhaus heritage, because his method was animated by the conviction that the whole personality must be involved in work: the designer's and the artist's activity must involve the mind, the body, the senses and the memory, and the unconscious urges.

Whatever Itten's weaknesses or follies, this essential truth remains to me the most relevant facet of the Bauhaus, and the exercises he evolved the only possible introduction to a modern formal language. In any account of the Bauhaus Itten must not be by-passed as Kandinsky and Gropius by-passed him in 1923. It may be that he represents the Bauhaus at its darkest. But then I think it was also the Bauhaus at its richest.

Two Houses by Eileen Gray

After the publication of her Centre de Vacances in Le Corbusier's book Des Canons, des Munitions? Merci: Des Logis ... SVP *(Paris, 1937) to coincide with the exhibition of her model in the Pavillon des Temps Nouveaux at the World Exhibition that year, nothing by Eileen Gray was published until a piece of mine appeared in* Domus *469 in December 1968. Her work was so diverse, so prophetic, that a cult was bound to develop round it sooner or later. In the meantime, I had had the privilege of contact with that remarkable lady, and the opportunity to explore her work in greater detail. There is now a considerable body of writing about her which is listed in the catalogue of an exhibition held at the Victoria and Albert Museum, London and the Museum of Modern Art, New York at the beginning of 1980. I have selected this article, originally published in* Perspecta *13/14, 1971, rather than my earlier essays about her, since it is the least anecdotal and comes closest to raising theoretical problems.*

For an architectural œuvre two houses, a few interiors and some unexecuted projects might seem relatively modest. In the particular case of Eileen Gray the modest quantity is in sharp contrast to the extraordinary quality: quality high enough to set her among the masters of the Modern Movement, however condensed her accomplishment. In particular it is the sophistication and assurance of her work which seems most surprising: her very first building designed in 1926 – though not occupied until 1929 – already displayed a full and original understanding of the language of the Modern Movement up to that date, and gave it an original interpretation.

This first building, a house at Roquebrune, was taken by Jean Badovici, the editor of *Architecture Vivante*. Badovici was, of course, well aware of all that was going on in modern design and would have been particularly familiar with what was going on in Paris. Through some of the time when this building was being designed he must have been working on the 1927 issue which published in detail the buildings at the Weissenhof colony in Stuttgart. When Eileen Gray met Badovici she was already involved in matters of design. She had been one of the earliest women students at the Slade School of Art in London just before 1900. Some time later – about 1907 – she moved to Paris to the apartment she still occupies in the rue Bonaparte. And

although for some time before World War I she had apprenticed herself to a Japanese lacquer craftsman in London, and had travelled widely – particularly by air in the early days of air travel – Paris has been her home since then.

Before World War I she had opened an atelier round the corner from her flat, in the rue Visconti, first making lacquer objects, then other furniture. At this time she also received her first commissions for complete interiors. In 1922 she showed a room at the Union des Artistes Modernes, which brought her into contact with other exhibitors, notably J. J. P. Oud; it was probably at his suggestion that the Dutch review *Wendingen* devoted an issue to her furniture, fabrics and interiors, when she exhibited again in the Union des Artistes Modernes, and opened a shop, dealing mostly in her own designs: various pieces of furniture as well as carpets and rugs, and some fabrics. There were some excellent light fittings and screens in lacquer, the material she employed so very originally and brilliantly.

The issue of *Wendingen* was introduced by Jan Wils, a member of the De Stijl group and the architect of Amsterdam Stadium; it also carried an article about her work by Jean Badovici, who was then already co-editor, with Albert Morancé, of *Architecture Vivante*.

Before this time her work had occasionally declined – naturally enough – to what is now called Art Deco. But even about her earliest pieces there is a modest elegance, a formal nicety and a sharp appreciation of the quality of material – whether poor or noble – which is nearer in spirit to the work of Adolf Loos, or even Mies van der Rohe than to Djo Bourgeois or Francis Jourdain.

The meeting with Badovici was to prove decisive for Eileen Gray. He appreciated the particular inclination of her talent and suggested that she should venture into architecture. There seemed to be no client at hand, however, and Eileen Gray decided to build for herself. She found two sites on the Riviera, one at Roquebrune, the other at Castellar; both were sloping sites which presented great difficulties as far as main facilities and the supply of building materials were concerned; but both commanded magnificent views. The first house to be built was the one at Roquebrune, the one which was to become Badovici's home. She began work on it in 1926; the house was not occupied until 1929, however, and was then also published in *Architecture Vivante* as the 'Maison en Bord de Mer'.

In this house at Roquebrune Eileen Gray's previous work is eclipsed and transformed, purged of any Art Deco velleities. How much this is due to Badovici's influence is

EILEEN GRAY *Tempe a Pailla* Castellar 1932–34, entrance from the road. The garage is built on what had been an old cistern, while steps beyond the gate lead upwards to the guest room level and continue to the living terrace.

EILEEN GRAY *E-1027* west end, looking up from the sun trap.

EILEEN GRAY *E-1027* Roquebrune 1927, main floor plan.

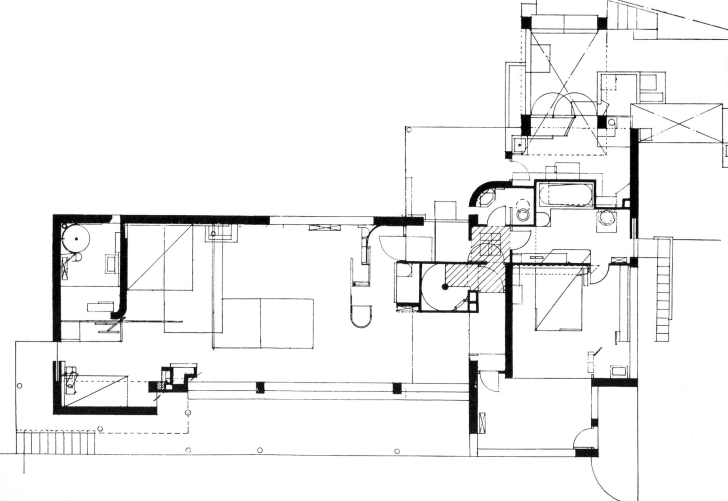

EILEEN GRAY *E-1027* living room with dining recess.　　　　EILEEN GRAY *E-1027* main bedroom.

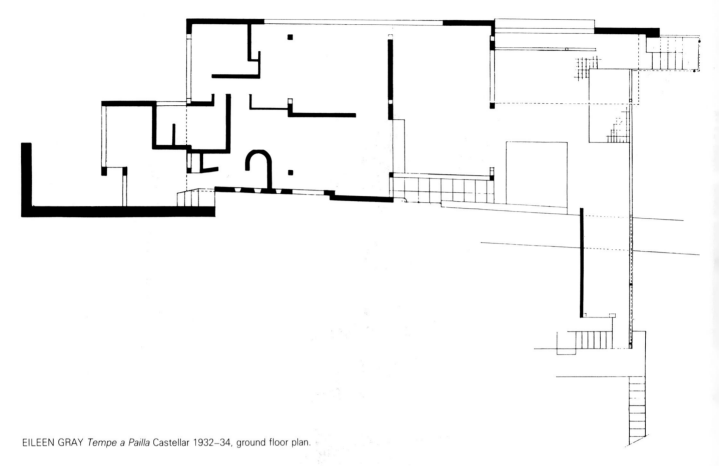

EILEEN GRAY *Tempe a Pailla* Castellar 1932–34, ground floor plan.

now difficult to tell; certainly he had a familiarity with all the latest developments of the Modern Movement which Eileen Gray herself probably lacked. The nature of this influence may be illustrated by the analogous case of a contemporary: Pierre Chareau's only interesting work in the early thirties was done during his collaboration with B. Bijvoet. But when Bijvoet went back to Holland Chareau's work lapsed from any distinction; Eileen Gray's on the other hand had from the outset been lighter and much more accomplished than Chareau's and simply took on a decisive turn after 1925: it continued to develop, and to grow in assurance.

The publication of the 'Maison en Bord de Mer' has a long preface ('De l'éclecticisme au doute') in the form of a dialogue between Badovici and Miss Gray. It contains an appeal (unusual for its time) against the over-intellectualising of architecture; for a dramatising of the essential forms to which *Sachlichkeit* had purged building. This dramatisation might be brought about, or at any rate nearer, if as much attention was paid to the design of interiors as was then paid to exteriors. Interiors had hitherto been neglected by the best modern architects: it is worth remembering that at the time she designed the house, Le Corbusier was still using Thonet chairs and club armchairs, and that it is almost contemporary with the Bauhaus masters' house.

Miss Gray also explicitly disassociates herself from the excesses of open planning, from what she calls 'le style camping'. The 'Maison en Bord de Mer' is indeed hardly an open plan at all. On the contrary it is almost reasoned out into a container for a carefully articulated way of life. The visitor approaches along the north wall of the house, to a porch which connects the hall and the kitchens (outdoors for the summer, indoors for the winter). In the porch the visitor has to turn around 180° before he can open the front door. This introduces him directly into the space of the main living

room, through a section of it screened by a hall cupboard. But this very large room (approximately 40' × 15') is further marked out into a recessed dining area next to the entrance, and by a fireplace at the further end of it, which screens an auxiliary bedroom in a recess. This has a shower-room adjoining it, screened from the main space by cupboards analogous to the ones which screen the hall space, so making it into a kind of boudoir.

The living room opens onto a terrace, from which it is divided by a range of sliding-folding windows which open out against two columns. The terrace is further screened from the outside by a set of engulfing awnings which shelter it against the southern and western sun. The entering visitor, who peers through the slatted blinds which screen the horizontal window strip nearest the entrance, may have his view entertained at four levels: at the same slats, at the window behind it, at the southern sliding-folding window and at the terrace awnings. Correspondingly, anyone inside the main living room knows himself to be separated from the outside world by an intermediate zone.

The bedroom may be entered either from the front hall through a bathroom suite or from an isolated atelier, but not directly from the living room. A spiral staircase leads down to a guest room and a servant's room under the pilotis, as well as to a sheltered terrace.

With all this, an enormous care has been taken over the surfaces, as much – if in a rather different spirit – as in Eileen Gray's earlier work. For instance, the main ceilings are not plastered, but are in painted exposed concrete, the roof slab being suspended from the beams so as to avoid the unpleasant details at the joint of wall and ceiling, and the cracked ceiling plaster. But it is not only the structural surfaces and the colours which are so carefully arranged. The house was conceived as a design problem in the spirit

EILEEN GRAY *Tempe a Pailla* living terrace.

EILEEN GRAY *Tempe a Pailla* view from the road.

EILEEN GRAY *Tempe a Pailla* view of the terrace showing adjustable metal blinds.

of the preface quoted earlier, and a whole range of furniture including the now famous wood-frame upholstered chair and the armchair in rolls of white leather (which Eileen Gray now calls 'la Chaise Bibendum') was created for the occasion. She also designed and wove all the rugs for the house: so that with its decorations and furniture, the house formed one of the most remarkable 'ensembles' of the time.

The fate of the house has been both kind and curious. Le Corbusier had befriended the fisherman who bought the adjoining site, and when this fisherman enlarged his house to include a small bistro, Le Corbusier built a small cabin adjoining it. Towards the end of the war he painted five of his major wall-pictures in the house, which then still belonged to Badovici, but has now passed to Madame Staalberg, who has treated it as the great heritage which it certainly is.

The other of the two houses, at Castellar, has had a much less distinguished fate: just after the war it was bought by

Graham Sutherland, who belongs to that anecdotal and calligraphic English artistic tradition which is implacably opposed to Modern architecture, indeed to any serious architecture which cannot be usefully considered as a ruin. And he has 'adapted' the house to his taste, so destroying its exquisite integrity. Yet the Castellar house, as I have suggested earlier, is a much more accomplished exercise. Again, the main rooms are on one floor and the house is built on a terraced hillside. While at Roquebrune the piloti rose out of the waterside cliff, at Castellar the smooth concrete walls rise, rather irregularly, out of a random rubble podium. The main approach is through the terrace this time, over a passerelle from the garden, and up an open concrete staircase from the street. The terrace opens onto two panoramic views. The blinds, which were used on one small horizontal window at Roquebrune, here act as a fully-fledged brise-soleil, much as the awnings had done at Roquebrune.

But they not only act as a brise-soleil: Eileen Gray was

already using the adjustable louvred metal blinds as separate structural units, since they run in heavy and very visible metal frames and assume great importance in the visual complexity of the house: at one point, the north-east view from the terrace, the inner space is separated from the outside with only a dwarf wall supporting an independent brise-soleil of the kind I have just described.

As at Roquebrune, such details are very much part of the whole organisation, as are the furnishings. The main bedroom, for instance, which faces the same direction as the terrace, that is, north-east – for the view – has a circular glass dome let in the ceiling to catch the sunlight. This opening may be screened with a counter-balanced circular shield. The main clothes cupboard in the same room, which serves to articulate the dressing-room area, has rounded ends, and opens by sliding half the metal 'capsule' horizontally. There are several further such fresh and brilliant touches even in this one room; the formal sophistication of the detail is backed by the use of colour and texture. Again, as at Roquebrune, everything bears the mark of having been carefully considered. The upholstery has not only been supervised by the designer, but she has designed and had woven the materials as well as the rugs and carpets. Those of us familiar with latter-day proceedings, when an architect may think it in order to dictate the whole furnishing and even the details of the decoration to his client for fear that he might 'spoil' his building by use, may find some comfort in these proceedings. Eileen Gray built for herself; the houses were original, carefully considered, and matched to an open, relaxed way of life. In spite of the concentration on the intimately useful detail, the overall form is sufficiently strong to survive the kind of harsh treatment implied by a series of frescoes of Le Corbusier (though not the grosser evisceration, which no building, however strong, could survive).

The same care which she gave to the houses she spent on the design of a tiny one-room apartment, 24' × 15' (i.e. a golden section), producing a habitable space which almost has the quality of a Moholy-Nagy 'light modulator'. The main space, 15' square, is a bed-living-room, with the kitchen, bathroom and hall neatly packed into the remaining 9' ×15'. The tightly packed uses are screened from each other both by a primitive form of flexible door and very ingenious perforated metal screens.

This room, more than the houses in a way, provides an example of the kind of dramatisation she had talked of in 'De l'éclecticisme au doute'. Her work is always modest, reasonable, yet so fresh and exquisite as to be exhilarating. In the Paris where Giacometti had been earning his living making wrought-iron firedogs, it could not have a great success. Indeed there is very little executed work after this: most of it is projects such as the prefabricated elliptical-section house (1937) and the sculptor's studio of 1937. Of 1937 too, the large model for the holiday centre for the Pavillon des Temps Nouveaux at the world exhibition (Le Corbusier's 'tent' pavilion), and some later schemes, as well as much furniture before the war and some commissioned interiors. There is some work after the war as well, but all this is outside my province.

It is the houses and the one-room apartment which remain her most important 'standing' achievement. A tenuous achievement it may be, but unmatched for a relaxed and elastic control of the visual ambience, control which fits both a style of living and a built form and yet is sufficiently independent from the latter to allow for a transformation to a radically different life-style.

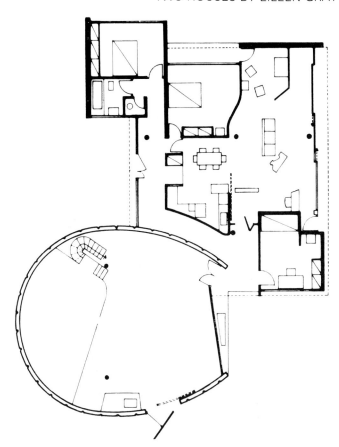

EILEEN GRAY *Sculptors' Studio* 1937, ground floor plan.

The Necessity of Artifice

Commissioned by the Institute for Architecture and Urban Studies in New York, of which I was then a Fellow, for their special issue of Casabella 359–360, December 1971, *this article deals with a perennial common-place of architectural argument which considers design as problem-solving. Incidentally, it also attempts to restate the language/building analogy not in terms of the merely structural and morphological parallels then in vogue, but by appealing to linguistic procedures which deal with rather complex statements such as those of rhetoric – methods which are being used (without necessarily being understood) in visual advertising. This concern was allied to my interest in the use of rhetoric by certain seventeenth-century architects, particularly Borromini.*

Ten or fifteen years ago the word 'pollution' was only heard on the lunatic fringe. This year every candidate for political office in the United States, and some in Britain, has been obliged to take some stance towards it. This change cannot simply be due to the mounting pressure from 'elderly radicals': the problem impinges increasingly on Everyman – too many stretches of beach are rendered useless to holiday makers, too many shirt cuffs are frayed to shreds in the sulphurated air, bronchitis is on the increase in spite of antibiotics. It is all too evident.

For some time now, no one, however remotely concerned with design, has been able to avoid the greater issue of urban blight (of which pollution is a symptom). And yet, even the dichotomy between midtown office space forbiddingly vacant at the weekend and the quasi-rurality of the suburb disguises the source of the trouble: the vast hinterland of industrial production and industrial waste which too often are excluded from the planner's talk and his practice. The hinterland is put outside the normal urban framework. The designer's model is still the metropolis which exchanges, administers, consumes: consumes products of the banished industry and of an agriculture from which it is entirely removed. The planner is too often concerned with exchange and too little with production.

The exchange and production metropolis was generated and compacted by economic and social forces which are no longer effective. Therefore industry has lately been moving into the open countryside well away from the city centre, carrying with it its own trail of suburban blight. The commercial hub of the metropolis meanwhile has been decaying under the gentle suasion of electrical communications, its vast paper memories condensing onto tiny spools of magnetic tape; the cosmopolitan population will not amalgamate into an undefined social porridge but is fissuring along the borders of new loyalties, around new centres of power. For the urban planner, for the architect, this is a confusing situation. Since decades now – since the garden city movement in England and Germany – the architect and the planner have been without a programme formulated by social establishments, and consequently, without a secure place in an organisation whose direction in building was sure. They have therefore taken upon themselves the ungrateful task of social planning which in present circumstances has even assumed the unsavoury name of social engineering. The word 'engineer' introduces a further misunderstanding. Architects and planners have for nearly a century found their essential concerns trivialised.

Seeing the culturally unfettered engineer and the quasi-scientific sociologist as their superiors, they have deliberately blurred the parameters of their competence so as to arrogate to themselves some of the esteem enjoyed by their apparently superior near-colleagues.

The architect and planner have both a much humbler and – ultimately – more effective role. It is not their business to solve the problem of society, indeed I very much doubt if (at that scale) it is their business to solve any problems at all. The duty of the architect and urban planner is to give physical form to a social establishment, to provide the screens which the passer-by outside and the user-participant within recognise as the demarcation lines of a social situation whether it is a bungalow or the city hall of megalopolis. His business is therefore in the first place with what he can manipulate: with the brute matter on which he will operate and with its surfaces, whose scansion will transform the inert material into a carrier of intentions. The screens which the designer constructs (and they may be anything from paper slides to huge stone or concrete walls) are the stage on which the action occurs. They are not part of the action, they cannot even directly influence it. Their relationship to it is always so varied and so indirect that the rules according to which they will develop have to be constituted independently of the more subtle and complex pattern of action. Which leaves yet another matter open and critical: the scansion of surface, although independent of action, has a relation to it analogous to that between a play and its physical setting. A stage set, however, although intended to accommodate particular movements and configurations (exits, entrances, trap doors, etc.) will have its more complex and varied analogues in any building (doors and windows, drains and electrical supply, air conditioning, etc.), but what will weld them together will be the designer's intention to create a coherent visual entity. When this kind of entity is isolated from the general milieu, it is called a form. As the social milieu cannot be differentiated, cannot be read without isolating establishments within it, whether they be families, communes or even poker games, so the world around us cannot be read, and therefore not understood without isolating forms and sequences of forms within it.

To speak of informal architecture, design – let alone urbanism – is to contradict oneself. In design there must always be the intention, conscious or semi-conscious, to present the actor with a legible set to act within or against. There cannot be design – and at the risk of committing a tautology I would say that no artifact can exist without design being involved somewhere in the making of it – without intention; and it follows, since intention is a voluntary function, that there cannot be design without artifice.

As I have tried to show, design always involves the conscious or semi-conscious making of a form or forms; nor can this happen without the imposition of artifice. But intention on the designer's part also suggests that his task must in some way be a subjective one. It is therefore his comment on both action and material which regulates the surface of the artifact, and the very word 'comment' in this context robs the architect or planner of any pretence at objectivity, in the sense of neutrality. Since what he does always involves comment, he cannot pretend to undertake morally or politically distasteful commissions without using his skill to thwart or condemn the working of that institution which he will attempt to house. In fact I would go further and say that since the built artifact comments upon the establishment in the act of housing it, only a cynical attitude to his work would permit the designer to feel himself free to comment negatively on an institution he is helping to shelter.

This is of course the old point about the rules of rhetoric being neutral while its practice cannot be so. Nevertheless, it is these rules which make the surface of the artifact into the kind of unit which the agent who uses it should find interesting. The designer's merit will depend on having interested, to some extent also entertained, perhaps even edified, the actor by the skill with which the surface has been manipulated into a statement: artifice again.

This artifice of transforming brute matter into a built statement must therefore be subject to the rules of some game: clearly it is in some way a syntactic procedure of disposing elements according to some rules. Even those designers who claim to rely on the eye alone as a judge of their efforts and their only arbiter, will if pressed confess – if not to obeying a set of rules – at least to a number of prejudices couched usually in terms of taste. The pressure will only have to be exercised because such designers, who claim to eschew any formal criteria, will have repressed their prejudices enough to claim to be acting by the light of nature spontaneously, or by the light of reason 'functionally'. Yet the results will inevitably be 'consumed' as syntagmata: that is, they will be read by the spectator following some rules of 'visual grammar' which seem to him applicable. There are several such grammars, and their rules apply to the time-honoured categories of scale, proportion, eurhythmy; and at another level there are the rules of reading which were codified by the ancient teachers of rhetoric, and which have

recently had such a vogue in the world of advertising. They entered advertising by the back-door of motivational so-called psychology; and may therefore be thought irrelevant to the more highly amortised business of building and product design, which should obey more respectable and urgent dictates of physical need and economic organisation. This dichotomy is very agreeable to the advertiser, who plays on the delicate imbalances of human personality in order to accentuate them and stimulate illusory needs which the acquisition of more or less elaborate consumer objects might assuage. But the truth is that the advertiser operates only because the rhetorical techniques have retained all their force and validity. The architect and urbanist must however operate in a way opposite to the advertiser; where the advertiser irritates, sharpens conflict, deliberately confuses, the architects' and planners' duty is to clarify, to reconcile, to fortify. It is only in this way that any relationship between the action and its container can be established.

Naturally, the appeals of the theorists of pop to the techniques of advertising and the nightjoys of neon offer attractive illusory solutions of current problems. Architecture cannot simply be the night-time release of tired workers and executives; it must be the constant ground of all our action and suffering. That is why the appeal to rhetoric is constant, why the human values cannot ever be abandoned for the joys promised by the dreams of a superabundant technological froth. That too would be an abrogation of the designer's responsibility: the answer to our present and future concerns cannot come from the automatic, unfettered developments of technology, from the night-time joys, from the sophistications of advertising, from the statistical musings of 'behavioural scientists' or any one of a thousand other patent remedies for the real enough ills of architecture. All of us in the business know that any building an architect will design makes very little impact on the blighted world which surrounds us; we are inevitably tempted by the easy, 'total' solutions to *all* our problems, all the more since the merchants of panaceas often have something real to offer in the current situation. But ultimately we must realise that the ills of architecture (in so far as they are not part of a total social pathology) must be treated from within our discipline: and can never be so treated as long as the liberty to choose and criticise is compromised by adherence to some illusory 'total' solution. Most urgent seems to me at the moment the need to restore the integrity and the necessary optimism of our discipline by renewing the full implication of the linguistic analogy.

The problems of pollution, or urban blight, cannot be solved by architects and planners in the exercise of their profession. As citizens, as human beings, as technicians too, they have a duty to exercise themselves in this matter. But their discipline has its own integrity; and however small the fragment of human environment with which they are concerned, the conscious, the 'savant' exercise of their skill is the real contribution which they can make to the creation of a valid human environment.

The Nefarious Influence on Modern Architecture of the Neo-Classical Architects Boullée and Durand

The edited text of a television broadcast for the BBC during the Neo-Classical exhibition in London, originally published in The Listener, *November 9th 1972. Were I to write it now, I would probably place much more emphasis on the distinction between my two anti-heroes.*

Modern buildings rely heavily on an insistent use of elementary geometrical shapes. Some, like the square, are easy to divide and quick to draw. Others, like the circle and the triangle, or solids based on them like the cylinder, are rather more awkward to manage. Yet the worst contemporary architects and industrial designers *will* use them. The idea has got about that elementary geometrical shapes are in some way better than more complicated shapes. We owe this belief to Neo-Classical architects, but it goes back much further. In the fifth century B.C., Plato had already formulated the idea that the regular bodies such as the cube and the tetrahedron corresponded to the elements of which the universe was made up, and that the sphere, being the most perfect, contained and united them all. These ideas were inherited by mediaeval philosophers and had a powerful revival in the Renaissance, when many philosophers and astronomers, believing that the universe was round, suspected that the Earth was too. When Raphael painted the philosophers of Antiquity in a great panorama called *The School of Athens*, he showed Ptolemy, the astronomer and geographer, and Zoroaster, the mythical astronomer, one holding a globe and the other an astronomical sphere.

These Platonic notions and their later developments were reflected in architecture. Renaissance church architects favoured the dome, which displayed in miniature the spherical vault of the sky, and for many philosophers the sphere was an image of God's perfection. But there was also another image of God's perfection: the human body. Scripture says that God created man in his own image, and like the Ancients, many Christian philosophers wanted to reconcile the idea of the perfection of the human body with the geometrical description of the universe. Artists examined the proportions of the human figure for secrets of universal harmony, and devoted a great deal of energy to speculating on the possibility of communicating this harmony by means of simple mathematical formulae. Renaissance architects thought that architecture could transmit the idea both of mathematical harmony and of man as the microcosm.

By the middle of the seventeenth century scientists had gone their separate ways, searching for those irreducible particles of knowledge from which they might build up new and specialised systems. Experiment took the place of speculation about universal harmony. And in architectural theory, too, the ancient orders were no longer sacrosanct. But the armoury of classical ornament went on being used by architects, although many could no longer accept it as the support or basis of a rational approach to the problems of building. Several seventeenth-century architects who wrote about theoretical problems justified classical ornament as a convention. They came to see it as a way of designing which was generally familiar and which was governed by rules: rules which were set up by ancient authority and thus guaranteed correctness of taste. A quarrel grew up between the 'ancients', who believed in some form of the Platonic idea, and the 'moderns', who were looking for some kind of empirical discipline. But even architects who seemed to follow the classical teaching closely could not accept it as universally valid. Nicholas Hawksmoor, for instance, who had worked with Christopher Wren on St Paul's, when asked to extend a mediaeval building, All Souls College in Oxford, did so in what he thought was a mediaeval manner. Most of his predecessors and even his contemporaries would have thought his design too clumsy and barbaric for a new building.

Meanwhile, travellers were bringing back stories of splendid buildings of a kind practically no one in Europe had seen. From China and India came accounts of vast palaces and towers of porcelain and alabaster and gilded roofs and fantastic ornament. What is more, China was described by travellers as a land governed by a benevolent despot through men of learning, the mandarins, who attained their position by merit alone. This sort of society appeared very attractive to people in France and Britain in the eighteenth century. Social reformers saw the Chinese not only as the rivals but even as the superiors of the ancient civilisations of Greece and Rome. Exotic buildings and artefacts were eagerly imitated, sometimes in rather fancy versions. Roman and Greek architecture had become one style among others, though it remained pre-eminent.

The next logical step, some designers thought, was to derive a form of ornament, not from Chinese, or Gothic, or Egyptian, or even classical models, but from nature itself – from rocks and shells and plants. This kind of ornament was established as another style, called Rocaille at first, and later Rococo. It was a style in which inventive freedom was made the servant of an ideal – the ideal of a *natural* pleasure.

ETIENNE-LOUIS BOULLEE *Salle d'Opéra* exterior view and section.

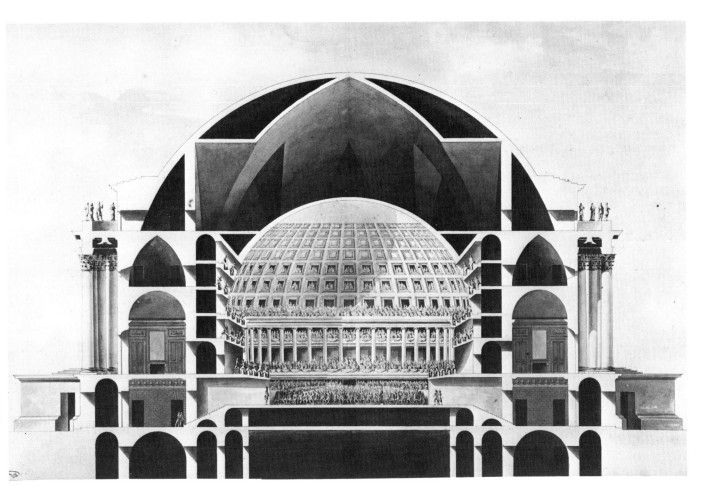

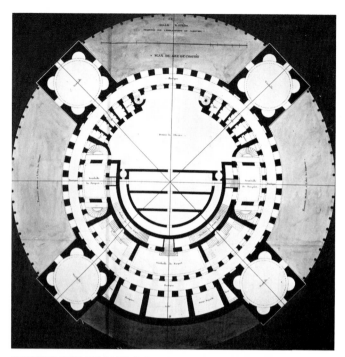

ETIENNE-LOUIS BOULLEE *Salle d'Opéra*, ground floor plan.

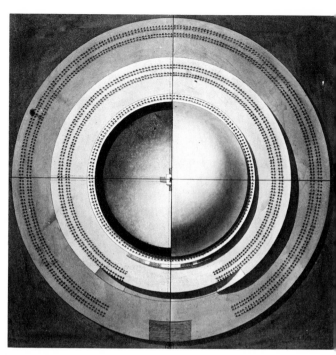

ETIENNE-LOUIS BOULLEE *Cenotaph to Newton*, plan.

Rococo artists such as Meissonier would design anything: they even redesigned nature itself. It was the style of a generation which had been released from the strict despotism of Louis XIV: from France it spread all over Europe and for thirty years it dominated fashionable life. But it was a spineless fashion. It catered to the fancy: it smoothed, it swerved, in the end it cloyed.

A new and powerful middle class was taking over Europe in the second half of the eighteenth century. They rejected the apparently frivolous Rococo style. France no longer led fashion. The bourgeoisie looked to a much more strait-laced England for leadership. The return to a sober classical mode was an inevitable reaction, which affected the aristocrat as much as the bourgeois patron who was setting the pace. But now the ornamental patterns and even the major forms had to be carefully examined and categorised by comparison with surviving examples, and this is perhaps the greatest difference between the Renaissance practitioners of a classical art and the Neo-Classical view of Antiquity. Even the most fervent Neo-Classical architects and designers were not quite able to believe that the particular way in which they were designing was the absolutely right way of working, either because it reflected the universal harmonies or because it was wholly rational. For them it had now become a matter of imagination and taste.

For me, the architect who best focused this conflict between the sober and edifying example of the Ancients and the challenge of a rational and empirical method was the Parisian, Etienne-Louis Boullée. So I suppose it's fitting that his greatest project was dedicated to the great philosopher-scientist of the time – Isaac Newton. Boullée was born in 1728, a year after Newton's death. He wanted originally to be a painter, but at his father's insistence he decided to study architecture. He had a long career as a teacher of architecture, first as a member of the Royal Academy of Architecture in Paris; then, when the Revolutionary Government abolished the Academy, he became a member of the new Institut de France and remained one of the most influential teachers of architecture in France until his death in 1799. Boullée actually built very little, mostly houses in Paris

and the suburbs for members of the nobility. He reserved his energies for vast projects which never got beyond the watercolour stage. A manuscript in which he outlined his ideas was left to the nation in his will but was not published until a few years ago.

Much of the book is taken up with his attempt to arrive at an understanding of his work from first principles and to set down universally valid rules for design, rules which would have the same cast-iron validity as Newton's. He concerned himself with the properties of solids and, writing at the height of the Rococo period, he looked first at irregular bodies. Their complexity and large number left him confused: 'Tired of the dumb sterility of the irregular bodies, I went on to the regular ones.' There he found the fundamental qualities – regularity, symmetry and variety – which, working together, would produce the image of order that he was looking for. The sphere, Boullée thought, unites all the properties of the regular bodies. Every point on its surface is equidistant from the centre, which means that from whatever point you look at it, no optical effect can alter the magnificent beauty of its form: it always appears perfect to our view. The sphere had other advantages too. Its majesty is enhanced by the fact that it reveals the largest possible surface to our view. It is the simplest of forms, because there is no break in the surface, and it is the most graceful since all its profiles are perfectly smooth. In short, it was the mirror of perfection: perfection for itself, not as a symbol of universal harmony.

The sphere became the dominant element in many of his projects: for instance, the Opera which he projected between the Tuileries and the Louvre. Boullée thought the Opera should be a temple of good taste, a temple of pleasure and Venus, where the charms of the Parisian women would be given their proper shrine. But he considered all sorts of practical problems as well. Eighteenth-century theatres were often destroyed by fire: his theatre was to be all brick and stone. The great peristyle which encircles the building isolates it, but also provides shelter for the servants waiting for the end of the show.

Some years later Boullée designed his cenotaph to

ETIENNE-LOUIS BOULLEE *Cenotaph to Newton* exterior perspective and section, night view.

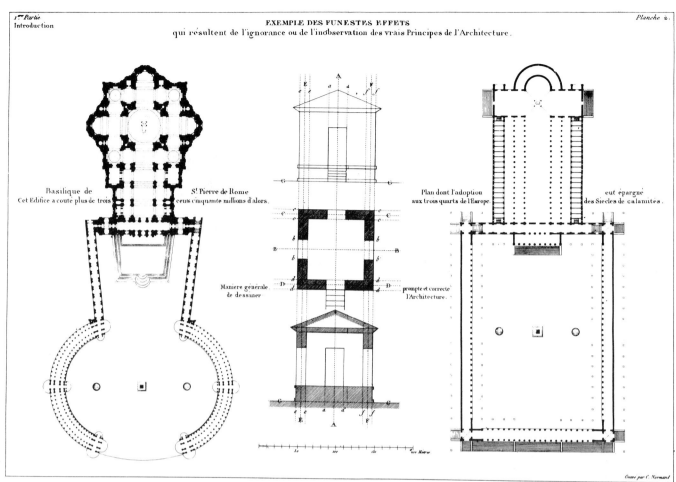

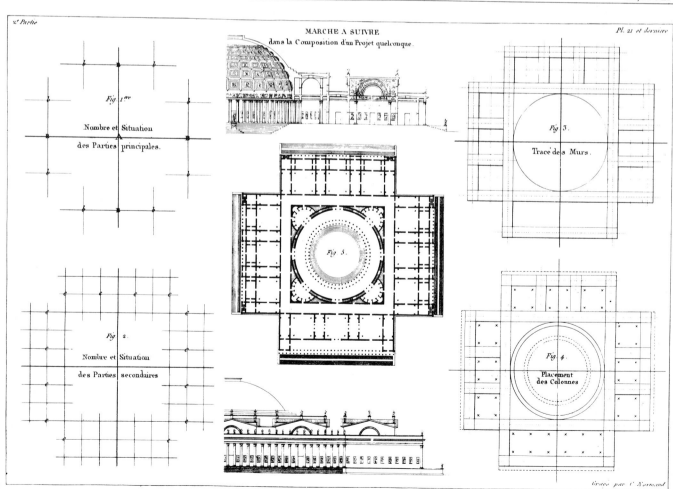

Newton, which was wholly spherical. He conceived it to be absolutely vast so as to match the stature of his hero. At night the dark sphere is lit by an ancillary sphere representing the Solar System as a series of lamps in constant revolution: 'Making use, Oh Newton, of your divine system to make the sepulchral lamp which will mark your tomb, I have raised myself, or so it seems to me, to the sublime.' At night the tomb was the daytime Solar System, but during the day the sphere represented the sky at night. The stars are represented by funnel-shaped openings in the vault which channelled pin-points of daylight. The enormous sphere had to be devoid of any ornament: Boullée simply encircles it with cypresses and flowers. Like the vast bald pate of some antique victor encircled with a wreath, the hemisphere, naked except for the ring of tall cypress trees, dwarfs the tiny visitor or worshipper. He arrives by a vaulted underground passage tunnelled through the base and comes out under the sarcophagus. The spectator is literally kept in his place. Isolated on all sides, he may only look on the immensity of the sky: the tomb is the only material object. His imagination is not invited to play with associations or allusions: it is overwhelmed by the sheer size and by the violent contrast between the narrow passage and the vast interior of the monument. Boullée makes the contrast so brutal because he thought the architect's business was not with fancy or illusion as Rococo designers had conceived it, but with the inflexible laws of reason best represented by elementary geometry, reinforced by the violence of the contrast.

Boullée built very little. His favourite disciple and pupil, Jacques Nicolas Louis Durand, seems to have built even less, and yet he was much more directly influential than Boullée had been. He lived at another crisis point of intellectual fashion, when the original energy of Neo-Classicism had flagged. The obsession with Roman and Greek Antiquity had been reduced to a formula, a useful formula but a dry one. For most of his career, Durand taught architecture to engineers. His lectures were published; their fame spread and architects from all over Europe came to hear him. His teaching became the basis of the so-called academic teaching of architecture all over the world – and its effects, completely devoid of any of the virtues which might have inspired him, are still with us.

Durand's essential teaching is simple. The discipline of the architect is made up of two parts: the first is a knowledge of elements; the second the knowledge of composition. The knowledge of elements, the analytical part, is straightforward – the various materials, their use and their combination into ever more complex features, walls, vaults, columns. For Durand columns meant the classical orders. They provide the architect with a useful variety of differently proportioned supports. Gone is all the stuff about the perfection of Greek forms: you might as well leave them out if you can't get a view of them or if you overload them

with decoration. But the core of his book is concerned with the knowledge of composition. Durand's composition follows fixed rules. He begins by stating the aim of his compositional methods, which is the obvious commonsense one of making buildings which are solid, healthy and comfortable. Buildings must also be economic. All writers on architecture had said something of the kind. Unlike most of them, however, Durand did not just mean cheap when he said 'economic', though he thought buildings should be built as cheaply as possible. For him 'economic' also meant symmetrical, regular and simple: easy to understand, not necessarily easy to build.

The elements discussed in the first part of his book must be composed into the simplest possible geometrical shapes: the square and the circle are preferred to all others. The whole building must be symmetrical, laid out on a system of axes and sub-axes. The minor elements are arranged within the system of axes with the help of a regular grid. This method of planning is still observed by most architects and some of the best contemporary architects call on assumptions similar to Durand's, even if they never state them. For some, the preference for elementary geometrical bodies is an arbitrary and empty shorthand, for others an almost hysterical seeking for a rigid order in our chaotic cities. Whatever the reason, we have now arrived at Durand's completely rational architecture with a vengeance. His belief that pleasure is derived from the economic working of the building is shared by most architects, if not all their clients. 'Decoration' and 'character', they would say, as Durand did, are just ways of inveigling the client into wasting money.

This is not what the great masters of Neo-Classical architecture had intended. They could not foresee what monsters an architecture which claims to be only reasonable, and wholly reasonable, might produce. We have got an architecture based on elementary geometry and on the belief that pleasure is a wicked luxury with which, being serious and reasonable men, we should have no truck. But as Goya, a contemporary of Durand, put it, when reason sleeps, it dreams up monsters.

J.N.L. DURAND 'Example of the baleful results of ignoring or of not observing the true principles of architecture' from the *Précis des Leçons d'Architecture*, vol 1, plate 2. *Left* Basilica of St Peter's in Rome – this building cost more than 350,000,000 (Francs?) in the money of the time; *Right* Plan whose adoption would have saved three quarters of Europe from centuries of misery; *Centre* General method of drawing architecture readily and correctly.

J.N.L. DURAND 'The correct sequence of operations in designing any project' from the *Précis* vol 1, plate 21. *Fig. 1* Number and place of the principal parts; *Fig. 2* Number and situation of secondary parts; *Fig. 3* The outlines of the walls; *Fig. 4* Placing the columns; *Fig. 5* The finished project.

ADOLF LOOS *Project for the Chicago Tribune tower* Chicago 1923.

Adolf Loos: the New Vision

This essay was originally written to preface the Italian edition of the writings of Adolf Loos, Parole nel Vuoto, *which I prepared for the publisher Adelphi of Milan in 1972. An amplified English version of the essay was published in* Studio International *in July/August 1973.*

Adolf Loos was not the finest architect of the century. But amongst twentieth-century architects, he was probably the only one (with the possible exception of Le Corbusier) to be a major writer.

His prose was not of a kind we associate with architects nowadays; they write as if they were 'important' people. Their style is usually hermetic and shrouds the questionable mysteries of their trade. They like to appear as demiurge master-builders; creators of the whole artificial world. Their work must rival the gigantic and discontinuous scale of the hangars at Cape Kennedy or the thrills of the Las Vegas nightlife panorama if it is to make the impact which they seek.

Loos would have regarded such ambitions as incomprehensible. It is true that he was a man self-confessedly modern, a man who worked towards a better and more vital society; or more precisely against a claustrophobic and faded one. But his own understanding of his modernity is already so remote as to need comment.

One key to it is his insistently patrician and even supercilious view of his contemporaries. This was not the superciliousness of the aristocrat, however: Loos was a professing democrat, even something of an egalitarian, in spite of his weakness for the ceremonial display of the Viennese court.

His family was unremarkable, though his background was a continuing influence. He was the son of a prosperous craftsman, of a monumental mason who had been very conscious of the dignity of his trade, which he had practised in Brno, on the border of the Czech and German-speaking Habsburg lands, the town where he lived and where Adolf Loos was born in 1870. Adolf was therefore forty-eight when the Habsburg Empire fell. He died in 1933, the year of the Nazi rise to power, a deaf man, broken in spite of his relatively young age. His writings were marked by the feeling summed up in their titles: *Ins Leere Gesprochen* and *Trotzdem* ('Spoken into the Void' and 'Nonetheless'). The sense of contradiction is inherent from the outset. Loos had been – surely more than his father even – aware of the nobility and worth of the paternal calling. But his father had died when Loos was just over ten years old, and his

veneration for his father's memory contrasted sharply with his distaste for his mother's ways, her drudging insistence on security and achievement. The army, the art school and finally the American journey liberated him, severed the family ties and formulated his resolve to become an architect. Already, when he was a student at the Dresden Kunstgewerbeschule, he showed his mettle. Unlike most of his contemporaries, he rejected the servitude of the fraternities and the brand of a duelling scar that went with it. It was not only his distaste for the philistine ways of most of his student contemporaries, but also a fastidious care for personal propriety and integrity which motivated him. And his civil courage was already firm.

The fastidiousness was already in evidence when he first went to do his military service in Vienna. Leather and silver objects of high quality became his passion. The designers of that time regarded surface as a provocation for the ornamental inventor. Curves, lines, inlays of varied materials covered all available plain surfaces. Instinctively, Loos already sought the smooth, the barely chamfered or edged. This passion for smooth and precious surfaces was an unconscious preference – which, as I will try to show, he later rationalised. His period at the arts and crafts schools had left him with an interest in ornament – as he recognises in one or two autobiographical pieces; but when he returned to Austria, his taste seemed to him to have been cleared by the sharp, clear Anglo-Saxon air he had breathed. And he rejoiced that the sensible Viennese bourgeoisie had rejected the fancy ornament which had become so popular in Germany and France. He was, of course, a mythomane. His idea that 'the American kitchen never smells of onion, that the American woman can prepare the most exquisite meal in a quarter of an hour; she twitters like a bird and always smiles...' could not be the product of much direct experience; in spite of the visits to Philadelphia cousins, his stay in America seems to have been taken up with nights washing-up in restaurants, living in the YMCA and poor lodgings, some journalism and occasional recourse to the breadline. But those three years in the United States decisively formed Loos' view of what he was about: he was to be an architect, and in that sense a builder like his father. But he was also to bring to Vienna the inestimable gift of Western culture; his little magazine (of which only two numbers appeared) *Das Andere* ('The Other') had as its subtitle 'A paper for the introduction of Western culture to Austria'. This Western culture had a curious physiognomy. Its structure could not be described;

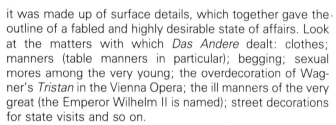

HENRY VAN DE VELDE *Havana Company Cigar Shop* Berlin 1899–1900, interior view.

OTTO WAGNER *Linke Wienzeile 38* Vienna 1898–99, detail of the facade with medallions by Koloman Moser.

it was made up of surface details, which together gave the outline of a fabled and highly desirable state of affairs. Look at the matters with which *Das Andere* dealt: clothes; manners (table manners in particular); begging; sexual mores among the very young; the overdecoration of Wagner's *Tristan* in the Vienna Opera; the ill manners of the very great (the Emperor Wilhelm II is named); street decorations for state visits and so on.

All the time, the manners of the Anglo-Saxon countries are proposed as a model, as a standard of reference. The right way to do things is the way they are done at the heart of civilisation, and that was either in London or in New York. By comparison with *their* ways, Austrian manners are found wanting at every point. Much attention is paid, for example, to the lack of spoons for the salt-cellars of Viennese restaurants. And, sometimes, this insistence is taken to extreme lengths: Loos rediscovers the aubergine (familiar in Europe since the sixteenth century) as the American egg-plant, and arranges to have American-type aubergine fritters served daily for a week in a named vegetarian restaurant in the hope of inspiring Viennese housewives and restaurateurs into emulation.

This may all seem very remote from Loos' central business of architecture. And yet for him it was not. Whenever he worked, he was always almost obsessively interested in how a building would be occupied. His great hostility to the Secession, the group of anti-academic Viennese artists who were the Austrian branch of Art Nouveau, turned on this point also. Art Nouveau architects and designers thought that a new style could be created for their own time in terms of an ornamental vocabulary, which would have no relation to historical ornament, but would be drawn entirely and directly from nature. Some went even further. They thought that this ornamental surface could be applied not only to walls, windows, floors, and pieces of

furniture, but also to clothes and even to jewellery in a scientific fashion, so as to stimulate or reflect emotional states.

In some ways, this attitude to ornament had its source in the psychology (and later the aesthetics) of empathy, a teaching still not wholly dispensable, according to which we 'read' our state of being into the objects which surround us, and in a particularly heightened form when these objects present the pressing claim to our attention which works of art inevitably do. While this idea stimulated the particular researches of certain designers such as Henry van de Velde, for whom Loos reserves his most withering scorn, the notion of a style which can be summed up in terms of its ornamental patterns is an idea formulated – among others – by the great German historian and architect, Gottfried Semper. Clothing, he believed, was the primary stimulus for all figuration. Clothing understood not only as protection, but also as the adorning of the human body. Semper was perhaps the first to consider tattooing among the arts of mankind.

Tattooing obviously fascinated Loos. In the most famous of his essays, the one on ornament and crime, he holds the Papuan up as an example of one who has not evolved to the moral and civilised circumstances of modern man, and who will therefore kill and consume his enemies without committing a crime. Had a modern – meaning a Western – man done the same thing, he would either be considered a criminal or a degenerate. By the same token, the Papuan may tattoo his skin, his boat, his oar or anything he may lay his hands on . . . He is no criminal. Tattooed men who are not imprisoned are either latent criminals or degenerate aristocrats. If a tattooed man dies free, this is because he has died prematurely, before committing his murder.

Horror vacui is the origin of all figuration. 'All art is erotic'. But man has evolved. And Loos proposes the axiom that the evolution of culture is equivalent to the *entfernen* of ornament from everyday things. Writing this essay as he did in 1908, it was easy to dismiss the elaborate confections of van de Velde and Otto Eckmann, or even Joseph Olbrich, as worthless. Art Nouveau was already a thing of the past. Loos' contempt for their efforts had proved justified, while art schools, ministries and professional bodies were still intent on the study of ornament. But even in Loos' triumph, there is an element of inconsistency. His shoes, he admits, are covered with ornaments. English-style brogues, one must suppose. Loos imagines offering his shoemaker a premium price for the shoes: a quarter more than usual, and the delight of the shoemaker at having such an extremely appreciative client. But were he to ask the shoemaker to make the shoes quite smooth, without any ornament, he would topple his shoemaker from the heaven he had raised him to by his offer into the deepest hell. The creation of ornament is the shoemaker's pleasure. And that, Loos thinks, is what makes it acceptable. 'I can put up with ornament even on my own body, if it is a witness to the pleasure of my fellow-man.' Brogue shoes, Balkan Kelims, all that is tolerable, even welcome. But, says Loos, I preach to patricians. And patricians are those who – unlike his shoemaker – go after a day's work to relax listening to *Tristan* or to Beethoven. And a man who goes to listen to the Ninth Symphony and then sits down to draw a carpet pattern is either a confidence trickster or a degenerate.

The particular hate for the ornamental patterns of the Art Nouveau designers had a further motivation. Loos wrote the moral tale of the Poor Rich Man, who had his house, which he had hitherto inhabited so peacefully and contentedly, made into a work of art, since he had become discontented living without art. And the architect had designed every detail of the Rich Man's home, covered every surface with elaborate ornament; he anticipated everything, even the pattern on the Rich Man's slippers. The day came when the Poor Rich Man's family offered him birthday presents, which they had bought at the most approved arts and crafts establishments. The architect, summoned to find correct places for them in his composition, was furious that a client had *dared* to accept presents about which he, the architect, had not been consulted. For the house was altogether finished, as was his client: he was complete. The Poor Rich Man was written in 1900, at the height of the Art Nouveau phase. Loos's was then an unpopular, minority view among the cultivated; he seemed to take up cudgels for the philistines who still preferred their saddlework and their silver smooth and unadorned. By 1908, the year in which *Ornament and Crime* appeared, the climate of opinion had changed. Even the Viennese leaders of the Secession, like Joseph Olbrich, were working in a sober, ornament-shorn classical manner. Olbrich's last houses (he died in 1910) and Hoffmann's buildings – such as his pavilion at the Werkbund exhibition of 1914 – align them with the more 'progressive' among the German architects: with Peter Behrens, Bruno Paul, Hermann Muthesius, Heinrich Tessenov.

But the 'shorn' classicism which they practised was not for Loos. They were the architects of – at that time at any rate – a confident bourgeoisie, which seemed to believe that the problems of Germany (and by extension of the rest of the world) would be solved in a reasonable way: that the Werkbund ideals of educated taste and good design would favour the expanding markets; and that all these good things would be fostered by the improving of art education on the English arts and crafts school model.

JOSEPH MARIA OLBRICH *Haus Feinhals* Köln-Marienburg 1908, garden facade.

KARL FRIEDRICH SCHINKEL Monumental entry with shopping arcade, Neue Wilhelmsstrasse, Berlin 1819.

The architects who held such ideas appealed to an architecture of reason for their precedent – to the architecture of the age of reason, of the age of taste. Classicism, the brand of classicism which had evolved in Germany and Austria in the wake of the French masters, and culminated in the work of Schinkel, was the favoured model. But the apparently arbitrary slavery of neo-classical architects to an historical past was rejected. A model, yes, but to emulate, not to copy. Ornament, in any case, was considered something abstract; the ideas of the eighties and nineties, the notion that ornament and line could convey a mood or even a message, were alien to them. To Behrens as to Hoffmann, ornament was a modenature which might accentuate the play of light over the surface, at the most an anodyne echo of a generalised melancholy for the past, a garnish for the essential geometrics which – so it seemed to them – reason had always dictated.

Loos, like many of the architects of the pre-1914 period, was self-consciously modern. I have already noted this. And he had other things in common with them. His generous, if sometimes misguided, enthusiasm for all things English, for instance. But he was untouched by the generalised Werkbund optimism. It was not through the reformation of untutored mechanics in art schools, however excellent, that good design would be achieved throughout society. In so far as good design was available, it was those very rude mechanics, the saddler, the silversmith, the upholsterer, even the plumber – but above all the tailor and the shoemaker – who already provided a repertory of excellent objects for everyday use. This was the early intuition of the perfection, of the superiority, of unadorned objects, as they had come from the 'unspoilt' craftsman's hands. Loos remained consistent in this: if you look through his interiors, whether private or commercial (he never designed a public building) you will find that he never used 'modern' designed

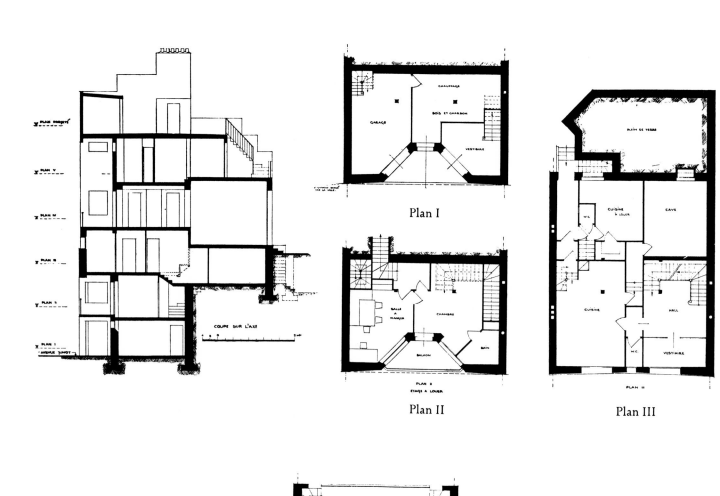

Plan I

Plan II

Plan III

Plan IV

Plan V

Plan VI

ADOLF LOOS *Tristan Tzara house* Paris 1926, section and plans. Plan VI is
the unexecuted top storey; the seventh plan is of the third floor as built.

furniture. His preference was for English style, for Chippendale or Hepplewhite chairs; or else for cheaper canework. Occasionally he used the standard Thonet chairs in bentwood, familiar from cheap cafés all over Europe. The armchairs are the usual cosy, sub-Biedermeier upholstery, even including the occasional Chesterfield. The floors were, for preference, covered with Oriental rugs.

I suppose that is why there are so few photographs of the house which Loos designed for the most famous of his clients, Tristan Tzara, in the avenue Junot, in Montmartre. To the street the house would have shown (had the projected top storey been built) a great white square set over a rubble stone base. The base contained the garage and fuel store as well as a central niche, sheltering the main door under a balcony onto which the windows of a flat for letting opened. This flat was entered from behind the building. The main apartment consisted of hall and kitchen looking through the windows set over the string course; the more important rooms in the huge niche, about half the height of the square and a third of its width, which cut sharply into the great white surface, a negative of the shape which he was later to perfect in the Müller home at Prague. It was set in the middle, so that a swathe of white, a third of the square's width, went round it on three sides.

The inner complexity of the plan was a typical Loosian solution for a difficult site. The complexity had its wit, as did the strangely highly-abstracted anthropomorphism of the facade, or the use of the common-place Parisian industrial detailing in the lower floors, the shape of the lower niche, again the inversion of his favourite English bay-window. It is a configuration not unlike Le Corbusier's exactly contemporary villa at Garches for Leo Stein: a blank facade, sparsely pierced to the street, and an open, glazed frame towards the terraces and gardens at the back. But Loos' complexity always remains hard, the spaces are never moulded, never the plastic, shaped interiors which Le Corbusier made them.

Repeatedly Loos asserted that the architect's business is with the *immeuble*, the craftsman's with the *meuble*. The architect saw to the inert volume, to the walls and ceilings and floors, to the fixed details such as chimneys and fireplaces (beaten copper was one of Loos' favourite materials). And here his haptic reading of buildings was most important.

Wherever he could, Loos used semi-precious materials on walls and ceilings: metal plaques, leather, veined marbles or highly veneered woods, even as facing for built-in pieces of furniture. But unlike his contemporaries, Loos never used these materials as pieces to be framed, but always as integral, continuous surfaces, always as plain as possible, always displaying their proper texture: almost as if they were a kind of ornament, an ornament which showed the pleasure providence took in making them, as the more obvious type of ornament would display the pleasure experienced by his fellow-men.

Curious, this feeling for the decorative effect of figuring in the arch-enemy of all ornament. Even more curious is his persistent use of the classical columns and mouldings. The crassest of these was his project for the *Chicago Tribune*, an unplaced competition project. It was an extraordinary scheme which consisted of a vast Doric column (the shaft alone 21 storeys high) on a high parallelepiped base. To Loos, however, the project seemed wholly serious. The building was to be a pure classic form, classic and therefore outside the reach of fashion, so that it would fulfil the programme of the competition promoters to 'erect the most

ADOLF LOOS *Tristan Tzara house* retouched photograph showing unbuilt top storey.

ADOLF LOOS *Haus Müller* Prague 1930, exterior view.

ADOLF LOOS *Kärtner-Bar* Vienna 1907, interior view.

ADOLF LOOS *Goldman and Salatsch building* Vienna 1910.

beautiful and distinctive office building in the world'.

It was to have been faced, column and base, in black polished granite. There would have been practical difficulties about this vast circular block, Loos' enemies suggested. But he was only interested in the creation of this great evocative shape in the urban context of Chicago: 'The huge Greek Doric column shall be built. If not in Chicago, then in another town. If not for the *Chicago Tribune*, then for someone else. If not by me, then by another architect', he wrote at the end of the competition report. And indeed on a smaller scale, he had persistently used classical columns. Perhaps the most important instance was the Goldman and Salatsch building on the Michaelerplatz in Vienna. This building caused a furore. The city building office tried to stop construction. Loos was permanently attacked by word of mouth and in the press (even if he had powerful defenders, such as Otto Wagner) and the acrimony caused him a period of illness. Now the building looks unremarkable, even tame.

But at the time, objection was violent on the very grounds which now seem inoffensive. The site is opposite the Hofburg, facing onto a square that had recently been enlarged, and which carried memories of the feudal past. Its lower storeys therefore, as Loos carefully explained, the storeys which housed the shop, were faced in marble. The facade, in consideration of the context, was decked out with Roman Doric columns. Tectonic columns, stone monoliths, their ornament finished by craftsmen. The windows above display level were 'Anglo-American type' bay-windows, to give the facade the requisite plastic quality.

The upper level was quite different. Above the marble cornice the traditional Viennese finish, stucco. Not moulded ornamentally, but treated for what it is in material terms, a skin, therefore quite unmoulded. Above the stucco, a final cornice, a heavy copper roof, which as Loos had foreseen, turned quite black, and which Loos also had to defend.

The concern in his polemic is almost always with the

symbolic reading of his buildings, whether built or unbuilt, sometimes in a quite crude way, sometimes more subtly. In the description of his project for the new ministry of war, he emphasises that the building was to be sheathed with black granite and framed with yellow terra-cotta mouldings, so displaying the Habsburg colours. He reasons rather differently about one of his most famous projects, the house for Josephine Baker in Paris. Of all Loos' houses, it is perhaps that which is nearest to his ideal, since his evocative intention is manifest. The sharply contrasted geometry of the volumes, the flat roofs, the large expanses of window-less wall are all deliberately exotic, almost African. As is the extraordinary facing of white and black alternating stripes of marble slabs. Above a plain podium, the windowless walls surround a swimming-pool, lit from a lantern in the roof: the water surface is on the top floor, just below the floor level of the bedrooms. The visitor comes in under the circular turret – a favourite device of Loos – up a grand staircase. Through a colonnade, a large piano nobile salon, a semi-circular stair-way leads to a foyer, from which, through more columns, the dining-room opens and the suite of bedrooms. Both have access to the swimming-pool. But at the lower level, that of the salon, a narrow passage is provided round the volume of water, leading to a boudoir and a tiny 'café' in the circular turret. The passage and the boudoir, moreover, have safety glass windows into the pool through which you might see the people bathing in the water.

A naughty extravaganza you might say. Of course. But Loos was convinced, secure enough, to allow himself that also. He had imagined a way of life in the house. The felicities of the plan all exult in the way the house was to be occupied, to be lived in. And do everything to ennoble it formally by a quiet unassertive wit. It is at this scale that Loos was at his happiest. The private houses are his masterpieces: they, the bars, the clothes shops, all buildings on a small scale – for the greater dimension of public urban

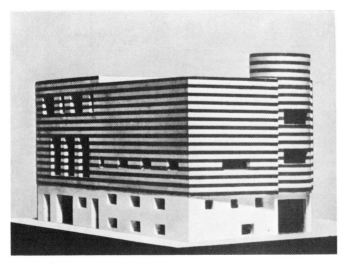

ADOLF LOOS *Project for a house for 'Josephine Baker'* Paris 1928.

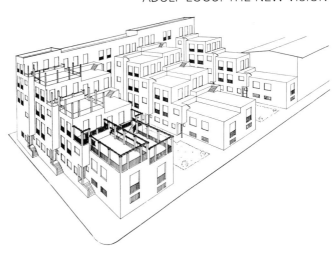

ADOLF LOOS *Group of twenty villas* 1923, perspective drawing. The roof on one house serves as a garden for the house behind.

building he could not quite master. Though perhaps this is not entirely fair to him. In 1920 he was appointed chief architect for the *Siedlungen* of the post-abdication, and newly republican Vienna. It was the nearest he came to giving positive expression to the Western civilisation he spoke of in architecture. There too he was consumed by one or two detailed ideas which he never fully worked out: the terrace house with weight-bearing party-walls, and light construction cross-wall (what he called 'the house with one wall'); the use of stepped terraces, so that the roof of one house could serve as garden to the next; the provision of access at every other floor, so that the terrace became in fact an *immeuble villa*, to adapt Le Corbusier's phrase. But his appointment did not and could not last. Only one of his *Siedlungen* was actually built (only partly following his plans) before he retired, disappointed and embittered, to Paris. It is too easy to say that it was fated, that he should have remained the architect of the individual villa. Although all his projects for great public buildings show him at his worst, the low income housing absorbed his ingenious talent, drew the egalitarian and the moralist in him to a full engagement.

However, although the failure was primarily political, there is in the projects a kind of *naiveté*, a concentration on the passage from one material to another, the lack of a sense of urban context for them, the absence, for want of a better word, of a sense of structure. After all, the pleasures of his architecture are the pleasures of touch. And yet he was dimly aware of a mystery beyond, a mystery which he could not quite name. 'All art is erotic', he had written in *Ornament and Crime*. The erotic element in art had to be sublimated, however. The man who scrawls explicit erotic signs on walls is, again, a criminal or a degenerate, like all tattooers of surface. And yet, ornament cannot be dismissed altogether, for in the end the business of architecture is evocative. In attempting to get closer to this idea, he fell into a strange figure. 'When, in a wood we come on a mound, six foot long, three foot wide, heaped up into a pyramid with a spade, then we become serious and something says inside us: someone lies buried here. *That is architecture.*'

Obsessionally almost (and in his later years ever more despairingly), Loos followed the ideal of an architecture which could communicate; communicate about this perfect way of life which seemed to him realised in the Anglo-Saxon lands, in his paradise. He never attempted a systematic view, a coherent theory of architecture, or of anything else for that matter. He was obsessed with immediate sensa-tions as ingredients of a perfect way of life. The quality of smell and of touch, the juxtaposition of textures, the passage of an inhabitant from one volume to another, all these he observed with a sharp and loving eye.

Beyond this, and more gropingly, he sought for an architecture which could communicate and reconcile man to his fate. Though again it was not man in general with whom he concerned himself, but the same inhabitant of his buildings whose senses he wanted to stimulate and soothe. And beyond him, the passer-by: every building of his is not a maze which traps a way of life, but a presence which communicates with its inanimate neighbours.

It is these two passions which make him so fascinating a figure: since he tried to capture and celebrate things which his contemporaries had taken for granted, and were discarding in the name of progress. And which (now that they *are* lost) we miss in a way our fathers, his contemporaries, would never have imagined.

The 15th Triennale

This text, originally published in Domus 530, January 1974, *has been cut only of the details which obscure its main polemic intention. Although it has had oblique references from the interested parties – Rossi complained of attacks from 'servile academics and reviewers of furniture and fashion' (I hope only the second refers to me), while Tafuri has reproved me for quoting him out of Scolari's introduction to the Rationalist exhibition catalogue (though not of misquoting ...) – I still await a direct answer.*

Like an ageing primadonna, every time the Triennale reappears, it seems a farewell: every Triennale, we are told by its critics, is so much worse than the others, that it must surely be the last.

In the meanwhile, its half-century has come round, at the 15th exhibition. Bad arithmetic apart – caused by wars and the uncertainties of peace – it's something of an achievement. A retrospective is very much in order therefore. Had the thirtieth anniversary not been celebrated so amply and so well (and with better arithmetic, at the 10th Triennale), this particular retrospective would have been more welcome. It is announced, at the top of the monumental staircase, by a composition based on the contrast between a full-size Citroën DS 23 and Arturo Martini's *Madonna and Child* of 1930 – to the same scale. It follows on, round the apse of the first floor of the Palazzo dell'Arte, rather tucked away, with all the material from the earlier exhibitions already the subject of revivals. All is exhibited against the background of rusty steel which – though handsome enough – may not have quite the associations the organisers wished to create. But it is certainly apposite. And agreeable, since it is one of the few things more or less well done in this generally deplorable show. It turns the visitor's mind back to the purpose of the whole enterprise, which began, after all, as the Milanese 'applied' answer to the Venetian display of 'fine' art; partly to stimulate exchange at the level of display and of discussion; but also to promote the best, and even commission interesting work. The Triennale certainly did all that in its time. And it informed not only architects, but their clients, both public and private, on what was going on. The climax came in the 13th Triennale. In a way, it was as near an exhibition which is itself a unified and coherent object as possible: a kind of carnival. And yet it was destructively ironic, almost cynical about the designer's part in the social fabric.

Then came the *dénouement*. In 1968, the Triennale, even more corrosive about the artist's and the designer's role than its predecessors, was nevertheless occupied by students and various architects, artists and designers who wanted to question the whole enterprise. The familiar generous gestures, the posturing, the noble words: it all ended in the squalor of defeat. I say squalor advisedly. The swing to the right in politics, the fostering of certain careers, are all well known and documented. As far as architecture and design are concerned, the operation certainly achieved a minor success: the crisis sharpened. Not that the vast barracks at the Défense or at Montparnasse, in the suburbs of Milan and Rome (or for that matter, New York, Chicago, Moscow, Bucharest or Warsaw) were instantly stopped: no, they continued to rise, occasionally slowed by a strike. Only the few designers who take the job seriously experienced the crisis in their professional lives: lines were drawn more sharply, opposing ideas were hardened. The protests died.

The few students who made a demonstration at the 15th Triennale opening had little impact: although I was present, I did not hear of the arrest of three of them until well after the event. The protesters of '68 were in 1973 either absent or among the exhibitors. And yet the protesters were right. One of them approached me to sign a manifesto. I wouldn't do this. Not because I thought he was wrong, but because his manifesto did not go far enough. It was against the Triennale, because the Triennale masked political manoeuvrings, because it masked the absence of the housing commitment of one party (as if the others had any serious commitment in the matter) and the closing down of 'scientific' research at the faculty of architecture in Milan. Naturally, I deplore the absence of housing policies; but I also know that there was precious little 'scientific' work going on at the Milan faculty, as I understand the word scientific. Moreover, I think that kind of research is out of place in a faculty of architecture. And in any case, I'm not against the Triennale in general – the Triennale which would accomplish the sort of modest aim for which it was formed.

I tell this autobiographical detail not because I have heartsearchings about my signature: long ago, I learnt the lesson of that cunning master, Martin Buber: never sign manifestos *against*, sign only manifestos *in favour*. If you put yourself into common opposition, you will always find yourself in undesirable company. I tell it because I am about to speak against this Triennale, and I wish to be quite clear that my opposition is less clamorous, but ultimately more radical than the students'.

Let me first praise what I can of the things I found inside the Palazzo dell'Arte. I have already said something about the retrospective show, but there is something even better: the exhibition of C. R. Mackintosh's chairs, lovingly, punctiliously reconstructed by Filippo Alison, and accompanied by a careful choice of the master's drawings. Are we sufficiently far from neo-Liberty already to accept these reproductions as we would the models of any historical building? And if – as will inevitably happen, they will be reproduced commercially, how are we to think of them? With the contempt we reserve for fake Louis XVI or fake Chippendale? With the matter-of-fact approval of perennial products like the Thonet chairs? Or with the nostalgic admiration we reserve for the reproductions of Le Corbusier or Breuer furniture?

You may find the problem a little ethereal: the truth is that I would be inclined to be empirical about this sort of thing, and wouldn't be above using a nice bit of fake Louis XVI myself, if it came to hand. But the distance from neo-Liberty brings me to the other matter, so conspicuous in this exhibition: the neo-rationalist revival, or the movement, the *Tendenza*, to use Massimo Scolari's term, which makes this appeal. It has been coming for some time, of course. Its theoretical basis, however, was formulated recently. Manfredo Tafuri, from his splendidly isolated monastery of the Tolentini in Venice, proclaimed the death of architecture. Some time later, he modified his opinion. Aldo Rossi's competition scheme for the cemetery at Modena was another focus: a rigid arrangement of elementary geometries, which still dominates the panorama (literally) in this exhibition. The conjunction is not accidental. Rossi, who heads the team which has organised the most important part of this exhibition, that concerned with 'rational' architecture and the building and the city, has often and loudly proclaimed the independence, the abstraction of architecture from all ideology, and from any 'redemptive' role, to use his word. His is a 'pure' architecture, form without utopia which at best achieves a sublime uselessness. These are Tafuri's words, his apologia for Rossi: 'We will always prefer, to any mystifying attempt at decking architecture in ideological dress, the sincerity of him who has the courage to speak of its silent and irrelevant purity.'

So that's it, then. Architecture may stay alive as long as she stays dumb. Dumb and beautiful maybe, but dumb. Those of us who refuse this condition are sternly set aside. Tafuri is right in a way, of course. Architecture is pretty dead. Even if the pessimistic calculations of the architect's share of the world's building volume made by Constantin Doxiadis (5%) is incorrect, the percentage can't be more than doubled. Of that (I speak optimistically), a small percentage – a tenth say – reaches the bottom rungs of mediocrity: which, *en passant*, cannot be said of the appalling Italian section of this exhibition, best forgotten. Architectural theory and criticism deal therefore with a thousandth of the world's buildings, on an optimistic estimate. Can it, does it matter to the world's population? Only if you accept that what that thousandth constitutes is the treasure-house of the art of building, the leaven which must infect the rest: that it has the function of poetry on all spoken and written words, that of purifying the language of the tribe.

Architecture is only worth doing, I maintain, if it can be understood in that way, if it is the passionate, involved attempt to exhort, edify, inform, influence the spectator/inhabitant by operating the visual apparatus of the art of building. Of course, buildings should not fall down: making them stand up is not part of architectural theory, it is an aspect of the technique starting from which architecture operates. Of course, buildings should be commodious, even

ALDO ROSSI *Cemetery of Modena* engraving, 1973, of the winning scheme designed in collaboration with G. Braghieri.

comfortable, if that is possible. It would be easy enough to reiterate the previous argument about structure. But a short visit to the Triennale architectural section, and a look at the catalogue will convince the reader that the architects of the *Tendenza* are not as concerned with commodity (function, as it used to be called) as one might assume. 'The indifference of architecture to function may be demonstrated in many different ways', so Rossi himself. 'Indifference to functional considerations' (I take it that is what he means by 'indifferenza distributiva') 'is proper to architecture: the transformation of antique buildings … is its sufficient proof. [This indifference] has the force of a law: … transformation of amphitheatres [Arles, Coliseum, Lucca] before the transformation of the [Roman] cities, means that the greatest architectural precision – in this case that of the monument – offers the greatest functional liberty potentially …'

Well. Here is as monstrous a *petitio principii* as one could wish to find. Has Aldo Rossi only looked at ancient buildings in Canina's engravings? Has he ever thought of how they were used? Or that 'the architecture of the Romans was, from first to last, an art of shaping space around ritual' (and I quote the most brilliant interpreter of Roman architecture of recent times, Frank E. Brown). Does he not remember, from his childhood, the procession of lights and incense at the reading of the gospel? Does he not realise that he was looking at the perpetuation of a Roman civil law-court's ceremonial over 2,500 years, or thereabouts?

The buildings of which he speaks, the amphitheatres, theatres, sanctuaries, baths, cannot be understood as

GERRIT THOMAS RIETVELD *Schroeder House* Utrecht 1924.

HANS SCHMIDT, PAUL ARTARIA, M. E. HAEFELI, C. HUBACHER, W. M. MOSER, E. ROTH and R. STEIGER *Neubühl Siedlung*, Zürich 1930–32.

LUDWIG HILBERSEIMER *Housing Estate* 1927, perspective drawing.

'types' in the way he uses the word at all. They are not void forms, repeated in and out of different contexts. They are living forms, elaborated over centuries of use, and polished by it as are the pebbles in a stream. The built forms act on the forms of behaviour in a dialectical process: they shelter a pre-existing behaviour, and can condition the behaviour that comes after, and the ways of thinking.

What is true of Roman buildings is equally true of – say the Villa Savoye or the Schroeder House. But I don't want to cite private houses only. Take Terragni's Casa del Fascio or Rietveld's Utrecht terrace housing, each tailored carefully to a way of behaving, and each now conditioning a second generation of users. But then Rietveld is not one of Rossi's heroes. His absence from the Pantheon, from the catalogue, from references is interesting, since we are offered a new culture hero, Hans Schmidt. A Swiss architect, best known for some private houses done with Paul Artaria in and around Zürich, his work on the Neubühl Siedlung there of 1930–32. He is a recent discovery (posthumous) and those who care for that sort of thing may localise him as one of the fathers of the *Existenz-minimum*, that odious concept which is now being excavated from the libraries. It is curious to find him celebrated in the hall of the Triennale architecture section with the humane and brilliant Ernesto Rogers, and with the ham-fisted Piero Bottoni, whose QT8 was brutally (and to my mind justly) condemned by Le Corbusier.

Beside them, uncelebrated in the little Pantheon, but appealed to constantly in the apologias of the *Tendenza*, is a more ominous figure: Ludwig Hilberseimer, the conceiver of those quite hideous *Groszstadt* schemes, the inflater of Mies, the man who makes the master's Chicago manner really unacceptable by multiplying the scale of everything by 100 and showing it up for the inhuman, monstrous imposition it is. And indeed the catalogue of the show, if not the show itself, holds up for our admiration a quite revolting Hilberseimerian concoction, the East German housing by the Halle-Neustadt collective. True, this is only held up as a shining exemplar of a working method, not of architectural achievement: but God keep us, say I, from working methods, however collective, which lead to this kind of result.

There is a point on which I am in agreement with Rossi: 'There is no ideological justification for bad architecture, nor for the collapsing bridge'. But what sort of ideology or anti-ideology is it which offers us the Halle-Neustadt housing for admiration? And there is worse. The questionable instances are multiplied. How do you justify Leon Krier's *sventramento* of Echternach, a charming mediaeval city, a disembowelling thinly disguised by the *Heimatkunst* facades to his buildings? And so it goes on, the catalogue of strange, tendentious exercises which the theory props up. *Sventramento* on a huge scale (Salvatore Bisogni's Montecalvario in Naples is a good example, done specially for exhibition in the Triennale: an updated version of Bramante's Vatican palace without the jousting, set at the foot of the Certosa di San Martino) is very much favoured. And this really shows the true nature of the *Tendenza*. Its rationalism is not that of Persico and Albini, of Terragni and Pagano. It is the 'rationalism' of Piacentini and Muzio, of Portaluppi and de Finetti, filtered through a Kahnian grid, sophisticated and chastened a little. At its best, its buildings are what Louis Kahn's would have been like, had they been seen by Sironi: *Tendenza* is a revival of the Novecento. And to be expected. How could we revive the Gruppo 7 before reviving Novecento? After neo-Liberty, the sequence re-quires neo-Novecento. Neo-Gruppo 7, neo-Quadrante are styles of the future.

Going round the exhibition, so deliberately tendentious, it is curious to see what is absorbed into the show: the *sventramenti* of Krier fit well enough; Costantino Dardi and Adolfo Natalini (when at his most apocalyptic) are also clearly of the company. But what is James Stirling doing in it? Or even Vittorio Gregotti? Even odder, what are the five New York architects up to in this *galère*, with their cabbalistic reinterpretation of the next historical phase due for revival (I mean the Persico-Albini-Terragni phase) or even more remote, their studied absorption of a Cubist plasticity into the Shingle Style?

This is a little unfair to the five architects who are not a homogeneous group. Certainly Michael Graves would not share the theoretical position of the Tendenza, and I suspect would want to contradict it; the same is true, to a lesser degree, of Richard Meier and even Peter Eisenman. Hejduk was perhaps nearest to them at one point. But even he is changing. Their almost decorative, small-scale use of the Cubist idiom and sometimes of the De Stijl techniques (in Hejduk's case particularly) is a deliberate attempt to achieve the sort of variation which Rossi and his followers also eschew deliberately. This is perhaps clearest in the matter of proportion. The *Tendenza*'s almost exclusive devotion to the three most elementary shapes – square, circle, equilateral triangle – gives their buildings a look of a willed rigidity. The Fibonacci series, or even a $\sqrt{2}$ system have a sweetness and elasticity which they might find worrying. How they countenanced the playful hesitations, the gentle proportions of the Americans, as well as their wayward theorising, is mysterious.

The architectural section of the Triennale has not even the merit of being properly tendentious: nor, in spite of Rossi's charming projection drawing, is it visually coherent. It is scrappy, almost shoddy, and I suspect polemically so, to show the proper contempt for the seductive techniques of earlier days. This is an exhibition for architects by architects about architecture, which is the architects' business. If laymen choose to intrude, too bad for them, it seems to be saying. I have spent so much space on the architectural section of the Triennale, because it is the most considerable and will certainly attract much attention, as well as exercise much influence, most of it nefarious, I suspect.

There remain two sections to be dealt with. The first is that concerned with industrial design – a blacked-out chamber, in which ranges of steps are picked out by small blue lights, like on an airport at night. In the chamber, some twenty television receivers each show a number of taped films from different countries. The show has inevitably to be silent, and the viewer must wander round and put on earphones, sit down and watch the films. It would take, on my conservative reckoning, at least ten days of continuous viewing during the exhibition's opening hours to see the whole lot through. At the time when I visited the mute television boxes, there was no telling what you could see on each, nor at what time. There were three other people in the room. Maybe some indication will be provided in the future of what is to be shown, on which box and at what time. The four of us wandered disconsolately about the hall picking up earphones, trying to find a movie to see all the way through. Our disorientation was a by-product of a misjudgment about levels of attention. Or was it simply a ruse – yet another move against consumer society?

One tiny show is worth a mention because it has a

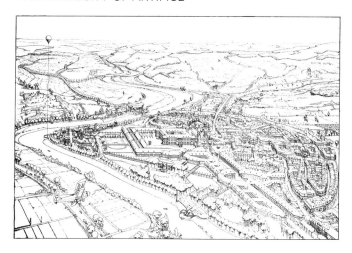

LEON KRIER *Scheme for Echternach* 1970, perspective view showing the extension of the Lycée Classique and the new pedestrian boulevard in disused railway land.

MICHAEL GRAVES *Mural for the XV Triennale* 1973.

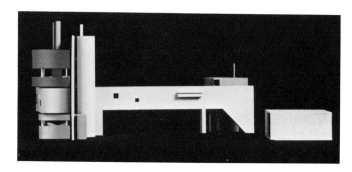

JOHN HEJDUK *Bye Residence* 1972–74.

maverick appeal: that of the craftsmen, squashed into a passage between the dark television room and that wretched Italian section. Here is a phenomenon which an inscription puts under the patronage of André Leroi-Gourhan (one of the greatest living anthropologists) and which goes counter to what the Triennale seems to be about. It is inevitably rough, haptic. It shows the product of studio potters and jewellers, not that of traditionally-trained country artisans. But it is the harbinger of a kind of protest against the consumer society familiar in the Anglo-Saxon world, and to which both the television displays of the 'international design' section, and the megalomaniac posturing of *Tendenza* are dumb. It is too small, nor is it in the context of this show sufficiently individuated to make it the focus of the protest that might have been.

So the visitor is offered the slurpy abundances of the Italian section downstairs, or the forbidding darknesses of the international design room: the alternative is the tatty hermetism, the prim certainties of the architecture section. To connect it with the upstairs rooms – the retrospective exhibition, the Mackintosh chairs, the national sections (in which the Japanese win) – there is a foyer and a stairway which is to be the scene of various happenings. Let me say at once, that however often Mr. Joseph Beuys takes his melancholy face (with or without hat on) up and down that stairway talking of Nietzsche or Zen, it will not redeem the sickly bathos of that environment.

Is this the last Triennale then? It certainly feels like it. The vein seems definitely exhausted. And yet there was a similar situation in 1957 when the whole thing seemed lost and off the rails. It was a time when student protest was gathering momentum. One of them, as a concession, was allowed to address the study centre which was to give the Triennale its new direction. I remember him a lost, untidy figure reading the students' condemnation of Triennale policy and their recommendations for the future, so fast that he was almost incomprehensible. When I questioned him afterwards about it, he confessed that he was afraid he would not be allowed to finish. The recommendations the students and many younger architects made then were, of course, ignored, though I suppose the 13th Triennale is really based on them. It came too late.

The Triennale is a hardy plant. It is fertilised by all that Milanese capital. Something will probably happen to rescue it from its *bas-fonds* of 1973. But as it is now, it has lost its function. Italian goods don't need the quality export fair at the Palazzo dell'Arte. The original worthy aims are out of context now. The forum function of the Triennale is duplicated many times over by conferences, exhibitions, festivals. The Triennale will have to transform itself, become something new: what that might be is not for me to say. All I know is that Milan continues unceasingly attractive and that the waste of talent and resources which a Triennale like the current one represents is unbearable. An alternative *must* be found.

Art as Things Seen

To stimulate discussion on the present state of art history, the Times Literary Supplement *commissioned this article for the issue of May 24th, 1974 specially devoted to the subject. The argument against any positivist history is as urgent as the argument against a positivist theory of art.*

Although the 'furniture' of this essay is contingent on its being written in London, the argument applies equally, it seems to me, to Buenos Aires, Rome, New York or Tokyo.

Reprinted with the kind permission of Times Newspapers Ltd.

History of art might seem to be a very popular subject at the moment. Major works of art are for ever being rushed about the world to be exhibited in various capitals where long queues form for hours to catch a glimpse of them; the sensational sums which television companies offered for the rights to show Sir Kenneth Clark's *Civilisation* series, and the vast audience it attracted, were widely reported; several departments of History of Art have been founded at our universities, and they do not lack for students.

All this is curious to observe, since it is the obverse of a menacing situation: in museums and in art galleries we witness what an American critic has called the de-aesthetizing of art, while architectural standards seem to fall in inverse proportion to the catastrophically rising volume of building. Inevitably many artists feel impotent, since they cannot act on such an environment with any real effect, and they take refuge in various forms of self-celebration, while the public, even the informed elite, avert their eyes from the

MORRIS LAPIDUS *Churchill Hotel* London.

present. Some implications of this state of affairs were demonstrated by the building, a few years ago, of the grotesque Churchill Hotel virtually next door to the Courtauld Institute, *mater et caput* of all our art-history learneries.

Is the intense public regard for the study of the art of the past (as against its indifference to what is happening in the present) symptomatic perhaps of some break, of a gap in our social fabric? And is there anything the historian of art may have to say, professionally, about the matter? To my mind it is his first duty. He operates, after all, in this very situation. His visual sensibility (his primary piece of professional equipment) is formed in it, nor is there any evasion from this condition into the past. That is why any historian of art worth his salt will be vitally concerned, even publicly concerned, about the visual quality of his environment. Not just about the export of an important old-master painting, or the destruction of some conspicuous monument – the sort of thing which will provoke the usual, and sometimes effective letter to *The Times*.

There is another aspect of the art-historian's immediate present which all this implies: the historian, after all, rarely concerns himself nowadays with the doings of contemporary artists. It is not for the artists that he practises his craft. The most vigorous, and therefore perhaps the most vital, consumer of the art-historical product is the art-market, of which London is the world capital. The aspiring art-historian's present is not only conditioned by the situation I have described, it is emphatically *not* a present of studios and academies (whatever their modern equivalent) but the present of auction-rooms and old-master galleries. These include, by now, dealers who specialise in Impressionist, Post-Impressionist and even the art of the 'isms', from Cubism to hard-edge abstraction. Few art-historians (even students) in my experience will venture into the more extreme galleries dealing in the commercialised detritus of the various forms of artistic activity for which it is often difficult to find a descriptive label.

Even if he has no other wish than to teach the history of their skill to aspiring painters and architects, the most vigorously independent art-historian will necessarily be conditioned by this state of affairs. It is the present in which both his sensibility and his craft are forged. In an undeservedly neglected book, *The Shape of Time*, the American historian George Kubler quotes the self-questioning words of his master, Henri Focillon: 'Le passé ne sert qu'à connaître l'actualité; mais l'actualité m'échappe. Qu'est-ce que c'est donc que l'actualité?' What I said so far was not an

Marcel Duchamp playing with bicycle wheel mounted on stool.

attempt to answer that great historian's question. There is of course a rhetorical aspect to it: it is in some way an assertion of the art-historian's dependence on his present which I have pre-echoed. In commenting on it, Kubler compares the activity of the historian, and of the art-historian in particular, to that of the astronomer: 'However fragmentary its condition', he observes, 'any work of art is actually a portion of arrested happening... It is a graph of activity now stilled, but a graph made visible like an astronomical body, by the light that originated with the activity...'

I doubt if anyone would object to the truism inherent in the metaphor. But it indicates a shift of emphasis, which many will find uncongenial: it shifts the historian's attention from the object studied to the activity which produced it. This is not an invitation to infer the activity from the object, a procedure which is often sadly misleading; on the contrary, if the historian is as closely concerned with the activity which produced the object as with the object itself, if he sees the object as the product of a traceable intellectual and technical process, almost as the attempt by the artist, in producing it, to interpret a particular situation, only then will he be able to 'read' the object. But if he does proceed in this way, he will find that those objects which are usually studied by the historian of art, and the others which he usually

rejects as being outside his concern or competence, will not appear quite so disparate.

I take the term 'historian of art' to mean historian of the visual arts, not historian of literature or music. The objects which interest him therefore interest him first as 'things seen'. But this very limitation implies an enlargement of his field beyond current practice. The old category 'works of art' has rather elastic limits, even if its centre is obvious enough: paintings, sculpture, monumental buildings.

But take the last of these categories: what exactly might 'monumental' building mean for our purposes? If it is whatever is considered worthy of theoretical treatment in the treatises, then the category should now include even rural cottages, which became part of the standard literature of architecture in the eighteenth century. Some years ago Sir Nikolaus Pevsner conveniently pointed out the difference between architecture and building: 'A bicycle shed is a building; Lincoln Cathedral is a piece of architecture ... the term architecture applies only to buildings designed with a view to aesthetic appeal ...' Since they are the opening words of his famous *Outline of European Architecture* they might have served as a useful categorisation. Yet shortly before the book was first published, Gerrit Rietveld designed a masterly little bicycle shed facing Utrecht Cathedral

– which suggests that the historian of architecture will even have to concern himself with trivia of this nature. But I would like to direct the reader's attention to matters connected with building which may, on first consideration, appear still more trivial. 'Architectus', preached St Augustine, 'aedificat per machinas transituras domum manentem'. What of these 'machinae transiturae'? Of scaffolding and pulleys and mason's tackle? Are they part of 'things seen' by the same token as the buildings themselves?

Of course, this will seem far-fetched. Only the 'domus manens' of Augustine's sermon is what the art-historian usually considers worthy of study. But half a century ago attention was already focused on what he would reject as trivial. Marcel Duchamp and the Dadaists exalted the *objet trouvé* (it's almost superfluous to recall that the original *objet* was a urinal) and since then the art market has followed: mason's tackle and architect's drawing instruments are already prized in antique shops, and will soon appear in the salerooms.

These last categories are special cases perhaps. But take the other side of the art spectrum: photography and the film. By sticking to the old categories, the historian will sever his links with such a vast area of contemporary visual experience that much of twentieth- and even nineteenth-century art will become inexplicable to him: not only in the sense in which photography entered the artist's studio in the nineteenth century, but much more intimately, as Walter Benjamin has pointed out in his *Brief History of Photography*. An *objet trouvé* cannot by definition be multiplied. But the artist must make a living; so that it can be recorded, and most faithfully, by photographs, which in turn become marketable. So the exponents of certain avant-garde (as they are still quaintly called) procedures paradoxically 'make' objects which they 'find' by photographing them, and it is these photographs, for preference rather imperfect ones, which constitute some of the detritus I spoke of earlier.

But the photograph, or the film, have revealed a whole area of visual experience which remained veiled until their arrival. The work of Muybridge, and Marey before him, revealed the long-suspected secrets of human and animal motion. Recently, Muybridge's photographs have been used by a number of artists, of whom Francis Bacon is the best known. But if I refer this example back to my original category problem: the 'domus manens' and the 'machinae transiturae', you will see that the art-historian's territory has been much enlarged. Not only the house you see through the scaffolding, but the scaffolding itself might become part of his concern. While on the scaffolding, the mason's tools, his clothes, and even his postures might be the object of his attention. When building was a much longer process, the design of scaffolding was perhaps inevitably considered more carefully; skill at devising scaffolding and centering was regarded very much as part of the architect's craft. Brunelleschi's centering for the dome of Florence Cathedral became perhaps the most famous piece of scaffolding in the history of building.

But now the situation has become reversed. Few architects would devote any attention to scaffolding, now that the building process has been very much speeded up. Scaffolding has in some ways been assimilated to packaging, if only because if often carries advertising. Yet packaging itself has become an art-form, both as a sales-container, which is the graphic and industrial designer's province, and also in the elevated form of an elephantine art-work in the hands of the Bulgarian artist Christo, who was recently

The building of the Tower of Babel, fresco by Benozzo Gozzoli in the Campo Santo, Pisa (now destroyed).

consulted about the scaffolding in which the facade of Milan Cathedral was wrapped for many months.

As for the workmen on the scaffolding – to continue with my metaphor – their posture has not been much studied, though it is clearly a province of art-history. Some years ago, in a monograph which did not receive the notice it deserved, *Gesture and Rank in Roman Art*, Richard Brilliant examined a special category of postures, those of Roman statuary, by reference to the known use of gesture as a code system, as set out in the ancient manuals of rhetoric. More than a century earlier, an antiquarian and a precocious student of folklore, the Neapolitan Canon Andrea di Jorio, made a study of gesture in ancient art and literature, and compared it with gestures in common use in the Naples of his time. *La Mimica degli Antichi investigata nel Gestire Napoletano* has escaped the attention of the historian in spite of the publicity given to it by Benedetto Croce and its use by anthropologists and linguists.

Of art-historians only Sigfried Giedion has given serious attention to posture as a proper subject for consideration, in the long section on comfort which is the centre of his *Mechanisation Takes Command*. He was, I think, the first to relate the development of various forms of furniture to the demands of posture, and to the changing notion of comfort it implied. This relationship is read as an indication of the changing conception of space, and our corporeal occupation of it.

Of course, the way in which Giedion treats comfort is not accepted as proper art-history by everyone. His passionate concern to assert the values of inner balance against the solicitous comforts of elasticity, his condemnation of the upholsterers' excesses, were thought to be alien to the sober discussion of the history of furniture: a minor art, in

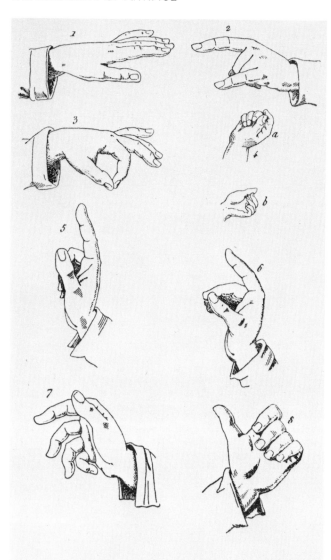

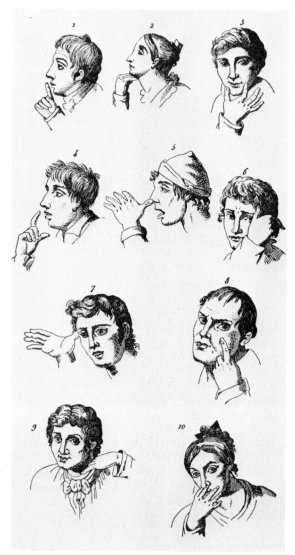

GIAMBATTISTA PIRANESI *Il Campo Marzio dell' Antica Roma* 1762, title page.

Opposite
ANDREA DI JORIO from *La Mimica degli Antichi investigata nel Gestire Napoletano. Left* 1. Could mean slowly, surprise, threat and middling depending on the movement of the hand and the context; 2. The 'horned hand', a sign of contempt, of something worthless (for the horn is empty), or an amulet gesture against bad luck, particularly the evil eye; 3. Justice and perfection, or threat; 4a. and b. Little; 5. The raised index can have a great variety of meanings according to movement or context; 6. 'Schiopetto' (a little gun): joy, dancing, contempt, familiar summons etc.; 7. Thieving, dishonesty; 8. Drinking (when pointing to the mouth) or indicating (behind oneself). *Right* 1. Silence; 2. F... off!; 3. Pretty!; 4. I'm hungry!; 5. Tee-hee!; 6. I'm tired!; 7. Silly ass!; 8. Squint; 9. Up the garden path; 10. Sharp. *Bottom* Mezzotint by the Baron Clugny de Nuis after a drawing by Gaetano Gigante. 'Well? What should I write?'. The seated girl, by leaning forward and putting her hand on her heart, explains that she wants to send a message of love to her absent husband and asks for one in exchange. The travelling secretary, by joining thumb and index, formulates the question. The standing girl disapproves of the message with her raised hand and indicates by rubbing index and thumb of the other that the letter should ask for money, not for love.

any case. Some would go so far as to describe Giedion's kind of history as social criticism rather than writing of history, not only because of his partisanship, which seems to them out of place in historical writing, but also because he concerned himself with a whole variety of objects (slaughterhouses, combine-harvesters, vacuum-cleaners, bread-loaves) which did not at all fit into the *genre* of 'art'. Yet Giedion treats all of them as 'things seen'. He treats each object as a microcosm, in which a complex situation may be summed up and examined. The chapter on the key, which he regarded as a model of his method, is a good instance: Linus Yale's invention of the tumbler-lock in the 1850s, and its English antecedents in the eighteenth century, are contrasted with the technical elaboration of orthodox locksmithing at the time. But Giedion recognises the archetype of Yale's invention in the wooden tumbler-lock, invented somewhere in central Asia perhaps, perfected in Europe during the Middle Ages, and brought to North America by the German or Scandinavian settlers; and shows the transformation of an archaic prototype into a highly mechanised device, in which the shift was as much a conceptual as a technological one, and which in turn transformed daily habits out of recognition.

A very remarkable visual sensibility enabled Giedion to formulate his account of an object so simple and so basic. But he understood very clearly that many by-products of such a development have important implications. The various forms of the burglar-proof key are not just a succession of problems reformulated at each failure. Every solution is itself a reinterpretation, a provisional summary: an object seen, represented in engravings and paintings, with implications which its inventor and maker may never have considered. The inadequacy of the problem/solution model as an account of artistic activity is never explicitly stated by Giedion, but it is certainly implicit in the book on mechanisation, as in his other work.

The problem-solving artist was very popular among 'scientifically' minded critics, and has been taken over by positivist historians. They have been known to speak of certain specific tropes, the *tondo* Madonna say, or the flying buttresses, as if there could be a perfect example of the type, a complete resolution of this formal or that iconographic device; if the artist's activity consisted of solving problems, then certainly, after a number of misses a hit would be scored, and the problem solved. When it comes to a complex 'problem', like that of the Gothic cathedral, no one has yet gone so far as to suggest that its features could be given a final resolution. In most Gothic cathedrals a number of problems, some technical and mechanical, others visual and conceptual, were acknowledged, if not exactly solved. But each cathedral is an object which is also a complex of interpretations, the result of a social 'great work', to borrow an alchemical term.

Describing the cathedral in this way is not an invitation to generalise about a category. On the contrary, it is only by paying the closest attention to his 'object', by considering its measurements, by observing the external and internal volumes, by seeing it empty and in use (if it still is in use), by 'reading' its iconographic programme in the sculptures and the stained glass, that the historian will be able to form any worthwhile notion about it. He may never look *through* his specimens; and must realise that whatever reading he may propose of the object of his study, the object itself will remain obstinately irreducible; sometimes it will continue to challenge interpretation even after it has been physically destroyed, like the great Parthenos of Phidias, known only through copies and imitations.

But it is not only great cathedrals or overwhelming masterpieces which maintain their challenge to the critic and historian. It seems to me that we should be able to accept the challenge of the humblest object. Most of my colleagues, for instance, would accept an account of fifteenth-century ivory or silver pastoral croziers as a suitable object for study, but would regard their method as wasted on seventeenth- and eighteenth-century hand-drills. Imagine though how rich the subject could become if accepted in Giedion's terms! The hand-drill could be considered as the successor of the fire-making bow, and related to neolithic stone drills. The adaptation of the drill to the hand could be considered, as well as the study of its articulation; and all this could be used to illustrate a host of ancillary matters.

Such a study would inevitably be critical. But perhaps that is endemic to proper art history, whose progenitor, Winckelmann, enjoined all artists to imitate the art of a period which he saw as the product of a society and a climate quite different from and superior to that of German and Italian society in his own day. The breathtaking grandeur of Piranesi's work lies in his transmutation of archaeological draughtsmanship into social denunciation; and so one could go on. Burckhardt's *Civilization of the Renaissance* is a work of social criticism, if only by implication; Morelli's political motivation is obvious; Semper's vision of the totality of art and industry goes counter to the practice of his day. 'Detached' and 'objective' art history as a refuge from the present is a fairly recent innovation; indeed history as a pseudo-scientific discipline, untainted by any partisanship, belongs to our own time and does it little honour. 'We must denounce such an attitude of mind angrily', wrote the French historian Henri-Irénée Marrou twenty years ago, 'as one of the worst dangers to threaten our Western civilisation, which seems destined to descend into an atrocious technological barbarism'.

Marrou specifically denounced the uncritical historian using a method 'whose logical construction is unknown to him, and the validity of whose rules he is unable to estimate; he is like a machine-minder who can only check the engine's working but would be unable to repair it, let alone build one'. He was writing of the historian in general; I have been appealing against what seems to me an even graver clerical treason by the historian of art. It is not only the lack of reflection on their method which seems to me very disturbing; but the unquestioning acceptance of the category 'art' as it was established in the debates of the seventeenth-century academies and canonised by the positivist historians of the nineteenth century, only to be taken over by the art market.

The art market itself is changing, as I have already suggested, primarily because the quantity of works of art which are still in private hands is declining fast, while demand for them rises. So the auction-rooms enlarge their repertoire: old theatre costumes, early cameras and gramophones, even vintage motor-cars. The recent revival of Art Deco offers an interesting insight into current developments. It has already produced its spate of nostalgic exhibitions and coffee-table books. Museums have begun to assemble 1920s and now even 1930s exhibition rooms. Cloche hats, I have noticed, have been looking very becoming (we are nearing the end of the Great Gatsby fashion craze at this very moment – which is all well enough, and in a way inevitable).

But this is exactly where the humblest of historians must begin to draw distinctions: cloche hats, yes; nude lady cigarette-lighters, no. The historian will remember that the Wurlitzer cinemas built in this country in profusion in the 1930s are the bastard progeny of a *petite noblesse*, the Dutch architecture of the 1920s, which itself descends from the work of Frank Lloyd Wright in earlier decades. But while such cinemas were springing up in a ring round London, Wright was still working and they were contemporary with some of his later masterpieces, from the Imperial Hotel in Tokyo to the Johnson Wax Factory at Racine, Wisconsin. It was the period, too, of Le Corbusier's best work. By such standards, by the standard of the products of the Bauhaus workshops, the work of the architects and designers of the 1920s and 1930s may be criticised and estimated. The criticism will have to take into account many criteria: the presence, for instance, of the effusion of Kitsch which drowns the quality work of the period. In doing this, the historian will be thrown back on his own sensibility: historical parallels will not serve him. Kitsch is not to the work of Le Corbusier as *rocaille* was to the architecture of Gabriel. The change which was effected on sensibility, the change so faithfully chronicled by Giedion and so magnificently denounced by Benjamin, is irreversible.

But the corruption of public taste which the very word Kitsch implies must be chronicled and accounted for. Without some love for it, the historian will be sterile. And yet he must be critical: to criticise Kitsch by the standards of the best work is not just like keeping Canaletto in mind when chronicling the minor followers of Carlevaris and Visentini: there is a violent break in quality, not a gradual diminution of it. The break corresponds to the rent in the social fabric of which I spoke at the beginning of this essay. Its healing is pre-conditional on its recognition. To affect this recognition the historian of art will have to turn away from the charms and entertainments of the art-market, and address himself again to the artists of his day. He owes them his existence, after all.

One Way of Thinking about a House

A general introduction, written as a preface to the first of three issues of the magazine Lotus *concerned with housing, and originally published as 'One Way of Thinking about a Home' in* Lotus 8, 1974.

In the Western Semitic alphabet – and therefore in all alphabets, since they all derive from it – the first two letters, *A, B,* show the essential acquisitions of civilised man: the domesticated animal, and the house: *aleph, beit.*

Aleph: written as *A* its origin isn't that obvious. But write it the archaic Phoenician or Moabite way, ▷ and garnish it further with eyes and ears, ▷ and its pictographic nature will show itself. It is a head of cattle, an ox or a bull; it is also the essential unit of counting, one. And it is male.

Beit is female; coming second in the alphabet, it stands for the number two. And its original meaning, as well as its shape, was *house.* The oldest Phoenician form, a closed shape with a tail, presumably represented a plan of a room and an enclosing wall. Since the earliest alphabetic inscriptions date from somewhere between 1500 and 1000 B.C. it should not be thought beyond the ingenuity of their devisers to have reduced the house to calligraphic plan-form. The earliest scale plans found up to date are more than a millenium older. The Egyptians had already nearly two thousand years earlier turned the house plan of the simplest form into a letter, or more properly, a hieroglyph: *h, hwt:* ⌷ , ⌷ , ⌷, is the form of the plan of an enclosure and is usually translated as home or mansion; it is most commonly used in combinations to suggest palace, temple, and so on. But the hieroglyphic repertory was much richer than any alphabet, and provided another character for house, *nht, nat:* ⌷ meaning a shelter, home, abode. The inevitable euphemism for the sky was of course house of the sky goddess: ⌷ . The sky-goddess was called Nut, and her name, like that of her male equivalent, Nu (not her husband though) was related to the simple character *nu:* ⌷ , fluid, vessel. It may be that the near identity of the goddess' name and the word for house was accidental: after all the sound had many meanings, some quite unrelated. Nut's consort was not Nu, a sky-god, but the earth-god, Geb, whose image she is often shown overshadowing. She straddled him, supporting herself on her hands and feet, while he held up her midriff, and her starry body was a canopy over him. Through her body, the sun travelled at night, entering at her mouth and being reborn the next morning through her genitalia. But she straddled also, painted on the inner lid of almost every mummy coffin, the body of the dead person, who travelled to his resurrection as the sun did through the sky:

> 'I pass through heaven, I walk upon Nut
> My home is the field of Rushes
> My riches are in the Field of Offering.'

The field of rushes was the Egyptian elysium: the sky which was Nut's body was also the soul's path, its way home.

The image of Nut made the coffin into the mummy's dwelling, as well as its guarantee of immortality. It indicates the feminine nature of the house as a female thing. The sense of it seems confirmed by the transformation, almost imperceptibly operated, from the Western Semitic ⨍ into *β* whose true nature as a pictogram is indicated by the soubriquet 'the provider, the nourisher' which it received from some hermetic authors; an implication which becomes obvious if you turn the letter on its side, like this: ∞ .

It's not much of a basis perhaps for grand generalisations. The letter-forms are mere indications of attitudes and beliefs. The world over, people have built houses of different shapes: heavy and square, light and circular. There are igloos, yurts, grass huts, rock dwellings – the catalogue could go on indefinitively.

And yet, through all these variations, there is an unavoidable theme: man comes from the womb, and he must return to the matter from which he came. The house which he occupies between these two unavoidable terminals of his journey must make reference to his condition and provide him with reassurance. So we find that the womb/tomb rhyme is a constant preoccupation of the house-builder. The variety of forms which houses take are the way in which their inhabitants make the peace between their condition and their place. The reconciliation is what dominates the vertical organisation of the house, from the cellar to the roof, as Gaston Bachelard (*La Poétique de l'Espace*, p. 35) has called it. The cellar is the dark, hidden, irrational part of the house: many peoples buried their dead under their floors or incorporated their bones into the substructure of their houses. The cellar, the undercroft, or just a hole in the ground was the repository of the family past, but also of its worldly goods. Where the individual house and not the social group holds the store of grain and oils for the household, this is most often let into the ground or kept in the undercroft, like those reserves of giant pithoi in the undercroft of the great palace of Knossos. The identity of the memory and the store, of the dead whose resurrection is a hope and the grain whose rebirth is a necessity, is one of the most ancient common-places of human belief.

Since men have abandoned nomad existence, by force of sedentary necessity, they have buried their past under their buildings. As each successive layer is added to the next, so another piece of the past is added to the stock of memories or repressed out of it. That is the dark and irrational part of the house. The roof on the contrary is its evident and explicit aspect. Its covering and slopes, its edging and seaming, make evident the way in which its inhabitants encounter the elements. Where it is seen from within, the structure of the roof, too, is a clearly intelligible constructional proposition. The roof is the head of the house – and since it stands between the inhabitant and the sky, it is also the sky's surrogate in the householder's little world.

The house in which you live, the house in which you were conceived, and in which, in your turn, you may conceive: that is a notion we urban dwellers moving at short intervals from one apartment to another have lost. And yet for those who live in the same place for many generations, the house is the setting for the primal scene. No wonder therefore that some peoples, such as the Dogon, see the house not only as its setting, but also as its representation: the plan of the house is the woman lying supine, the structure of the roof or ceiling is the man's rib-cage, the four pillars which usually support it, his arms and legs. This is a 'reading' of the structure which seems to invert the Egyptian order in which it is the goddess Nut who was the sky and overshadowed her husband Geb. But then, the reader must realise that I am not referring to an invariable scheme, but to an invariable expectancy in the householder and in the passer-by, who do not always look for the same meaning reiterated but always expect their environment to interpret the invariant essentials of their existence. Maturation is, among other things, the ability to confront the primal scene, the parental coitus which is the image, in turn, of the mating between earth and heaven, the type of creation. That is why the house not only exhibits symbols of it in its very structure, but building it is accompanied by rituals which reveal the image; and even worksongs which accompany the building will touch on cosmogonies, on myths of creation, of which the building of the house is itself a much reduced terrestrial acting-out.

I have spoken of individual houses so far. But, their ordering into collective groups, into villages and towns, more often than not reflects, on a larger scale, the ordering of the family dwelling. There are indeed peoples who never build for the individual family, or whose collective dwellings are much more important than their individual ones: but for the majority of the human race, the generalisations I have offered hold. The smaller and closer the individual house moreover, the looser may the organisation of the collective appear. But as the individual house is incorporated into the structure (the tissue of the collective dwelling), as the village grows into the town, so the inhabitants come to expect of the collectivity some of the things which their proper dwelling once supplied adequately. That is one meaning of the intimate relation between house and temple, an essential relationship. The temple comes to assume some of the sacred functions of the house, and even drains them. The form of the city may sometimes do it as well. The relationship between house, temple and city is a trinitary one: as the city grows, so its quarters will assume the intermediary functions. The temple turns into a cathedral, its intermediate representatives in the city quarters are the parish churches, and the unity of the quarter is summed up again on a smaller scale in the house. This kind of organisation becomes increasingly important as the town grows denser, as dwellings are imposed on each other and organised into flatted apartments. That is how the old functions, proper to the house, come to be increasingly transferred to 'representative' buildings.

Consider how even the familiar Latin word domus carries overtones which are interesting in this context: so often it is flatly translated house (casa), and yet it means something much more like the English 'home', and is often used almost synonymously for 'family'. Though it is also the word which signifies the physical substance of the house, and has a close connection with a whole range of words in other Indo-European languages which refer to construction (timber, Zimmer) as Emile Benveniste has pointed out (Vocabulaire des Institutions Indo-Européennes, I, p. 293 ff). On the other hand, dominus quite clearly means 'man of the house, master of the brood': so that the word covers the whole range of ideas connected with the house. And both domus and dominus move out of their original scale to signify 'palace, temple' and 'lord, emperor'. However much it was extended, the original meaning stayed. In the end, the function of the house is irreducible.

Perhaps the special case of the house of the dead will make my meaning a little clearer. Many peoples, as I said earlier, buried their dead under the floors of their houses: sometimes they were secondary burials, as at Catal Hüyük, for instance, where the Neolithic townsmen seemed to have exposed their dead to vultures before burying their skeletons. At other times they are simple primary burials; often in the womb position, with knees drawn up under the chin. There are cases where the meaning of the burial is emphasised by burying the corpse head downwards. This position was already adopted in the old stone-age burials, as in the famous skeletons in the Grotte des Enfants at Grimaldi. The notion underlying the practice is evident enough: the dead were returned to their mother, the earth, in the position in which she conceived and nurtured them and from which they would be reborn. In Egypt, too, where the dead were often buried in this position in the hot dry sands which preserved the corpse uncorrupted for centuries, there appeared, long before the creation of a dynastic monarchy, coffin burials of a near-uniform type. The coffin quite obviously represented a sizeable house. With the appearance of ambitious structures over the tomb, the articulation of the wall surface which had been devised for the coffin was simply enlarged in scale: the coffin to the mastaba; and again, later, when the mastaba was transformed into a pyramid, the wall articulation now enclosed the whole of the pyramid precinct and was therefore much larger than the original private house on which it had been based.

Even earlier than the Egyptian timber-house coffins, hut urns appear in the fertile crescent. The notion of cremating the dead and burying their remains in a model of a house is as diffused as the cremation rite itself. Where cremation is not practised, house models are used, as they are in China and among certain Amerindians, to deposit ancestral relics, or offerings to them. The Greek and Roman world took over such practices from a remoter antiquity, though the practices had the context of very different beliefs. The type of sarcophagus current in the classical world was that of a house with pediments on the narrow ends; the origin of the model was sometimes emphasised by the use of such ornaments as corner acroteria or columns on the body of the sarcophagus. Such great marble tombs were, of course, for the rich only. But even the very poor were often buried, when they were not cremated, in a supine position with a little roof formed over the body with actual roof tiles. Such simple practices survived well into the Christian era, and the survival of the practice testifies to the power of the type through the changes of belief. Variations on the type may be followed through varied contexts, but its power rests on the fact that the origin of the practice is not an arbitrary association, but a necessary and a positive one.

Another and a parallel notion has equally wide currency. Hut urns are often associated with another type of burial, particularly cremation burial; in biconic urns. In iron-age Italy, there is a whole gamut of practices and forms which links the hut urn with the biconic one. When the covers of the biconic urns are not helmets or cups, they may take the form of hut-roofs or be crowned with tiny hut models, or again, the whole upper part of the double cone may take the form of a hut. The urn itself is often modelled in a rudimentary way with references to the human body: a face, for instance, inscribed on the upper part. All these variations associate the dead with the house, but also with another powerful idea to which I have made reference: that the hut, like the body, is a token of universal wholeness. The implication of the biconic urn — a form which is found everywhere between northern Europe and the Amazon basin — and its association with the roof returns me to the theme which I mentioned earlier: that the urn represents the underworld, the undercroft; and the roof the world above. The person buried in a biconic urn, whatever its transformation, is enclosed in a microcosm, in an organic model of the universe. Its very completeness, its symbolic reduction to a tiny scale, is a guarantee of immortality.

But the notional identity of the house and the sarcophagus is underlined in the classical world by another practice. The Greeks and the Romans no longer painted the sky-goddess on the inside of their coffin lids, but they often varied the roof shape and sometimes made it an image of the deceased. In fact, the image of the dead person, sometimes — as in Etruscan sarcophagi of a dead couple reclining on the sides of the roof — re-emphasises the essential notion of the identity of house and body.

Two-Dimensional Art for Two-Dimensional Man: on Klein and Manzoni

Originally a review of the Tate Gallery show of March/May 1974 written for Domus, *the anecdote of its delay is worth telling. It was held up for several months, and then rejected – a thing which practically never happened in the course of ten years' collaboration with that magazine – on the grounds that it contained a factual error: Klein did not hurt himself in the 'Man in Space' exercise (the catalogue of the exhibition said he did . . .), and for the unworthy suggestion that Klein might have disposed of the gold ingots for his own benefit.*

The suggestion seemed to me wholly reasonable. After all, the curious activities whose remains made up the exhibition were Klein's full-time work, and I didn't see why he should not be able to make a living out of it.

Nevertheless, I was at that time becoming involved in the Venice Biennale, and wanted to establish my own critical position publicly and unequivocally. I therefore offered the article to Casabella, *who agreed to print it as it stood, with an open letter to the editors of* Domus *which explained the lapse of time between review and exhibition, as well as my particular interest in the publication of the piece. Some weeks later, I received a telegram from a member of the editorial staff asking me to withdraw the article 'to avoid useless polemics'. My cabled answer 'that 'all polemics are useful' remained unanswered, but at the insistence of the editors of* Domus, *the open letter was withdrawn by the editor of* Casabella. *Since the matter touches nearly on my parallel concerns in architecture, and my view has in no way been modified by intervening events, it seems to me that this article, eventually published in* Casabella *398, February 1975, can stand as a rider to 'Art as Things Seen'.*

There are one or two museum galleries in the world whose retrospective exhibitions with their catalogues have the force, for the art world, of a full-scale canonisation in St Peter's.

There is the Museum of Modern Art in New York, the Musée National d'Art Moderne in Paris, the Stedelijk Museum in Amsterdam, and the Tate Gallery in London. Often the canonisation comes to the living: this time two dead artists are celebrated, Yves Klein, Klein le Monochrome, and Piero Manzoni. Both achieved fame in their lives, both died very young: Manzoni at thirty in 1963; Klein, a year earlier, at thirty-four, epically. His heart-attack was brought on (so the catalogue tells the visitor) by the shattering realisation that Jacopetti's *Mondo Cane* was not entirely devoted to him.

'De mortuis nihil nisi bene'. I speak no ill: it is his widow and his admirers who register this sad incident. Anyway, it is not about the dead that I really want to speak, but about the living. The living who have put on this large and sumptuous exhibition; in spite of all their good will (which I don't wish for a moment to question), this turns out to be a sad and squalid affair. The sadness was summed up for me by the sight of one of Piero Manzoni's 'magic podia': a square base with sloping sides, with two inner soles, the foam rubber kind you put inside your shoes, stuck down on the top in a conventional 'statue' position. Obviously what Manzoni meant you to do, is to stand up there and be a statue: but at the foot of the base, there was a large printed notice, PLEASE DO NOT TOUCH OR STEP ON THE BASE. Of course, it would be rather funny if someone did step on it, and it broke. But it's not the sort of joke exhibition organisers relish: besides the base is meant to be there for a month! On one of Klein's more complex exhibits, a scribbled note urges you not to mess about with the blue powder colour deposited under four hanging blue rods, with another of the blue canvases hanging in the background. But is that what Klein would have wished you to do, *not* mess about with that blue poster colour? Emphatically, no. Here is the making of a do-it-yourself anthropometry.

PIERO MANZONI *Magic Base* 1961.

'Anthropometries', I remember, used to be called 'Suaires' in the old days. Naked ladies, daubed in Klein's favourite colour, usually a bright, poster-colour ultramarine, would rub themselves against blank canvases to the tune of his monotone symphony, performed by a number of musicians, in the presence of the artist, of course. The show held a promise of the sort of *frisson* you might get from ladies wrestling in mud (very popular, I am told, in Hamburg).

It's too easy to accuse Klein of commercial speculation. Clearly the making of an 'Anthropometry' could be an expensive public spectacle, and the result could be put on show afterwards. But that is irrelevant now. The 'Anthropometries' remain: large canvases, daubed with recognisable bits of female anatomy, poor remnants, as Klein himself said, of a ritual. All his obsession with ritual, childish though it was, is carefully chronicled in the exhibition and in the catalogue. Gone are the days when, as Erik Satie said, it was not honourable to have refused the Legion of Honour, but rather to have done nothing which would deserve it. For Klein every decoration and diploma mattered: his much vaunted membership of the Knightly Order of St Sebastian (I wonder what the Bishop of Sens, who signed his diploma, thought of it all?), his special postage stamps, his lectures at the Sorbonne, his letters to famous people (not always answered!), all are part of the persona which this exhibition displays. And, of course, the chronicling of all the mini-events is essential to its manufacture.

Occasionally, Klein had to pay for this process in person: as when he threw himself off a 5 metre high wall to transform himself into a 'man in space' montage and got hurt in the fall. Of course, this is where the story goes awry. He should have remained unscathed. The master of judo (which he really was) should in some way have carried the whole operation out with a faultless elegance. The rituals should have been perfect, yes, but also demanding on all the participants. That is not how they were. Take the instance of Klein's symphony, which was to induce transcendental states: heard on tape at the exhibition, it is a low-pitched buzz, overlaid by the noises of a nearby building site, by the shuffling of feet, by snatches of conversation.

In a more public ritual, Klein's clients would burn one of his cheque-shaped receipts which entitled them personally to an 'Immaterial Pictorial Sensitivity Zone', and for which they paid in gold: half in ingots, half in gold leaf which Klein would scatter on the water (while being photographed, of course). The fate of the ingots is not discussed: which mars the ritual. All that gold seems a lot to pay for the pleasure of burning a piece of paper on the quays of the Seine in the company of Klein and an expert witness (Klein insisted that they should be museum directors, art critics or such-like) while he not only got off with the ingots but had the fun of throwing in the gold leaf. Still a great many clever and talented people did go through with it, and may be seen photographed in the catalogue wearing their overcoats (since most of these happenings seem to have been arranged in cold weather). The pastime may seem harmless enough, and an interesting subject for a sociological study. But not all Klein's activities were so impermanent and ritual.

For some years, Klein collaborated on the decoration of the new city theatre at Gelsenkirchen. To say that this building was mediocre would be grossly flattering to it. But this was a matter of indifference to Klein. He was at no point concerned with the visual aspect of the world around him. His own 'things' when they were actually in some way 'designed' showed it clearly: as did the vulgar, crass life-cast

YVES KLEIN First public exhibition of 'Anthropometry', March 9th 1960.

YVES KLEIN *Immaterial Pictorial Sensitivity Zone* No. 05, Série 1, January 26th 1962. Klein exchanges 20 grammes of gold leaf with 'buyer' Dino Buzzati.

YVES KLEIN *Immaterial Pictorial Sensitivity Zone* No. 06, Série 1, February 4th 1962. Klein scatters the gold leaf of 'buyer' Claude Pascal on the river Seine.

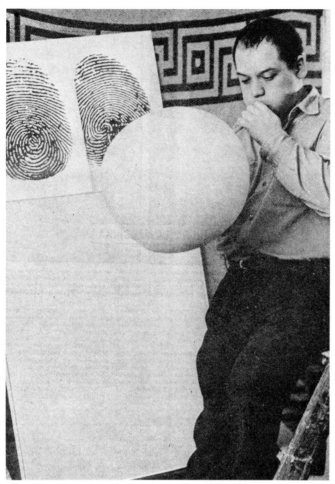

Piero Manzoni creating *The Artist's Breath* 1960.

Piero Manzoni with the *Artist's Shit* 1961.

of Klein's friend, the artist, Arman, coloured the usual ultramarine and mounted on a gold-leaf background. Klein was right to protest when Pierre Restany derived his procedure from that of the Dadaists: their activities were characterised by a black humour, by elegance and by their opposition to certain social conventions. Klein was highly, almost obsessively conventional, dapper in dress, avid for financial as well as social recognition, technically inept and totally earnest. The elegance which the Dadaists conferred on their products he reserved for his diminutive person.

To return now to Piero Manzoni, with whom I began: he saw himself as a disciple of Klein in a way: the catalogue of his part of the show registers their first meeting, and the impression it made on him. But Manzoni was a much more skilled operator, and was that much more elegant (I use the word quite deliberately) than Klein. The 'achromes', which he produced throughout his brief career, being basically white to pale grey, were never as abrasive as Klein's cheap poster-colour ultramarines; and the events he excogitated, like the artophagy (or perhaps more correctly, graphophagy) sessions in which guests were invited to eat hard-boiled eggs marked with the artist's thumb-print, and therefore raised to the status of works of art were wittier, homelier than any of Klein's solemn ceremonies. For my part, if I had to eat art, I'd much rather consume one of Ricardo Miralda's and Dorothée Seltz' delicious-looking objects. Maybe I just don't like hard-boiled eggs enough.

There were other products: balloons of the artist's breath, or balloons the purchaser could inflate with his own (pre-sumably inferior) product. There were those famous tins of artist's shit (made in Italy ...) which were sold for their weight in gold; there were to be inevitably also marketed assemblies of the artist's pee, sweat, and blood. But he didn't get that far. All this concentration on the artist's bodily function is analogous to Klein's obsessive neatness, to his pin-stripes. It focuses attention on the artist, away from his products.

It's all in the Duchamp country, of course. That first signed urinal of his, the 50 cc. of Paris air have their progeny in this kind of proto-conceptual art. I don't really want to quibble about nomenclature, so perhaps I should qualify what I mean. Take another one of Manzoni's inventions, the single line. Manzoni sold lines of various lengths. They come in plain black boxes, in metal boxes, even in a lead one (I think) for a line 7,200 m. long; though the simplest were the empty boxes which 'contained' an infinite line the spectator/purchaser had to imagine himself.

These again have obvious Duchamp precedents – the 'Three Stoppages' – much as Manzoni's signing of his friends and giving them certificates to signify that they were 'living works of art' is analogous to all that play Klein had with certificates and gold leaf. In fact, the Manzoni catalogue tells the pathetic story of Manzoni knocking on Klein's door, and on being opened to, saying: 'You are the monochrome blue, I am the monochrome white, we must work together', but, the catalogue adds laconically, 'no working arrangement followed'.

This art-historical parenthesis returns me to the exhibition: Manzoni did not make his bases collapse under innocent, would-be 'works of art'; he meant anyone who stepped on them to be transformed in some way: that was their magic. If you put the base in a museum and stop anyone getting on it, then you rob them of the possibility of 'working' at all; they become impotent, pointless art-objects.

But museum authorities are not interested in whether things 'work' or not; they want objects. If quizzed, they would no doubt tell you that high insurance costs ... that irresponsible people ... that children ... that dirt ... and show their disregard for the artist's intention: or would they?

In so far as Manzoni and Klein belong to one exhibition, had analogous aims, are their intentions betrayed in this way? They were both, it has always been clear, purveyors of concepts. Not the disembodied concepts which conceptual art proper purveys: Klein and Manzoni both needed to incarnate their concepts in objects. They lived by their art, and concepts are rather difficult to sell. And they manipulated the situation in the early days of the happening, as well as the usual art-market mechanism: numbered editions and hand-made this and that. Manzoni's shit, for instance, is even advertised as being 'free from artificial preservatives', though I shall never open a tin to find out if that's true.

Their objects are made rare, like old-fashioned works of art, equally ungainly, always showable, but essentially undemanding. Their concept (in the old academic sense of *concetto*) was always brutally simple. Once you had seen the conceit, you are left with the physical encumbrance of the object in which it is incarnate. If you bought it, you could be reminded that you understood the conceit each time you looked at it. Apart from the rising investment value, it held no further surprises. This is even true of Klein's plainest blue canvases, if you take them out of the context of a collective exhibition, and hang them among other pictures in a drawing-room. Its possessor was visibly the owner of a 'work of art'; but of a work of art which was uncritical: it held nothing up to his inspection, it did not seek to make any real impact on the visible world. In that sense, even the most abstruse practitioners of Arte Povera were (yes, it's in the past already) more vital.

Now, you may say, it's all very well for me to be carping. What is a poor artist to do? Duchamp and Malevich had got down to degree zero as far as painting is concerned. There is no way out. Only the immediate gesture can create the work of art, and that, as Duchamp told us, must be the 'artist's gesture' – the gesture for which he is responsible only to himself. Now I don't think this is true. I don't think all that printing of cheque-forms and receipts has anything to do with immediate gesture, or even with rituals: nor do I think that Yves Klein is innocent of the gross perpetrations at Gelsenkirchen because he is an artist. It's an awful building, and his blue sponge wallpaper is part of the awfulness. There are many ways forward from the zero which was reached fifty years ago: the understanding that everything is art is perhaps the most important of them. Klein and Manzoni worked against such an understanding. In the present climate, I cannot accept the operating of the art-market in the interest of exhibitionist personalities, however charismatic, as an entertaining and harmless diversion. It is a camouflage for the sinister forces which degrade the quality of our lives, and to tolerate it means that you accept the alibi of the despoilers of our visual environment.

PIERO MANZONI *Line of Infinite Length* 1960

PIERO MANZONI *Artist's Shit* 1961.

Ornament is no Crime

The title of this essay (much as Loos' well-known one which it travestied) was equally ironic in intention; since the essay was written to introduce a discussion of architecture and the other arts in a special issue of Studio International, *September/October 1975. If I have a regret about something I published, it is for the unfortunate and precocious use of the term 'post-Modern Movement style' which I applied here to the work of Paul Rudolph. However, let it stand.*

There was a time when the painter and sculptor had a clear idea of their link with the architect: they were all three 'visual' artists. The art of the painter and sculptor, however, was imitative of nature: that of the architect was only partially so. Architecture imitated, yes – but imitated culture. Monumental building reproduced the *necessary* forms of a primitive but rickety construction in permanent and noble materials. In so far as it came to imitating nature, it was the proportions of the human body which the architect abstracted in his measurements.

This view of the art of building, consecrated by theorists since Vitruvius (and he had drawn on much older sources) had an enormous vogue at the end of the eighteenth century. With a change of century came a change of attitude, shown by a double attack on the old view. Architecture, some said (with Goethe and the poets), did not imitate primitive construction: architecture imitated nature – the sacred wood, the cave-shrine. In this novel argument, the old belief that architecture was based on the proportions of the human body (which had been the mainstay of the advocates of nature) was forgotten. But even this modified form of the natural argument was contradicted by a new and important breed, the Polytechnicians. Architecture, they maintained, did not imitate anything. Architecture was dressed-up construction. The Polytechnicians did not – at any rate at first – ever advocate that construction should appear shamelessly naked. Decency, propriety, convention – society, in short – demanded that naked construction be covered, and that covering was ornament.

Ornament had once meant that which makes decent in supplying a missing essential. 'Modesty', the French Academy dictionary defines, 'is a great ornament of merit'. That is not what the Polytechnicians meant. Ornament was not supplying that which was good in itself with its essential complement, but covering the unacceptable. The cover catered to trivial pleasure. Architecture was concerned primarily with necessity, and its true essential beauty depended on a direct and economic satisfaction of man's most urgent, physical needs. The beauty of necessity satisfied reason alone; much as the beauty of association and sentiment could appeal only to the imagination. Here was a dichotomy which was to grow more divisive throughout the nineteenth century.

There were two kinds of architecture: that of the poets and that of the Polytechnicians. They often overlapped, and in any case the public came to consider them suitable for different kinds of building. The poets concentrated their attention on historical, and therefore nostalgic, ornament; the Polytechnicians maintained that if beauty must be specially catered for in building, it was through proportion. Not the old musical consonances of universal harmony, dear to Renaissance and Baroque theorists, but three different and separate kinds: that simply derived from the properties of materials, and that derived from economy which is the desire for the greatest possible simplicity of geometry (and justified their insistent use of the circle and square); and, as a mean, that old-fashioned kind of proportion which was associated with classical orders – and therefore with a repertory of decoration – and which was considered *useful* in that it would, by clothing structure with convention, spare the users of the building the shock of the unusual. This last proportion was thought to be of purely local application in Europe and the Mediterranean. Builders in Persia, China or India would have no call for this kind of packaging and could rely on materials and economy alone to furnish them with all they needed.

As the disciples of the Polytechnicians spread throughout Europe, to the Far East, to the American West and to Africa, they carried this doctrine with them. It is, of course, true that the nineteenth century was the great age of applied ornament. But as the century went on, the merely conventional nature of ornament was increasingly evident, and increasingly despised by any vital artist. Even those whose practice involved them in the most elaborate ornamental inventions theorised in terms which were not unsympathetic to the Polytechnicians. There should be no features about a building which are not necessary for convenience, one of them wrote; construction and propriety and all ornament should consist of the enrichment of the essential structure of a building. Such ideas now seem a strange justification for a full-blooded return to the imitation of English architecture in the late fifteenth century. But such theories were advanced as a justification of Gothic and classical, Hindu and Moorish and even Chinese. The appeal was ultimately to the polytechnic justification of ornament as a shock-absorbent package, particularly necessary in an age of structural innovation and functional specialising and diversifying. It was, however, self-destructive in the end, when the justification of ornament by convention would appear threadbare or even cynical. The process was expedited by another, and rather different development: throughout the nineteenth century, artists who had earlier been uprooted from their guilds and gathered into academies were schooled in the disciplines of taste. Art schools grew from the academies at the time when the Polytechnics were created. In the schools, artists shifted their attention from creating objects intended to edify, move or excite the spectator, and concentrated on an authentic expression of individual vision, in which the artist's relation to the spectator *through* the object became increasingly less important, as artists moved into that kingdom which has come to be known as Bohemia.

There were protests. The Pre-Raphaelites made stained glass and tapestries for William Morris. Puvis de Chavannes painted a fresco-cycle in the Paris Pantheon. But these were exceptions. The view of ornament as a conventional dressing was welded to a notion of style. A style was conceived from about the middle of the century onwards as a complete and integral 'expression' of an epoch. It was, of course, most easily characterised by its surface features, its ornament.

Although various attempts had been made to devise a repertory of new ornament for the coming epoch, these were hampered by the kind of devaluation I have described. Some of the more adventurous innovators conceived an ideal point in time such as fifteenth-century England or Renaissance Italy to which architects might return, since it was a point of fusion; and took original development beyond it, first having achieved a satisfactory emulation of the chosen historical style.

The final attempt to create the total artistic vesture for the new age lasted about fifteen years in all. It had various names: Art Nouveau, Jugendstil, Stile Liberty and so on. At its height, one of the most influential architects of the time wrote: 'there is no doubt that the point may and shall be reached when nothing visible will be created without receiving an *artistic* baptism.'

It is a good description of tensions. But, of course, the aim was soon seen to be unattainable. And this gave rise to the final triumph of the Polytechnicians in a destructive attack on all ornament. It was summarised in the essay 'Ornament and Crime' by the Austrian architect, Adolf Loos, which first appeared in 1908, the argument of which was insistently recapitulated through his work. To Loos pleasure in architec-

ture is – ultimately – pleasure of the imagination: but it is the whole architectural object which must engage the imagination, having also satisfied reason, however. For Loos, the only ornament which is licit is that which expresses the maker's pleasure: of the upholsterer (mouldings and brass-work on furniture), of the nomadic carpet-weaver (patterns in oriental carpets), and the shoemaker (brogue shoes). It is an expression of the maker's pleasure, *not* a concession which indulges the user's eye. True pleasure in one's surroundings for the civilised man (defined by Loos as a man who listens to Beethoven's Ninth or to *Tristan*) is in the smooth texture of objects designed to perform their job with least fuss: the saddle, the smooth silver cigarette-case are examples obviously liked, as he liked the products of engineering and industry. They cater to the pleasures of reason and of the senses. Ornament – all art in fact – had its origin in the obscene, magical scrawl of the cave-dweller. The art of modern man is not concerned with the instinctive needs which were satisfied by such daubs, but is addressed to the higher faculties. In so far as architecture has to do with feeling and imagination, it is the whole mass of the building which does so, not any of its details.

Loos was not entirely consistent, but his attack was symptomatic, and was echoed by other writers. The sociologist Georg Simmel, for instance, writing in the same year as Loos, in 1908, suggested that ornament, being related to the individuation of objects, may subsist in craft, but is out of place in industrial production, and must in any case be identified with the greatest possible 'generalisation' since style and elegance depend on the lack of individuality.

Within a matter of months of the publication of that fateful essay on Ornament and Crime, the man who Loos sometimes regarded as his arch-enemy was commissioned to design a theatre in Paris. This theatre was to be an epic building. Van de Velde recounts the story in circumstantial detail in his memoirs, though, he did not finish it of course: the original project was modified by Auguste Perret, who had been invited as a concrete expert, and ended by ousting van de Velde as van de Velde had ousted the previous architect, Roger Bouvard. The men who had maintained their part in the building, however, through the three architects' régimes were the painter Maurice Denis, a pupil of Cézanne, who had been commissioned from the outset of the whole enterprise to paint the auditorium ceiling (and acted as its impresario), and the sculptor, Antoine Bourdelle, who was to do the panels on the facade and the decorations of the foyer. The decorative continuity, which had been van de Velde's main preoccupation, was broken by Perret. For the flowing Art Nouveau lines, for the broken and coruscating surfaces, he substituted a smooth, severe, clipped, 'French-classical' manner, much more to the taste of the committee which had originally commissioned the theatre than van de Velde's decorations. The divisions it marked between the articulations and the artists' works were also more to the taste of Bourdelle and Denis. And it marks a break in European taste from which there was no going back.

Perret, of course, had used ornament before, in the elaborate flower-design ceramic facing of his own flats in the rue Franklin, which was done in 1902–03; there, he already declared his independence of the current Art Nouveau linearities, his faith in a new material, reinforced concrete. He used it as a skeleton, inducing a modular severity which he chose to interpret in a 'classical' fashion. But the abundant use of sculpture and painting in the

A. W. PUGIN 'Factory chimneys, Government preaching halls, Zion Chapels' from *The True Principles of Pointed or Christian Architecture.*

Théâtre des Champs Elysées was not something he normal-
ly favoured; here it was part of the commission, and
Bourdelle and Denis were there before him. He was to work
with Denis again on the church of Our Lady at Raincy, done
in 1922–23, where Denis was responsible for the coloured
windows which fill the panels between the shorn and
elongated classical colonettes. Although he went on designing churches based on the Raincy idea, this was the only
other time he willingly collaborated with an artist of importance. 'That which is beautiful does not need decoration,
since it decorates', he used to say, according to an admirer:
and so elided the problem. (Perret meant something more
like 'dignifies' or 'gives decorum' than the English word
'decorate'.) And, of course, in the twenties a rather specious
distinction grew up between the work of sculptors or
painters, 'works of art' used 'decoratively' and the repetitive
ornament produced by mere craftsmen. Perret did use both,
and that in spite of his noble aphorism. He never wholly
abjured the hammered and inlaid ornament of the shorn
classicism I spoke of – even after the last war, in the
reconstruction of Amiens and Le Havre, he did not renounce
the detached colonnades, the apparatus of details derived
from the style of *le grand siècle*. In the meanwhile, his old
opponent van de Velde had become converted to a similar
creed, if not a similar manner; the belief, as he put it, that
'the rational conception produced the silex or cut onyx tools
and weapons ... [it] is the inexhaustible, and ever-cool
source of all that strain, which – through the ages – has born
witness to the existence and constant vitality of a style
which never ages, which is and shall be of every age.'

It was this ageless modern style which van de Velde was
introducing to the Paris public by way of comment and
almost of protest at the time of the decorative art exhibition
in Paris in 1925. That exhibition was as much the apogee of
Art Deco as the 1902 Turin show was of Art Nouveau. And
the whole of what came to be called the Modern Movement
was a protest against its pervasive influence.

Now the Modern Movement eschewed ornament with
the greatest acerbity. But it did not quite dispense with the
more or less 'decorative' work of art. Mies van der Rohe, the
harshest of the Modern Movement formalists, not only
employed sculptures by Kolbe and Lehmbruck as the only
photographable inhabitants of his building, but also modelled
the figures in his drawings on Lehmbruck's sculptures. Le
Corbusier employed work by Jacques Lipschitz and by
Léger, and in his later work – *faute de mieux* sometimes, as
he himself knew – his own paintings and even sculptures.
Of one building of that period, the Spanish pavilion at the
Paris exhibition of 1937, little is remembered. But the
painting which was specially done for it, Picasso's *Guernica*,
has become the best-known single twentieth-century
image. It also contained the mysterious painting by Miró
(*Rebellious Catalan peasant* or *The Reaper*) and the mercury
fountain by Calder, which stood before it, is fairly well
known. The building itself deserved better than to become
the Sistine Chapel of the twentieth century. But it is entirely
dwarfed by the works of art which it sheltered, and which
were in part commissioned by the architects and sometimes
– as was the case with the mercury fountain – even
attributed to them. Such buildings represent the upper tip of
what you might call 'architects' architecture' for the thirties.
The minor masters were, of course, much more thorough in
their eschewing of the visual 'irrelevance'. The generalised
belief that whatever was beautiful did not need to decorate
because it was itself *décor* was extended. It was beautiful

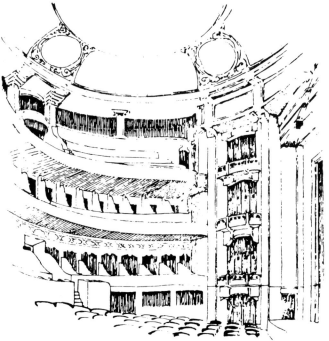

HENRY VAN DE VELDE *Théâtre des Champs Elysées* Paris, original projects
for the facade and auditorium, 1910.

Opposite
AUGUSTE and GEORGES PERRET *Théâtre des Champs Elysées* Paris
1911–13. *Top left* facade and corner with decorative panels by Antoine
Bourdelle; *top right* auditorium with ceiling painting by Maurice Denis and
balcony extended across the front of the loggia; *bottom* foyer.

because it served its purpose most directly. And therefore that which served its purpose most directly could in itself turn into an object *à émouvoir*; the archetype of such an object was, of course, the technological product, which had radically altered the means at the artists' disposal in the twentieth century. It had been regarded as a slave until the middle of the nineteenth, when it became an enemy. The volume of technological objects grew, however, and the dialogue with machine production altered in tone. The enemy of the nineteenth century became the master, the *deus* (doubly you might say) *ex machina*. God-created (as against man-created) nature became muted, trivialised. The menace to twentieth-century urban man was no longer drought, storm and flood. The great dangers came from a different nature: from the boom-crisis economy, from the methods of secret persuasion and of oppression, and from the omnipresent destructive forces we have devised: gases, bacteria, nerve-drugs in drinking-water, the BOMB; or even from the increasing malfunctioning of our ingenuities: pollution, overcrowding, jamming, the rising flood of detritus.

Artists were not able to absorb the technological product into their work and had therefore to account for it by irony: naming, indicating and quoting. It started gently with collage and frottage, and was speeded up by R. Mutt's famous fountain choice – of which so much has already been said. This attempt to absorb the industrial and exalt it into culture was a much more powerful and hazardous piece of magic than we can now realise. But the magic wore off (with the war), and had to be renewed. The efforts ranged from solipsist inflatable defiance to the total immersion of Ulm; from the admiring imitations of Tinguely to the rebarbative *longueurs* of Warhol. The work of the artists stood apart from the rational normality of what was built and inhabited. Buildings increasingly became images of technical production, from which the world of the imagination was banished. But while the artist had less and less truck with society – and therefore with rationality – architects and designers strove earnestly to assimilate their procedure to that of the mechanic. In the heroic days of De Stijl, of the Russian Constructivists and, to some extent, in the later years of the Bauhaus, the very leap into the realm of quantity was exciting by the desperate nature of the exercise. Unfortunately, its consequence was anything but exhilarating. The pressing of all imaginative effort into the mould of pseudo-rationalism (of the particularly naive positivist brand which went on in the late thirties and immediately after the war) has convinced the architect's most important clients, the world's various civil services and the boards of the large companies, that the answer to their problems in terms of what is now called 'built form' (that is, architecture and building) will be a good social service provided that they are presented in tabulated form, and the quantities show some positive result, however dottily calculated. Hence the various products of 'systems design' and its even dottier by-products (some of which, such as the work of the Ulm school) have even entered the murky penumbra of modern mythology.

Production is the result of our dialogue with nature: and the process of dialogue and production is what we call culture. Not an adequate definition perhaps, but it does something to tie up the diverse dictionary meanings of worship, tillage, selective breeding, training and education; and distinguishes it from the towny, even bourgeois qualities of civilisation. The truth is that technology is 'Son of Culture', as they say in the titles of horror films, but culture has not learnt to take account of its vast offspring, at any rate not on a conscious level. The sad, playful attempts in the forties and fifties of our century to produce a generally acceptable and machine-based (as well as machine-made) ornament is a warning of the futility of any short-cuts. We are witnessing a similar and equally futile exercise just now: the revival of what has been called the 'Cinema Style'; the ornamental jollities of Odeon cinemas and Lyons Corner Houses in this country aping the majority of twenties and early thirties skyscrapers in the U.S. But the revival raises the problem, which derives from a sub-cultural phenomenon: the shift in the social pattern of taste to a dictatorship of the working-class, more specifically the Anglo-Saxon working-class, which was exemplified by the cult of the Beatles and the Stones, and the graphic style of Alan Aldridge. The style is already past its peak, although its sources – the film strip-cartoon – are a permanent feature of our society, and cater for the same kind of irrational pleasure as the 'Cinema Style': the pleasure which appeals through the medium of a market populism; the people like it because they buy it, *ergo* it is good in itself because the people are good. Yet the critical shift from a bourgeois to a working-class cultural mode has made the joys of cinema interiors seem exotically remote.

The attitude has its sociological and by implication (as often happens nowadays) its philosophical apologist in the work of an American sociologist, Herbert Gans, whose *Levittowners* has counterattacked the many critics of American suburbia. It concentrated on the life of a commercial suburban development, one of a successful chain based on mass-produced, relatively cheap housing (marketed in various styles for the same house) by a large industrial building contractor on the East Coast of the States. Levittown – as these suburbs are called – has become a slogan as well as a commercial enterprise. It covers the range of attitudes which maintains that everyone has the right to their life-style provided it is within their means and not actively anti-social; that no pundit has any right to tell them otherwise. And in particular not the planner and architect, whose real business is to provide a suitable packaging for the given life-style, including the ornamental patterns which the inhabitant may choose for himself.

Inevitably, too, the attitude acquired a high culture architect as its advocate. He is the triune person of Robert Venturi, Denise Scott-Brown and John Rauch. On his own, when Robert Venturi wrote *Complexity and Contradiction in Architecture* (1966), he replaced the Miesian paradox 'Less is more' with the jibe 'Less is a bore'. His appeal against the purism of the old Modern Movement, against the uniformities and the boredom of the Masters was to an architecture of variety, and (as the title implied) of visual and volumetric complexity. Lutyens was quoted almost as often as Le Corbusier; and above all 'Main Street', which had been the cynosure of so many 'purist' critics (Venturi attacked Peter Blake in particular), messy, disorderly, commercialised Main Street was *almost* all right.

His next step was perhaps foreseeable. If Main Street is almost all right, then it can be made wholly so by putting it in inverted commas. So that is what Venturi did. 'Ugly and Ordinary' is how he describes the building he wishes to design. Note the inverted commas, however. Not ugly and ordinary, but 'Ugly and Ordinary'. These buildings are high culture, to be judged by the same criteria as 'architects' architecture', just as the Rolling Stones put themselves

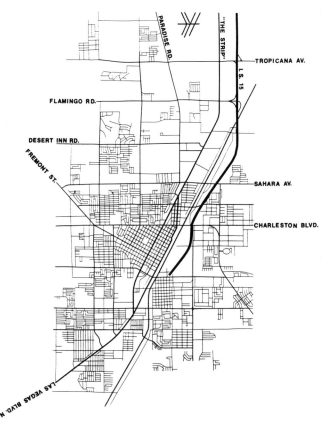

Las Vegas street map, 1972, showing the strip in relation to the rest of the town.

'The Long Island Duckling' from Peter Blake's *God's Own Junkyard.*

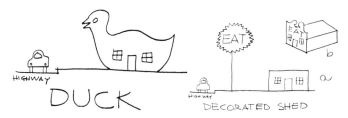

'Duck and decorated shed' from *Learning from Las Vegas*. The duck is defined as the special building which is a symbol, whereas the decorated shed is the conventional shelter with applied symbols.

between inverted commas when they made *Sympathy for the Devil* with Jean-Luc Godard.

The slogan of the ugly and the ordinary is not intended to be a critical judgment on their architecture, although it derives from a jury comment on a competition scheme of Venturi. Unfortunately, even in their second apologia, *Learning from Las Vegas* (1972), they do not offer a higher transcendental idea than variety as a justification for their approach. No idea there of variety for …? Variety is presented as good in itself, and the book sets as many posers as it answers.

Learning from Las Vegas was, you might say, the architectural tail of the comet which had Tom Wolfe as its flashing head. The analytical jeremiads which were the favoured U.S. kind of journalistic sociology, excellently purveyed by Vance Packard and William H. Whyte Jr., had its architectural equivalent in the post-Modern Movement style of Paul Rudolph. Naturally, he became the Venturis' favourite target. But architecture is more expensive than clothes or even customised motor cars, and architectural fashions follow behind other fashion manifestations which are cheaper, more volatile and more sensitive to the change of social tone.

The cult of Levittown as a representative of American suburban life combines the self-sufficiency and individualism of the generation which grew up in the fifties and early sixties and is now saddled with the universal paraphernalia of wife, children, mortgage and job. Levittown makes a premium of individuality within the suburban milieu. The variety which Venturi exalted in *Complexity and Contradiction* is available in Levittown, as it is on the Las Vegas strip, although it is a quite different product from the arcane complexities of Lutyens' plans.

But the counterposition of Las Vegas and of Levittown is interesting for another reason. The study done in *Learning*

from Las Vegas deals *only* with the strip. Not a word is said of Las Vegas housing. Though if you look at the Venturis' plans of the town on which the strip is marked for your admiration, you will see that it is virtually square: and yet in the book, the parts of the town beyond the facades of the strip do not appear, except at the edge of one or two aerial photographs. Their attention is entirely focused on the eccentric volumes of the casinos and hotels: but even more, on their signs.

The variety of the neon and other electric signs is, of course, what continues to fascinate so many journalists as well as the architects and designers who make Las Vegas part of their grand tour. And yet Tom Wolfe, who had popularised it, also had, all those many years ago, a warning for them: his first hero of the Las Vegas adventure, whom he called 'Raymond' and who – 'although not a typical Las Vegas tourist' – is a 'good example of the impact Las Vegas had on the senses', demonstrated that the impact, augmented by alternating doses of amphetamine and meprobamate (taken with alcohol), had induced a state of toxic schizophrenia.

The Venturis have now transferred their attention to the much more anodyne varieties of 'customised' Levittown housing, which indicates a duality (unresolved and perhaps unresolvable) in approach. On the one hand is the public space of Las Vegas; on the other, the private one of the speculators' suburb. Variety is the one transcendent value to which they pay any service. Yet in the first book there was a pervading assumption that variety had no meaning without a unity to which it is subsumed.

In the later studies there is less talk of unity. In the Las Vegas study there is a crucial attempt to classify all building into two major classes: ducks, that is buildings which are three-dimensional, volumetric envelopes for a given function (a drive-in in the shape of a vast duck was illustrated in a

97

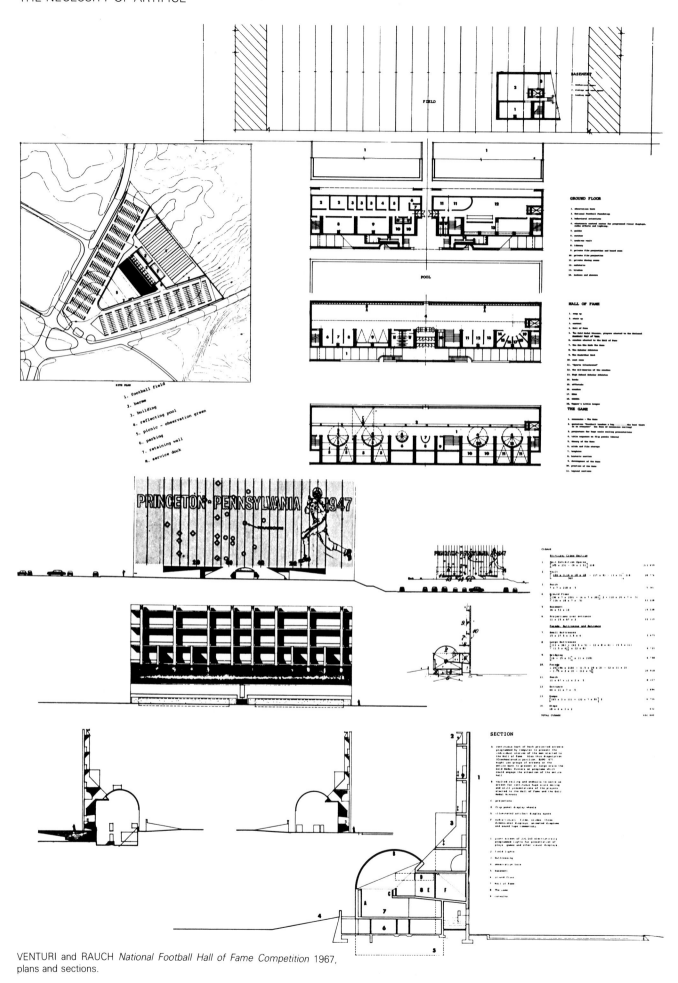

VENTURI and RAUCH *National Football Hall of Fame Competition* 1967,
plans and sections.

VENTURI and RAUCH *National Football Hall of Fame Competition* 1967, side view of the model.

book by Peter Blake, *God's Own Junkyard*, which he ridiculed); and 'decorated sheds'. Venturi maintains that most modern 'architects' architecture' is 'ducks': buildings in which the symbolic form is the organising principle of structure, volume and programme. While their validity in the past (Gothic cathedrals) is unquestioned, the Venturis propose as the type of a modern building the decorated shed, in which the shelter is dictated by utilitarian considerations, while the symbolic bits and pieces are stuck on to the front: facades, billboards or signs. Assertively, Venturi has carried his theory out in practice. Decorated sheds, 'ugly and ordinary' is what he claims to build, though he also produces the occasional duck: there is after all no ban on ducks in his theory.

The dual classification, with its emphatic preference for the decorated shed, does, however, raise a most important issue; and it may be worth looking at one of their buildings in some detail to state it. This oldish scheme (1967) is useful since it embodies the approach at a level near parody. It is the competition design for the National Football Hall of Fame near the Rutgers Stadium in New Jersey. The scheme is a low (three-storey) vaulted gallery with an atrophied grandstand towards a playing field at the back; but the important feature is the vast electrified billboard (Bill-Ding-Board), the size of a full-size football pitch, more than twice the height of the hall proper, and running its full width. The triangular piazza in front, the building and the pitch are isolated from the surrounding roadways by a parking lot about twice the total area of piazza, building and pitch. The shed is therefore decorated with a vengeance; and isolated in the New Jersey urban sprawl in a way which makes it part of the suburban landscape, camouflaged indeed as an uncritical object

among others. Here's the rub. This acceptance of the culture of the shed and the billboard, which *Learning from Las Vegas* has theorised, is an acceptance of the product of technology as the incarnation of some natural force immanent in machine production; it is therefore presented as being outside the critical, judging reach of any cultural criteria. In that way, the Venturi argument is strangely parallel to the Loos argument. Needs dictate the shed; the shed should not be transformed into 'sculptured' volume which is more expensive and less directly related to their direct satisfaction. So far the argument has much in common with Loos' more sophisticated justification of engineering works against the tortuous effects of architects' insensitivity to the deeds of men and of nature. But the Venturi argument adds a rather heavy makeweight, which inverts the result. Since variety is an essential human need and buildings need in some way to say what they are, this extra need and the labelling requirement is fully satisfied by sticking the most varied matter on to the building itself: and you have the new architecture, which has moreover the great virtue of looking just like all other buildings.

So concerned are the Venturis to emphasise the unity of their buildings with all that surrounds them that the distinction between the '*almost* all right' of Main Street and the presumably 'quite all right' of the Venturis' work is often blurred; though it is probably discernible in the way the ugly and ordinary have been complex and contradictory.

I say this without malice: it is the Venturis' favourite approval words which I have used to qualify their own work. Since they have become the best-known architectural office (among the younger ones) in the Anglo-Saxon world, the whole problem of ornament has now been identified with

99

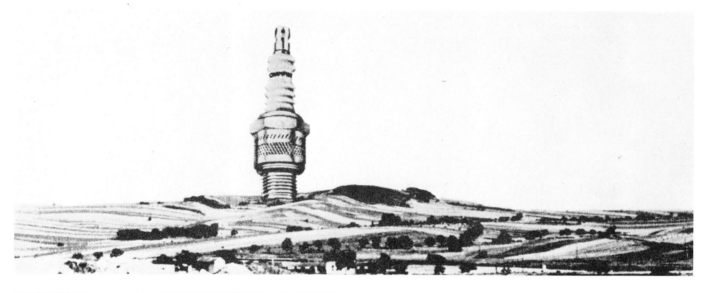

Above
HANS HOLLEIN *High-rise building* 1964.

Left
HANS HOLLEIN *New York skyline collage* 1962.

Below
CLAES OLDENBURG *Soft Toilet* 1966.

CLAES OLDENBURG *Hard Switches* 1964.

their formulation of it. But in fact it has been about for some time. Some ten years ago, the Zürich Kunstgewerbemuseum presented the argument for and against the thing visually, through an exhibition. And the problem has been re-appearing in quite different ways. Notoriously, certain architects as different as James Stirling (air-conditioning plant in the History Faculty Library at Cambridge) and Richard Rogers and Renzo Piano (service ducting on the exterior of the Centre Pompidou in Paris) have been using services in a way which suggests that they have formulated the problem, at least to themselves. More crucially, it has been explored by the Viennese group: St. Florian, Pichler, Abraham, Hollein and others. For lack of space, I shall arbitrarily take Hans Hollein as the representative of the group. He has none of the populist propensities of the Venturis, though he, too, is concerned with the ordinary, if not the ugly. In particular, he has elevated the method of ironic choice into an exercise which he has called 'Everything is architecture'. Among his media, he has included an atomiser for making 'instant environment' and a box of varying pills for transforming environment 'from inside yourself'. Many of his more tangible projects involve the changing of some piece of technology (a sparking plug, an aircraft-carrier) into an enigmatic but architectonic object through a change of scale and context. These buildings are all ornament; the very thing that is anathema to the Venturis. In condemnation of such things, they quote an aphorism of Pugin's (from a book he published in 1843) deploring '... ornaments that are actually constructed, instead of forming the decoration of construction'. In fact, Pugin meant the aphorism to condemn 'decorated sheds' of the kind dear to the Venturis, as the first part of that aphorism makes quite clear: 'Architectural features are continuously tacked on to buildings with which they have no connection, merely for what is termed effect ...'

To tag 'Eat Here' on to a café or diner is not what Pugin meant by 'the decoration of construction' at all. What he did mean is that ornament must be integrated with the way the building is built, as well as the way it is used. The whole unity, as he conceived it, would then become a kind of social operation. This kind of building he set up against the decorated sheds which his contemporaries purveyed. For him then, as it is for me now, the problem of architectural form was not one of packaging: nor could problems of ornament be solved by 'sticking' suitable labels on to neutral packaging.

And yet, at the formal level, both the Venturis and Hollein have something in common with an artist whose irony, whose sense of scale, have made him turn to constructions which are – more or less – urban and monumental complexes: Claes Oldenburg. His technique has always been one of irony: the edible hardened, the metallic made floppy, the household or even the hand-held turned into a vast monument. But always, as he himself has said, he is concerned with a reversal of expectation in his reshaping of the tangible (tangible-untouchable is a most important pair of opposites for him) commonplace.

This is where, perhaps, the Venturis' design is nearest to being critical, in the only sense which makes architecture worthwhile. Their buildings, unlike the creations of their more successful and more generalising contemporaries, are at their best eminently touchable. Hollein, too, is concerned with this bodily quality: almost obsessively. That may be the most important indicator of the way forward in architecture. And it is a way architects cannot take without the help of the painters and sculptors. If only because we must all acknowledge that, in a negative way at any rate, Loos was right: ornament, as the nineteenth-century architects and critics understood it, is wholly dead, beyond any hope of resurrection. We cannot rely on any kind of convention: the world of tangible form has to be learnt anew. Architects never think of buildings as tangible objects, except at the one direct point of contact, the door-handle. And yet buildings are not only enclosure; they are also extensions of ourselves, like clothing. But being more stable, more permanent, more important in fact, they are subject to the importuning demand that we, and by that I mean everybody, make of objects: that they should enhance, enrich, improve with our handling of them. This, it is increasingly clear, will not be done as long as there is a general social assumption that reasonable returns is all we require of products. On the contrary, they must engage our imagination. And they will not do so until architects and designers have really begun to learn the lessons which the painters and sculptors have to teach; and, moreover, have learnt to work together with them, make use of their work not only as analogue, but also as adornment. But such a development will only be valid if it is seen to be necessary, not gratuitous: as long as it will be seen not as a problem of ornament or not ornament, but as a problem of meaning.

'A Band Moves', nomadic African bushmen moving from one place of residence to another.

Learning from the Street

An edited version of the first section of a history of the street which was submitted to the Housing and Urban Development Administration in Washington in 1974, but never published.

With 'The Sitting Position' and 'Thinking about a House', it may be taken as an exercise in applying the same method at three different scales: the household object, the architectural object, the urban object.

Originally pulished in Lotus 11, 1976, it has now appeared in a highly edited version of the H.U.D. report (MIT Press 1978).

I am grateful to Dr. Suzanne Frank for her work on the etymology of the street and road, as well as for her continuous assistance in the preparation of this essay.

For nearly a century, the street has been under persistent attack from several directions: the designers of Siedlungen and Garden Cities; the CIAM modern masters; local government and welfare architects of Anglo-Saxon/Scandinavian countries have all attempted to postulate forms of urban settlement in which the street was deprived of its past function or analysed out of existence. There has been a correlative attack by those followers of Haussmann who have subordinated all functions of urban settlement to the street itself, particularly to the street as a carrier of traffic. The most extreme of these was the Spanish urbanist, Arturo Soria y Mata, who envisaged a street-city linking Cadiz and Petersburg, Peking and Brussels; he arrogated to the street all those urban functions which it had never performed previously and therefore, like his fellows, overcharged it to breaking-point.

Such movements were closely linked – in time at any rate – with the growth of a 'zoning' theory of planning. The modest attempts made by the builders of improved industrial settlements to site factories downstream or downwind of housing developed into a varied series of hypothetical zoning schemes. These took up the city divisions which were as old as urban dwelling but elaborated and schematised them; so for instance the density of dwellings to ground area was zoned, to result – incidentally – in the strict socio-economic class division in cities; or again, the zoning of height in relation to built-up area produced the serrated outlines of most American high buildings.

The latest refinements of these regulations have tended, lamely, to restore the integrity of the street pattern, but no consistent theory of either how or why it should be done has been developed. Other zoning regulations dividing the town or settlement by function have had a radical effect on the street pattern. This is most evident in the case of housing. Wherever the functions of exchange and commerce have been banished or 'ghettoed' in housing estates, the rift between public and private space has been widened disastrously. Most housing is nowadays built in some form of slab or point block. Internally, communication in these blocks occurs in vertical service-transport shafts, horizontally in access galleries or corridors which are sometimes dignified with the name of 'internal streets': while the terrain around high-rise dwellings becomes at best lawn or park, at worst paved space, euphemistically labelled 'playground'. Very rarely is such ground given over to participatory activities by the inhabitants of the high-rise blocks, such as allotments. Intermediate public space which could be regarded by the citizen as something quite different from street paving does not really exist. The space round high blocks is therefore treated by the inhabitants as alien ground, undignified by the pleasures or uses which they expect of the street.

It is perhaps the fate of fudged and ill-considered utopias to end in squalor quickly. But the speed with which Gropius' slab skyscraper in the park, which seemed such a splendid ideal to a Western European and even American haute-bourgeoisie only twenty or thirty years ago, decayed into the horrific square miles of Lefrak towers has left planners rather breathless: the shabby utopia had become the exemplar for the biggest boom in world history. The Gropius model might even with justice be called the CIAM model; it is to Le Corbusier's credit that he not only formulated an important modification of the mammoth *redents* of his Ville Radieuse in the *immeuble-villas* of 1922 and 1925; moreover he provided them with large areas of semi-public and service space to act as the in-between layer for the public and the private realm.

Neither Le Corbusier nor even Gropius, however, seriously considered urban problems outside the zoning straight-jacket. There is perhaps some mitigation in Le Corbusier's attempt to make real internal streets in the various Unités as well as ample and festive public entrance spaces for the blocks; though such efforts were from the outset frustrated by various market and regulation troubles. Their visible as well as conceptual remoteness from the ground, from circulation, robbed them of some of the qualities which the old-fashioned street not only has but is also seen to have.

In spite of the utopias, the building booms, the functions of the street have only been modified not altered out of recognition in existing cities however powerful the technological innovations: rail, motor-car, elevator, television. The expectation of daily human contact which the street uniquely offers: and offers in a pattern of exchanges without which the community would break down, is inhibited at the risk of the increasing alienation of the inhabitant from his city. The cost of this alienation is not easily calculable. It contributes to social stress generally; it generates waste space and therefore urban blight, one of whose by-products are the rising crime rates. The community pays for this in an impoverishment of its life, in the destruction of public and private property, in the increasing cost of policing. Any cost calculation of street renewal (though this goes for urban renewal generally) in terms of fiscal effectiveness alone is not only socially – it is economically shortsighted.

The state of affairs described in the last paragraph has concerned sociologists for several decades. Unfortunately, their discipline is not prescriptive: they describe, classify, determine causes. They do not 'solve' social problems. The

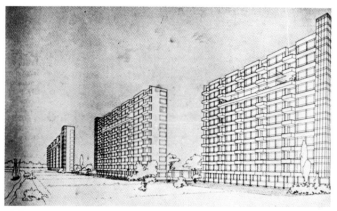

WALTER GROPIUS *High-rise apartment buildings in a lakeside park* 1931.

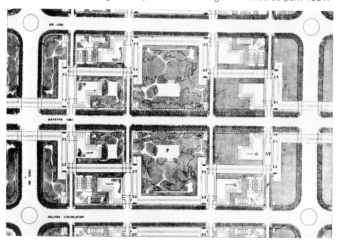

LE CORBUSIER *Immeuble-villas* 1925. Entry to the apartment blocks is by private access roads, each with its own parking facilities (ST). Each block is also provided with a garage (G). The ratio built area:cultivated area is 15:85.

LE CORBUSIER *Unité d'Habitation* Marseille 1946–52.

decisions which lead to a change in conditions are political, and to a lesser degree, formal. The sociologist cannot even tell us with any certainty what the social consequence of a given formal decision might be. He can only tell us, like a historian might, how certain social conditions and certain formal configurations of plan and volume were related in the past. Since such a relationship subsisted in the past, in our past, he can tell us about ourselves and hope that with greater self-knowledge our political decisions might grow more mature and more rational.

Paradoxically this is particularly important at the moment because of the very strong impact of technology on street use. Both building and transport technology have had their transforming effect on it. Inevitably therefore anyone concerned with the development of the street must postulate models for the future development of *city* patterns as well as *street* patterns. Urban renewal programmes which are only remedies for street pathology are inadequate in the present situation. The urbanist must envisage the pressure he wishes to exert on technological progress in terms of his own vision of the most desirable future for the city. Of course, this raises the hoary problem of the urbanist as an elite specialist opposed to the operation of the General Will. This very unreal objection need only be answered by those who equate the operation of the stock-market with the common good. The urbanist is not in the position of a despot, however benevolent, but rather in that of a motor-car engineer who can choose whether he thinks it more proper to develop ever faster and larger motor-cars, or whether the consumer watchdog has a case and he should be thinking in terms of less powerful, smaller, safer and cleaner vehicles. The decision – which of the two tendencies to follow – may be called economic but is ultimately political.

*   *   *

I should like at this point to consider what we expect of the street. The very words we use to describe it reveal something of our expectation. For the street is human movement institutionalised. An individual may clear or mark out a path in a wilderness: but unless he is followed by others, his path never becomes a road or street, because the road and the street are social institutions and it is their acceptance by the community which gives them the name and the function with which I am here concerned. The two words we use most commonly indicate a polarity. The word *street* is derived from the Latin *sternere*, to pave, and so relates to all Latin-derived words with the *'str'* root which are connected with building, with construction. It suggests that a surface is distinguished from its surroundings in some physical or at least notional way. It recurs in many European languages: the Italian *strada*, for instance, or the German *Strasse* suggest an area set apart for public use and can include spaces with simple, limited demarcations without necessary connections to other streets. It does not necessarily lead anywhere in particular therefore, but may finish in a plaza or in a blind-alley.

Road, on the other hand, suggests movement to a destination and – incidentally – the transporting of people and commodities on foot, by pack animal or vehicle. *Ride* is its Anglo-Saxon root (O.E. *ridan*) and it denotes passage from one place to another. In this sense, it is identical with the French word *rue*; *via* in Latin and Italian, which is related to the Latin word *ire* and derives from the Indo-European

word for bring, lead (Sanskrit *vahâmi*, from which *veho*, *Wagen*, and *waggon* also derive) is exactly analogous to *road* and *rue*. There are many other words to denote forms of passage-way in English, as there are in other languages. All of these, however, whether described individually or classed into broader categories, elaborate the essential duality suggested by the two primary words. *Alley*, for example, always implies a narrow passage; *avenue*, a wide street with one or more lines of trees; *boulevard* again suggests a tree-lined street and is derived from the widespread custom of adapting sixteenth- and seventeenth-century defensive earthworks within the expanding street pattern of eighteenth- and nineteenth-century towns. I should like to isolate three groups of words to suggest three different ways of considering the street. Firstly, *terrace*, *row*, *arcade*, *embankment* or *gallery* display the way in which the street is physically constituted by its context.

A second group includes words like *path*, *track*, *parade*, *promenade* and *mall*, all of which are connected with ways of proceeding on foot from picking out a route on totally unmarked ground (*track*), to sauntering along a well-defined, marked way, suggested by the word *promenade*; it even includes the walk through a path beaten by a recurrent walking game: *mall*; or the street along which races are regularly run: *corso*.

The third and last group relates entirely to vehicular traffic and to the legal and engineering matters it involves: *street*, *highway*, *artery*, *thoroughfare*, are such words. The term *high street* or *main street*, commonly a name of the principal street of many English and American towns, still carries the suggestion that a long distance route passes through a settlement, a built-up area. Often, before the days of bypasses, that is exactly what happened.

Variations on the ways in which traffic lanes are described have multiplied: and will continue to multiply as long as the volume of traffic grows and the legal complications which attend it increase. Both building and transport technology have contributed to transforming the fiscal and the legal notions connected with the street. What has lagged behind, however, is our understanding of the street as an essential carrier of communication, a thing deliberately created for that purpose and likely to continue in it. An essential attribute is that it is the most important component of the urban pattern: a pattern which is only consumed, learned, acknowledged by street use. All its qualities point to its being a channel for communication. A channel which has been purposively made, always according to the rules of some 'art', whose physical properties are always registered, criticised, altered according to such rules or by some other superimposed rules of another game: or even by deliberately breaking rules and so acknowledging them negatively. The extension of sea and air traffic seems to have abstracted the most obvious kind of communication, i.e. getting from one place to another, from any tangible connotations. Nevertheless, air routes (particularly when they are much frequented) assume some of the notional characteristics and present some of the problems of terrestrial streets, which is also true of certain sea routes: they all share a recognised starting-point and a definite aim.

But city histories often account for their growth and prosperity by their standing at the cross-roads of two trade routes: one is tempted to assume that such routes do not have stated goals but will go on crossing other trade routes indefinitely. It is as if a continent were a grid of such routes which lead further to ports and sea routes. A city grid plan

Paving of a Roman road, the via Appia, from Giambattista Piranesi's *Le Antichità Romane.*

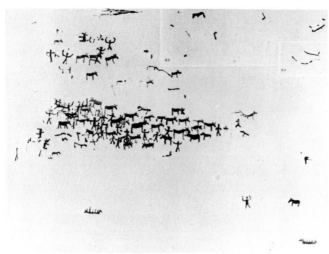

'The hunted herd as road-makers', rock carving, Nämforsen, Sweden.

Cleared site with pile of stones to mark a track of the Yantruwanta tribe, south west Queensland.

also implies that the town street will connect with the road outside the gate, or end in a blank wall or waterside: in a few exceptions there might be a square or a monument to impede and/or focus the street's progress.

Starting-point and goal are therefore not necessary physical attributes of the street or road, but its notional attributes. These notional attributes impinge on physical structure: it is clearly essential for the street user that – at whatever physical level its surface may be situated – its edges and boundaries may offer the user sufficiently similar yet varied exit-points to identify his particular aim with clarity. The unmediated passage between private and public which is such a common feature of the twentieth-century street seems to me to violate the primary condition of social intercourse in an urban milieu, which was previously assured by some form of private-public intermediate area: porch, gate, cortile, colonnaded street.

The very word street, as its etymology suggests, is a delimited surface: and therefore any part of an urban texture which is an extended area outlined by buildings on either side. But the manner in which the notion of road or street is embedded in human experience suggests that it has reference to ideas and patterns of behaviour more archaic than city building. Some light is thrown on this by the way in which pre-literate societies, especially those with very elementary forms of shelter, use the street, and also by the way in which children treat the space of play, suggesting a metamorphic notion of the street.

Track is the word which suggests the most basic course along which movement may take place. To the uninitiated, whether they are members of an alien tribe or children excluded from a game, a track may even be invisible, may appear to be an undifferentiated part of a featureless landscape: but to those who are aware of its presence, the track will be evident. It may be marked out by small heaps of pebbles, by broken branches, or carved signs on trees, all tokens which signal the passage. At the most 'primitive' technological level, the signals may show passage from one water-hole to another. On a huge, monumental scale, the pilgrimage churches on the route to Compostela or the spires of the major cathedrals of Western Europe form an analogous tracking system in a countryside whose roads must otherwise have seemed undifferentiated. To the traveller who relies on landmarks, the sight of the spire provides a visual and ideational reference both to the way he is to follow and the faith he holds true. On a much smaller scale, there are passage-ways which assume, if only temporarily, definite characteristics of the street analogous to those followed by the pilgrim wayfarer. Such are the ceremonial areas of the several tribes in the Darling river valley of Western Australia called *Bora* grounds. These are sometimes just mounds of earth connected by a narrow passage which is bordered by shallow banks. Such ceremonial grounds were used for a number of purposes such as peace-making (the passage from war to peace), but their main use was for initiation rites. The track is specifically intended to mark a route for the boy who is being instructed about the ways and beliefs of his tribe. Lining the path are images cut with a digging stick directly in the ground, so that the way is always varied by the incidence these 'illustrations' suggest. Along the path and sometimes within the ground, living trees are carved on the bark as sign-posts or pointers in the ritual pattern. Too little unfortunately is known about the value users attach to such images.

In Central Australia, an even more explicit usage is the

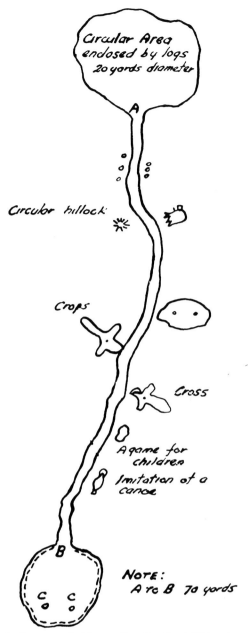

Diagram of a *Bora* ground in Moreton Bay, New South Wales, drawn by John Oxley, October 1824. This particular ground was used for peace-making, but is closely analogous to grounds used for initiation ceremonies.

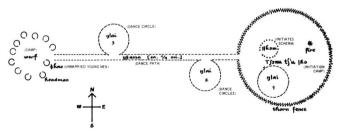

'Kung *werf* and its initiation enclosure connected by a dance path from which two dance circles open out. Note the exact orientation of the path.

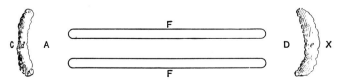

Diagram of an *Apulla* ground for Arunta initiation ceremonies. 'A' marks the place where the men sit, 'C' the place where the women sit and 'D' the place where circumcision is carried out. The path is between the parallel banks ('F'), bracketed at each end by windbreaks of thicket ('*d*' and '*e*').

Dendroglyph or incised tree, New South Wales. The trees are carved with tribal totems to mark ceremonial grounds or graves.

Bora ground showing the images carved with sticks which indicate the path.

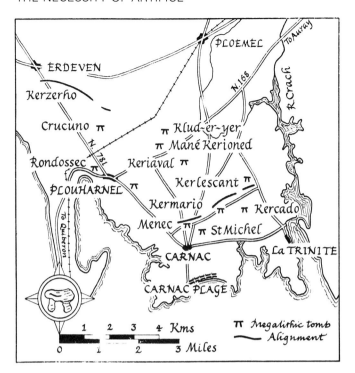

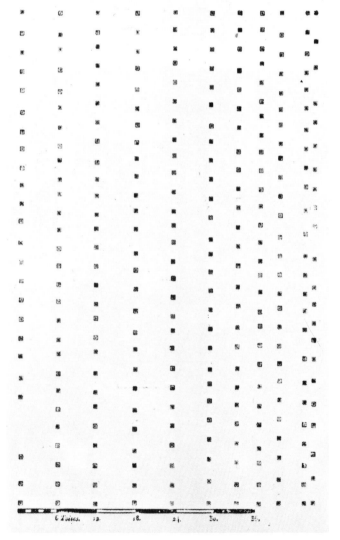

Carnac, Brittany. *Right* Megalithic alignments. The processional arrangement of stones suggests ceremonial purpose; *Top* Location of the main Megalithic sites around Carnac; *Above* Plan of the alignments according to La Sauvagère, 1764.

Avebury circle, and Stonehenge, inner circle.

construction of the *Apulla* ground: parallel lined banks are bracketed at either end by windbreaks of thicket. They are made for the circumcision ceremonies which are the climax of Arunta initiation.

Initiation is a prominent feature of Australian Aborigine life, though it is characteristic of social life generally. In Australia, it is visibly connected with the construction of special grounds involving signalled ways or roads of an elaborate nature in otherwise uninhabited territory. In all initiation, there is always a handing-down of group secrets, most often closely linked with an account of the human predicament. In many 'primitive' societies, there is also an explanation of the way in which the tribal heroes communicated such matters to their descendants and an explanation of the ground as a picture of the sky world.

The Darling valley tribes, like the Arunta, 'build' little more than windbreaks as shelter. In South Africa, the 'Kung build villages of very fragile shelter which may be moved and altered every day according to the mood of the inhabitants. These same tribes, like the Australian Aborigines, build initiation enclosures which are linked to the village proper by a straight dance path usually about a quarter of a mile long and orientated in an east-west direction as accurately as possible. Their ceremonies are performed between the village and the initiation ground. The passage from one to another is the crucial feature of the ceremony.

In certain societies, in large tracts of Polynesia for instance, and perhaps in the archaic Greece of the epic poets, the subject matter of initiation is itself a path, a way to escape the perils to the soul on its way to the underworld. Such customs suggest that human passage has always been metaphorically understood as part of the progress towards the 'great perhaps' at a level where the notion of street or way was totally divorced from built form as its containment. Megalithic fields and avenues represent still another kind of marked passage-way. Although their builders worked at a much higher technological level than either the Australians or the bushmen I described earlier, yet their use is unfortunately much more difficult to explain than that of the *Bora* or *Apulla* grounds, since no societies have survived with analogous constructions still in use.

The most spectacular of all such Megalithic groupings are the long lines of densely-packed stones, eleven thousand of them, at Carnac in Southern Brittany. Although various astronomical explanations have been put forward for these constructions, yet there can be little doubt that such fields were built for a purpose important not only for a local group, but for a much larger gathering at a national scale and immemorial traditions associate them with processional and even perhaps initiatory occasions.

The efforts needed to build the megaliths of Carnac or Avebury or the many others found throughout the Mediterranean, Western and Central Europe, India and Polynesia, certainly require a labour-force recruited nationally. They suggest therefore the existence of national or even interna-

tional travel routes, and this is further exemplified by the differing and sometimes very distant origins of the stones used in the construction.

The road or path may well pre-exist conceptually the permanence of human settlements. This may even be true of trade routes as a major channel of exchange. The transmission of certain definitely localised goods, amber for instance, obsidian or cowrie shells, suggests routes extending over thousands of miles in the old and new world millennia before any permanent form of building appeared along them.

The development from the notional street to the street as a surface and therefore as an object, particularly within the more permanent, explicit settlement, was a millenniary process.

Although apparently remote, but nevertheless relevant, the interpretation of the life cycle as a way of progress governs many children's games. Throwing and skipping patterns devised by children may even have analogies with the dancing steps tapped out on the *Bora* grounds. On still another scale, re-enactment of the daring which is rewarded and the chance which is a hasard in daily experience, is also implicit in dice and token games such as monopoly, snakes and ladders, or the *gioco dell'oca*. Most of these have a further metaphorical quality, since in some way they represent a model of society. Which in turn suggests that society itself is an entity, a landscape through which you may metaphorically proceed.

From its inception therefore, the road must be taken to have had both metaphoric and cognitive importance beyond its more obvious use. This nature of the street is witnessed by its innumerable proverbial appearances: everybody knows that the path to salvation is straight and the gate into it narrow. Movement along a set way, and even the delimitation of the way as an extended public space are very deeply embedded in human experience. That is why the persistent prophecies of the end of the street's function as a *locus* of human communication have not been fulfilled. The invention of movies, the telephone or television have not radically altered the need for the casual encounter as an essential element of human contact. It is perhaps a recognition of it that the drop-outs of the fifties, like the hippies of the sixties, organised themselves into various subcultures limited to city areas, mostly downtown, and based on the street. The great ecstatic festivals (such as Woodstock) establish a new pattern of seasonal movement in the subculture rather than of day-to-day activity, which remains essentially city-based.

I believe that the use of the street as a *locus* of personal exchange and communication can be promoted and that it is the business as well as the interest of public authority to promote such use, to which its more obvious functions, the carrying of traffic and the exchange of goods, should – at any rate conceptually – be subordinated. Failure to do this will not result in the death of a city: the large complexes of buildings will not be abandoned in a hurry, even if all services fail. But what is likely is the growing alienation of the city dweller from his physical environment which, along with the all too familiar social problems, may also produce a decay of services with the growing hasards this involves. At the present juncture, the mere treatment of the street at the face of the buildings which edge it will not do much good. In the modern city, and this is particularly true in the U.S., the street has become a three-dimensional phenomenon. One inevitable by-product of nineteenth- and twentieth-century

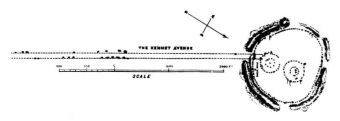

Avebury, Wiltshire, plan of the Avebury circle and Kennet Avenue.

change is that this conceptual emphasis has to be translated into terms of built form. In some ways, the builders of the *gallerie* and of nineteenth-century department stores were more acutely aware of the implications and possibilities inherent in the changes than most twentieth-century planners. The piecemeal relegation of urban motor traffic to buried lanes and the raising of a pedestrian platform above this, on which a promenade is built, ignoring the traffic below, is an image with disturbing psychological implications: that of repressing the whole problem of mechanised traffic. Any solution of urban street problems in terms of multi-purpose streets will inevitably involve the city and the state in political decisions which might turn out to be unpopular in the short run, however necessary, since they will be decisions about limiting private movement in favour of public, even if the elements of the three-dimensional street construction, the oblique mechanised surface carriers such as escalators, are already in use widely in the subway stations of most metropolitan cities, in department stores and shopping centres: but in such locations they are always denied their true status and treated as a kind of staircase. They will only assume their proper function if they are liberated from this subservient status.

All these political matters have a corollary: that the provision of even the most minimal permanent 'social' facilities (street surface, sewers) involves major *formal* decisions on the part of public authority, in the sense that sewer and street surface must be in the public domain and are usually co-axial. The private domain is therefore determined very often by the street sewer layout and consequently all internal planning, whether by authority or by public speculator, or even by individual owners, is dependent on the initial decision about the layout of services.

If you extend the public domain into the third dimension, you are at once faced with the inevitable complication of a services network allied to structural support, which involves the developing authority, or the major private developer, in transforming services and surface into built form. In a three-dimensional city, therefore, the in-between realm, the belt between private and public, will assume an even greater importance. That is why we need to be clear about the nature of the street and its life, its apparent indestructibility. And that is why we must examine carefully the historical genesis of present street forms, as well as the conceptual origin of the street. It will teach us the limits of our possible intervention, but also the scale at which our intervention is essential.

Europe, main routes of exchange in amber, mid-second millennium B.C.

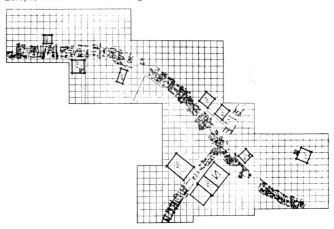

Novgorod, Russia, intersection of High and Serf streets at level 25 (laid 1006 A.D.).

Opposite
Biskupin, Poland, remains of a breakwater, ramparts, houses and corduroy circular road and cross streets of an early Iron Age settlement. Excavations conducted by Professors J. Kostrewski and Z. Rajewski.

Lodoli on Function and Representation

Although I had deduced the existence of Fra Carlo Lodoli's Hospice for the Pilgrims at San Francesco della Vigna from the old literature, it was only when I consulted Augusto Cavallari-Murat that I discovered that having made the same deduction, he had visited the courtyard of the monastery and photographed two windows which he imagined to have been by Lodoli. I was fortunate enough to visit the whole building finally, mutilated as late as the 1950s.

The conception of representation, as it was formulated by Lodoli in the context of the ideas of such thinkers as Vico and Leibniz with whose work he was familiar, seemed to me to require close examination.

Originally published in the Architectural Review, *July 1976.*

The Franciscan friar, Carlo Lodoli, was called the Socrates of architecture in his day – partly for his quizzical method of teaching and teasing his contemporaries, and partly for his refusal to commit himself to print. He had lived in eighteenth-century Venice as a peripatetic teacher, and spoke much about the radical reformation of building and of architecture. He liked the term *function* and he seems to have coined the expression *organic architecture.*[1] But as his papers were confiscated on his death by the Venetian state inquisitors (who left them to rot under a leaking roof in the Venetian prison known as the Piombi after the covering of that leaky roof) we have no direct means of knowing how he would have set his ideas down; and since it had often been said that no building by him survived, there was no means of telling what he wanted his ideal architecture to look like.

In itself, this might seem a murky by-way of eighteenth-century intrigue. But Lodoli was an important figure in many ways. His political and philosophical influence in Venice was great, and difficult to estimate;[2] and his name has recurred in connection with architectural theory since his death until the time when, in the early days of the 'white architecture', he was adopted as one of the founding fathers of all functionalism and rationalism. This reputation was largely based on the 'received' version of his theory published in an *Essay on Architecture* by the most popular of his pupils, Count Francesco Algarotti.[3]

But there was an alternative – more complex and more circumstantial – account published by another disciple,

CARLO LODOLI *San Francesco della Vigna* Venice, north side of the courtyard. The right hand arch of the cloister was walled in at a later date.

Andrea Memmo.[4] What is more, the one building by Lodoli whose design Memmo describes in detail, the hospice for the pilgrims to the Holy Land, has partly – if bedraggledly – survived, and is easily accessible: you go through the north transept door in San Francesco della Vigna in Venice (the church best-known for its facade by Palladio), cross the cloister, and find yourself in a little courtyard. The windows which face onto it are so odd that they arrest the attention of anyone used to seventeenth- or eighteenth-century Venetian architecture. And if you have read Memmo's book, you will know that you are looking at the architecture he spoke of, built with scientific solidity and with an elegance which is not capricious.

The little building does not fit the version of Lodoli's doctrine filtered by Algarotti; his *Saggio*, which appeared in 1753[5] was written in an ironical, detached manner, by an author who obviously thought that he was setting out excessive and eccentric ideas: 'If Lodoli has a paradise for martyrs to his creed', he once told the importuning Memmo, 'I would not hesitate for a moment to be counted among them'.[6]

Poor Lodoli had no such paradise; Algarotti was his opposite in character. The friar was harsh, aggressive, a social irritant. Algarotti moved about courtly Europe, deftly, inspiring sentimental devotion in both men and women. His longest, firmest and most useful attachment proved that of Frederick the Great; he stayed in Berlin for two extended periods (1738–42 and 1745–53) as the royal favourite, and was created a Prussian count. Memmo's busybody insistence that Algarotti become the spokesman for Lodoli's ideas was motivated by the belief – which proved fully justified – that it was the surest way of getting them a European public.

But Algarotti insisted on writing his essay quite independently of Memmo and Lodoli, and he did so with an irony which has deflected the influence of the ideas he purported to champion. He began in a complimentary enough manner: there is a philosopher – Lodoli is never named but called 'a philosopher' throughout the essay[7] – whose teaching is popular and catching and who manipulates the Socratic weapon with admirable skill, threatening the very laws promulgated by Vitruvius. The cornerstone of the 'philosopher's' teaching (I continue to paraphrase Algarotti) is the maxim that nothing should be put on show (*in rapresentazione*) that was not *in funzione*, a working part of the structure; and this maxim leads the philosopher to condemn much ancient as well as modern architecture. 'Function and representation' says Algarotti, turning on his hero, 'are not identical in building, but often in contradiction: as in the venerable matter of stone reproducing wooden construction ...', which had been familiar since Vitruvius, and was a staple argument, discussed or simply repeated in every architectural book ever published.[8]

Were it not for the tensile (fibrous) strength of wood, and had ancient architects worked in stone by Lodoli's maxim, 'all spans would have been very short, and the grace of the orders unknown'. But fortunately, like painting and poetry, architecture is an art, even if not entirely one of imitation. The primitive hut was of wood; its wonderful structural properties had recently been confirmed scientifically. Wood was inherently strong, and easy to work: the material best suited to resolving the paradox which bedevilled all art, the reconciling of unity with variety. Had stone become the exemplary material, the resulting architecture would have been boring: all arches and rusticated walls. The 'philos-

PIETRO VITALI *Carlo Lodoli* engraving after Antonio Longhi, or perhaps after Alessandro, the most celebrated Venetian portrait painter of his day. Presumably, since it was the frontispiece of Memmo's book, it was the portrait he mentions as being by the hand of Sig.abate Longhi, son of the late painter Pietro who also painted him several times, the most like being the one in the possession of N. H. Andrea Quirini (vol. 1, p. 83). There is another in the Accademia in Venice showing Lodoli holding a pair of steel-tipped brass compasses and a folio volume, while another volume falls open beside him showing a drawing or engraving of an Ionic capital. It is inscribed: 'Frater Lodoli in Apologis Conscribendis et in Architectonica haud inter supremos annumerandus Alexander Longhi pinxit'.

opher' wanted either bare walls, or coarse rustication, and banished the beauty of the orders. 'The two things which architecture requires', Algarotti now comments on what the 'philosopher' said, 'are solidity within and beauty without. Stone is essential for the first; for the second wood alone can provide the models. And if it leads to deception, what does it matter provided beauty is achieved? ''Che del vero piú bel e la menzogna''' Algarotti quotes[9] and argues that architecture is in any case 'the result of luxury masking naked necessity'.[10]

But as he has undertaken to set out the ideas of another – the 'philosopher' – he feels obliged to end with a compliment: all is not well with building, and the 'philosopher's' rigorous method, though it may destroy – figuratively, at least – some venerable buildings, may also bring about a much-needed improvement in building methods. All building trades should therefore be grateful to the Socrates of architecture ... and so on.

Algarotti showed Lodoli up, he did not really interpret him. At first – according to Memmo – Lodoli refrained from comment.[11] Pressed, he produced another parable, about meeting a hunting friend of his who insisted that he accept the gift of a fat pheasant. Being on an errand, he left it in a well-known cook-shop. When he returned for it – he was going to present the pheasant to another friend – it was nowhere to be found. Further inquiry identified the culprit: 'an apprentice who thought that the bird was part of the day's cooking plucked and trussed it, and fried it in the same pan as the rissoles and fritters for which the shop was famous'. Since Lodoli told his little story before a good many people, it was bound to get back to Algarotti, and it contained a double insult: treating the new Count as a cook-shop apprentice, and comparing his other effusions to cheap rissoles and fritters, quite inferior to the friar's pheasant.[12]

Whatever may have passed by word of mouth, Algarotti's essay became instantly popular, as Memmo had expected: it was read and it was quoted. The most important carrier of the Algarotti version of Lodoli was Francesco Milizia:[13] both in his *Lives of Famous Architects* and in his *Treatise on Civil Architecture*. It was presumably in the *Lives* (a very popular book indeed) that Horatio Greenough read 'quanto è in rapresentazione, deve essere sempre in funzione',[14] and the whole doctrine of necessity as the true source of ornament and of beauty. And from Greenough the tag that form follows function passed to Sullivan, to Wright and into the common-place of architectural talk.[15]

But Lodoli's ideas were not quite as jejune as Algarotti made them out. There is an alternative version given, long after Lodoli died, by Andrea Memmo. As the frontispiece to the first edition, Memmo used a portrait of Lodoli by Alessandro Longhi, engraved by Pietro Vitali.[16] It shows the philosopher eyeing the spectator through a port-hole, outlined by an inscribed frame with architectural tit-bits above and below, and two tablets on either side of the frame. Their inscriptions are a convenient summary of Lodoli's doctrine: 'Devonsi unire e fabrica e ragione e sià funzion la rapresentazione', says the frame; 'Ut eruas et destruas', one tablet, 'Ut plantes et aedifices' the other, quoting the prophet Jeremiah[17] 'to throw down and to destroy ... to plant and to build'. The implication of the mottoes is clear enough: the Socrates of architecture would root out and destroy, rejecting current – and past – building, uniting theory and practice. *Funzion* would then be identified with *rapresentazione*. Modern translators take that phrase to suggest that what goes on inside the building (in the planning as well as the structural sense) might show on the outside. This is not quite Lodoli's intention.[18] Both terms of the adage had a precise enough meaning when Lodoli coined them, and were much bandied about in scientific and philosophical controversy. Function, the first, had recently been re-coined. Not that the word itself was new: it derived from the Latin *fungor*, I perform, and had been used in a number of European languages to mean activity or performance in general, or the specific activity of certain things or persons, particularly the carrying out of any ritual or ceremonial action. Since the sixteenth century, it had been opposed to 'structure' by biologists. Health, for instance, was best defined by

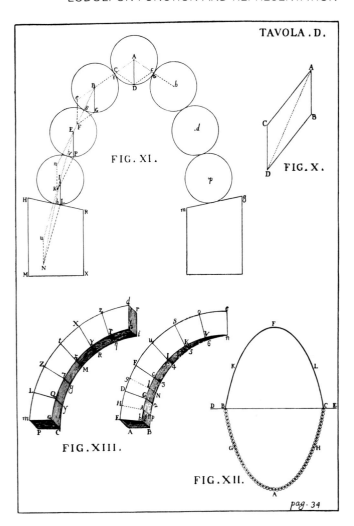

FIG. XI.

FIG. X.

FIG. XIII.

FIG. XII.

TAVOLA . D.

pag. 34

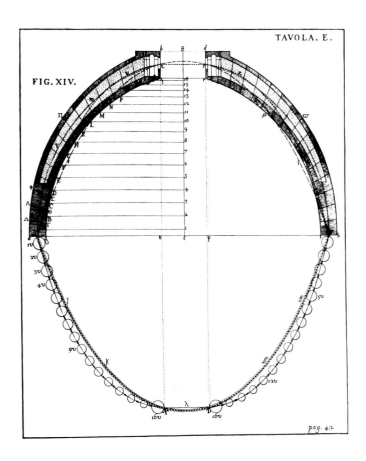

TAVOLA . E.

FIG. XIV.

pag. 42

Top right
GIOVANNI POLENI *Memorie Istoriche della Gran Cupola del Tempio Vaticano* plate D. *Fig. XI* the arch of spheres, showing the factors passing through the points of contact between the spheres; *fig. X* the parallelogram of forces with its vector; *fig. XII* the sphere-catenary and its inversion, the rigid parabolic arch; *fig. XIII* Stirling's Voussoir joints applied to an arch and to the section of a dome.

Right
GIOVANNI POLENI *Memorie Istoriche della Gran Cupola del Tempio Vaticano* plate E, figure XIV. The meridian axis of the dome of St Peter's compared with the mirror line of a constant catenary, and of the catenary produced by the actual material loading of the dome.

reference to the proper fulfilment of bodily functions, rather than to any structural modality. Later, towards the end of the seventeenth century, mathematicians took up the word to signify 'une quantité composée de quelque manière que ce soit de . . . grandeurs variables et de constantes'.[19] Or, to put it in terms of the actual problems to whose solution it was used: 'When one variable (y) depends on another (x) then y is said to be a *function* of x. Thus the distance of a moving body from its starting point is a function of the time; the attraction between two magnets is a function of their distance apart; the tension of a spring is a function of its length': and its graphic *representation* is a curve related to two co-ordinates.[20]

The word *representation* has come up inevitably, but again has rather complex implications. Its use had been specified in the French Academy of Science to have a meaning much stricter than the one in which I have just used it, to signify not just any concept or object, but specifically an analogue of some natural phenomenon which might be handled experimentally, or at least diagrammatical-ly. Writing in the *Histoire* of the Académie des Sciences, as its permanent secretary, Fontenelle put it explicitly, in reference to underground explosions: 'The best means to explain the working of Nature is to imitate it, and give (so to speak) a representation of it, by producing the expected effects from known causes which are put into operation. From then on, guesswork will be eliminated, and natural causes will be seen to have the same (or at any rate very similar) effects as artificial ones.[21]

This passage is quoted with great approval by the Marchese Giovanni Poleni in his book on the dome of St Peter's. Poleni was one of the great engineers of his time, and is too little known. The book on St Peter's is not only interesting for its account of the experiments which led to the reinforcing of Michelangelo's dome with extra chains as a result of surveys and calculations: but also for other experiments, which included the testing of a model of the dome to destruction. The book furthermore contained an account of the history of the basilica from its origins, a criticism of his predecessors' efforts, and a more general history of mechanical science from its Galilean origins.[22] In particular, Poleni was very interested in the mechanical application of the catenary curve, which is a representation: since it is produced by an even chain or cable hung freely between two points, and is a function of the span and the length of the chain. This particular curve had become very interesting to a number of mathematicians: La Hire, David Gregory and James Stirling, as well as the Bernoulli brothers and the great Leibniz.[23]

It was probably Leibniz who gave it the name (after the Latin *catena*, a chain – or the French *chainette*). Poleni also attributed the inversion of the catenary curve into a rigid arch to Stirling, though it had already been formulated by Gregory, as had the implication of constructing a catenary arch of spherical elements. Though Stirling seems to have resolved a problem formulated by La Hire: that of finding a form of arch whose members would stay fixed without recourse to friction or adhesive, by proposing that they should be of uniform weight, and their joints perpendicular to the tangents of the catenary. All this is reported in Poleni's book, with several problematic deductions.[24]

Lodoli was, of course, well aware of such researches, and of the experiments which they involved. He was, in any case, a close enough friend of Poleni to have known them at second hand. But both presumably read about them in the

GIOVANNI POLENI *Macchina Divulsoria* in the Teatro della Filosofia Sperimentale in the Palazzo del Bo, University of Padua. After the Poleni bicentenary booklet of the Accademia Patavina di Scienze, Lettere ed Arti, Padua, 1963, p. 86. The Paduan authorities, which at the time of first publication disclaimed all knowledge of this piece of apparatus, have now located its pieces, disassembled and wrapped in brown paper in a store-room to which I have not yet managed to gain access.

same publications,[25] and probably discussed them with Nicolas Bernoulli when he taught at Padua, as well as with James Stirling, during his Venetian peregrinations.[26]

Poleni also wanted to generalise his procedure on the dome of St Peter's: to this end he founded a 'Theatrum Philosophiae Experimentalis' for the University of Padua in the Palazzo del Bo. It was opened in 1743; but presumably the machinery employed there had already been made and used earlier.[27] One, a *macchina divulsoria* for testing various materials, was intended to provide builders and engineers with tabulated results of experiments. The machine illus-trated in Peter van Musschenbroek's *Cours de Philosophie Experimentale* is too like that devised by Poleni for their experiments to have been quite independent;[28] the same is true of their deflection-measuring instruments. Memmo boldly attributes the *macchina divulsoria* to Lodoli's genius, and claims that he did in fact draw up resistance tables, which perished with his other papers. The only surviving *divulsoria* was built by Poleni and is in the physics museum of the University of Padua to this day. On this point, at any rate, Memmo's memory may not be entirely accurate, some forty years after the events. But what he does describe, and that in the most particular detail, is the building which Lodoli designed as a programmatic application of his theories, and which, as I said earlier, was supposed to have been destroyed.[29]

Memmo's account of this building is very circumstantial, and in this matter, at least, he seems a most reliable witness: 'It was only a poor conversion of a friars' hospice'

ex
Fabrica
et
Ratiocinatione
Vitruvius

TOMO
SECONDO

CARLO LODOLI *San Francesco della Vigna*, one of the destroyed doors showing the wedge pieces half way up the imposts, the impost sections curved and 'catenaries' in the arch over the door as well as in the threshold, presumably tenoned into the blocks under the door jambs. Frontispiece from *L'Architettura di Jacopo Barozzi da Vignola* etc., vol 2, published by Giovanni Ziborghi, Venice, 1748.

he writes, to explain the lack of 'generosity, magnificence, fine planning, comfort and elegance'. This hospice, he goes on, opened off the main cloister. It consisted of five or six rooms only, en suite, so that the doors of the rooms had to be kept open all the time. The first thing to do was to create an open gallery wide enough for two persons to pass each other abreast; and since there was not enough money for a stone structure, he built a wooden gallery, the outer wall of which sloped outwards and up, since men are wider at the shoulder than at the foot. 'Not only did those passing each other have no difficulty, but even the porters who carried the luggage of the travelling friars on their shoulders could pass each other.' The sloping wall had other advantages so 'that when rain overflowed the gutter, it would not flow down the wooden wall'. Memmo describes other details: oblique lancet windows under squinches to light the dark vestibule, balconies opposite each room, and so on. All these things were thought at the time to be 'irregular' and therefore reprehensible by *professori*.[30]

What however did meet with approval – and was even imitated – were the doors and windows of the cells and passages. These were not, Memmo reiterates, the doors and windows of some great palace, but for poor friars' cells. The method Lodoli adopted was to put right obvious defects. To start at the threshold: this was usually made of a simple slab of stone; the door jambs rested on either end, and also on the bits of wall directly below, while the central portion of wall under the opening became a kind of leftover (*ipomoklion*, Lodoli called it).[31] Pressing up, this central part breaks the threshold in the middle, as may be seen in many cases. The great Galileo observed on something very similar; he described a column which was laid on its side; those who feared that it might break under its own weight wanted to add a third wooden block under the middle to the two which already supported either end; but the column broke on this very block, since the other two, having been put under it much earlier, had become quite soggy with moisture.

Some architects, ignorant of statics, seek to remedy the defect by leaving a course of stones out below the middle of the threshold. But stone is not elastic like wood or string; the walls on either side will settle unevenly, and the threshold will still crack. 'Those who have understood the eternal laws of lithology, statics and mechanics', Memmo goes on, 'need no more evidence to recognise the error in practice'.

Some have sought remedy by making the threshold of several pieces: 'the great Palladio among others, in the portico of coupled columns, much admired, which surrounds the first courtyard of the Monte Cassino monks on the Island of San Giorgio Maggiore in Venice, which used to be called *Memmia*.[32] But, like the others, Palladio did not reckon that the wall under the columns (or the door jambs) would sink, while the central piece (which bore its own weight only) seemed to rise: and as you may observe in that great portico, the result is unsightly.'

How did the philosopher-lithologue remedy the defect of thresholds? He divided the threshold into three pieces: the first was as wide as the span of the door or balcony opening, so that it did not bear any of the weight of the door-frame. Being shorter, and not loaded, it was more likely to resist, as everyone will recognise. Nevertheless, he wanted to increase its energy, shaping it in the middle to describe a catenary curve; and to prevent it rising in the manner of Palladio's thresholds, he joined the central piece to those under the door jambs with a mortice and tenon. 'Here, all you critics' (Memmo addresses his readers) 'you have something to make fun of: a wholly new, wholly Lodolian invention, which might become a norm for other occasions. You might well devise some better way of representing those three pieces by appropriate ornament, which would have been inappropriate in that beggarly place, and which their subtle deviser had no means of getting executed.'

'Even if you consider only these first letters in the alphabet of beams, you could take the matter much further – as I hope you will – so that I could learn from you. And although criticism is a very different matter from creation, yet even your criticism should be supported with some scientific observation, since in criticising you claim to be wiser than the one whom you criticise.'

He (Lodoli) – so Memmo goes on – made the beams in various ways. The one by which you enter the hospice he wanted to have in fairfaced stone and ornamented. He enlarged the central piece almost into a semi-circle, and had a bas-relief cut on it, showing the holy Protector of the Jerusalem friars;[33] but so that it may be seen to be an

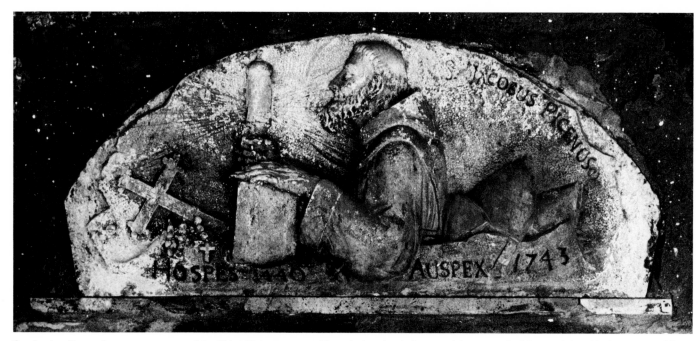

San Jacobus Picenus by an anonymous sculptor. This tablet was removed from the hospice during one of the many rebuildings and placed in the western cloister of San Francesco della Vigna. Unfortunately, no sign of the vines remains, nor any indication of how it was set.

attachment, he set round it four rather elaborate wine plants, which hold it up like a frame or a cartouche. Here is an appropriate enough ornament for you! Had he been able to let his fancy run free in the palace of some great lord, he would surely have decorated its beams with various allusions.[34] 'Other doors were spanned with segmental brick arches or catenaries, with a stone keystone or not – as was required. Observing that many imposts or jambs split about half way up because of their disproportionate length, and were thrust in by the wall (which, when unable to transmit its load directly downward, pushes in laterally) he also made them of several sections, securing them into the wall by means of suitable horizontal pieces, which were in turn wedged into the vertical sections of the door-jamb, and therefore became completely immovable. One such door, all friarly that it is, was printed in the second volume of Vignola's architecture, which Giovanni Ziborghi published in 1748, and without signing it, dedicated to him [i.e. Lodoli].'[35]

'Let the people exercise their imagination, let them reconstruct it according to the description I have given. Let them even seek out Ziborghi's book – but I don't want to give a picture of it here, so that it is not seen before the static rationale on which it was designed is understood. I fear that if it is not considered thoughtfully, and looked at by those who have not read this book, it will be compared with examples considered most beautiful, such as are found in great palaces and churches, and will therefore be condemned out of hand by the judgment of the material eye, and this book, which justifies this and other innovations will remain unread.'

'Since I was not obliged to observe such petty economies, in my week-end house in Venice', Memmo continues, 'or in that great palace which was built to my design in a most important city,[36] I was able to soften the Lodolian osteology of doors and balconies; and could entertain myself listening to the ignorant who maintained that Father Lodoli's work in the world consisted in approving the new way of decreasing beams from floor to floor according to the diminishing load they carried; superficially they got the cause of true function and its correct representation. Who knows whether, dif-

ferent curves having been found pleasing (and acquiring the support of a named authority, which the crowd respects more than the reasoning which it does not understand) the scientific curve may not come to please, and be imitated brilliantly in later days.'[37]

'Father Lodoli was also concerned that great care should be taken about the joining of those stone slabs whose office is that of defending us from water; and in his ingenuity he realised that these stones should be more firmly fixed, so that the joint should never open, nor the water seep through to make (as often happens in the joints of a cornice or gutter) some stain or deposit. Since he had to make two windows into a small closed courtyard of the same hospice, and wanting to put a capping over them so as to defend them from the rain, which might open the casements, he thought of two ways in which to modify the usual pediments (whose middle joint so often opens) by lapping one sloping piece over the other at the joint.'

'However, even this invention which he called a crooked *tuppé* [a wig askew] did not please him, when I, who had never done any architecture, suggested to him – a suggestion which he adopted with pleasure – that it might be managed better by drawing for him, on the site, a little ornament over the joint, which could be varied according to the size and nature of the building.[38] Let others improve on what we have done, devising further innovations to avoid the disadvantages we observed. And let them be content if I stimulate them to work independently, instead of inviting them to copy a none too happy – even if considered – example provided by the philosopher-architect, who abjured it at once, realising he could have done better. I would be only too happy, he would sometimes say, if I were compared to that Francesco Squarcione who was the master of the famous Andrea Mantegna: who knows if the successor of the Mantegna of architecture won't turn out to be its Correggio?'[39]

Function and *reason*, as well as *representation*, are words that recur throughout this text. They are inscribed round the frame of the portrait. And as if there were any danger of missing their relevance, the foundation tablets record on one side the date, 1743, and on the other, half the portrait motto: the tag from Vitruvius augmented: *ex fabrica et ratio/cinatio/ne*.[40] The tablets are now in the dark passage which Memmo mentioned, and barely visible. But the motto is repeated inside the engraving of that singular, all friarly door which Giovanni Ziborghi had published with Giovanni Pasquali in Venice in 1748. It is an edition of Vignola with a very short commentary, following the French example of the *Vignole de Poche*,[41] which had been taken up in Italy a few years previously, and printed together with an elementary book of instructions on mechanics. As a frontispiece to the mechanics sections, Ziborghi printed an engraving of the door, with the same inscription within it. And in the preface explained that his aim was simple, and agreeable to Lodoli: firstly providing a model of the five orders, removed from the shameful abuses of the day, so that men's imaginations might be brought back within the boundaries of nature; and in the second part to set out the incontrovertible principles of mechanics which will help to separate truth from error.[42]

Lodoli, who had been a censor of books for the Republic, may well have been shown the book before publication;[43] and Ziborghi was right in associating him with a fusion of antique example and the newly formulated principles of mechanics. Yet the little building, miserable as it is – Memmo's apologies are perfectly justified – suggests that he was after something more ambitious: the invention of new ornamental forms based on the *nature of materials* to use the cant modern phrase, but more accurately (and according with the terminology favoured by Lodoli himself) to display the energies inherent in them by a translation into a geometrical analogue. Ornament, however, should be not only appropriate to the material, but also to use and situation, as Lodoli's interest in the bas-relief of San Jacobus Picenus, and its framing within the arch showed. The little hospice was intended by Lodoli as a 'primitive', Squarcione-like exemplar in a new architecture, displaying the novel way in which ornament could be devised.

Memmo wrote his book many years after this building was designed, when he was a successful Venetian statesman, and *bally* or ambassador in Rome for the Republic. Although it had been circulating in manuscript,[44] only the first volume of the book appeared at the time of composition, the whole work being published much later. Memmo, however, seems to have had a very vivid memory for the events he recorded.[45] In any case, the building is still standing, and what remains after numerous alterations (the last about 1950) is much as he described it. If any proof was needed that Lodoli's teaching was more faithfully conveyed by Memmo than by Algarotti, here it is.

Emphatically Lodoli was not the enemy of all ornament Algarotti had made him: he had had a much more subtle attitude to the imitation of the past than Algarotti allowed him. Lodoli was not a 'typical' enlightenment figure. True, the experimental activities, which led to his ideas about structure and ornament, testify to his self-confessed devotion to the Baconian ethos and to Galileo. But there was another and different Baconian to whom he was also closely related: Giambattista Vico, the Neapolitan philosopher, lawyer and rhetorician, to whom the *verum* and *factum* of Baconian experimental philosophy had an important corollary: that the touchstone of the verifiable or knowable was what we and our like had made. And that therefore historical, and not geometrical knowledge could provide us with the only real certitude.[46]

Lodoli taught his students not only Bacon and Galileo, but also Hobbes, Puffendorf – and Cicero, the very thinkers to whom Vico also appealed.[47] Moreover Lodoli taught his pupils the independence of Italic and Etruscan institutions of Greek precept – an idea to which Vico had given great force in his book *On the Ancient Wisdom of the Italians* and which he was to refine through the various redactions of his major work, the *New Science*.[48] But if Italic institutions seemed as independent to Lodoli as they did to Vico, he suggested a further parallel to the history of architecture; as the Etruscans derived their institutions from the East, so they might have found a true stone architecture in Egypt, from which their Tuscan order derived, an order which, unlike the Greek Doric order did not imitate wooden prototypes.[49] The whole matter of the orders had, in Lodoli's view, been confused by Vitruvius' blinkered and excessively philhellenic attitude. Lodoli's view was not shared by many of his contemporaries; but it was conveyed forcefully to a young artist-architect on whom it made a great impression: Giambattista Piranesi.[50] Piranesi defended this view through voluminous writings and a thousand engravings. Through Piranesi, and through the many he influenced, like Robert and James Adam (who managed the remarkable trick of domesticating Piranesi's manner) certain Lodolian derivatives percolated into European, and more particularly Anglo-Saxon architecture; though others, notably George Dance, absorbed something more robust from Lodoli, through Piranesi again.[51]

But the received version of Lodoli's ideas was not Piranesi's, or even Memmo's: it was Algarotti's version, only marginally mediated by Milizia.[52] The forgotten hospice, which was seen by few among his admirers even, and modestly disowned by its designer, was not to provide the object lesson for the Correggio of architecture.

And yet, through what has come to be known as the Adam style, through the *architecture parlante* of Ledoux, certain ideas, certain themes on which Lodoli insisted, were absorbed into European architecture. A century after his death, the two terms he coined, *organic* and *functional*, were also given a new currency, but in a context which he would have found hard to recognise. To him, *organic* referred primarily to the human body; and *function* was the mechanical working of the forces within the structure translated into graphic terms, terms which were needed to draw the attention of his contemporaries to the urgent problem of inventing a new way of modelling surface in accordance with the scientific knowledge of material and force. He had attempted to provide a rough specimen of his method. His enemies sought a different architecture: 'juxta textum Vitruvii et mentem Newtonii',[53] as Poleni had wanted. The heroic re-working of surface appealed to forces of unreason which Vico, alone among his contemporaries, understood.

ΙΣΘΜΙΑ

GOTTFRIED SEMPER *Der Stil* vol 1, page 15, the wreath.

Semper and the Conception of Style

An augmented version of the paper read at the symposium sponsored by the ETH, Zürich in December 1974. From Gottfried Semper und die Mitte des 19. Jahrhunderts, *edited by A. M. Vogt, C. Reble and M. Fröhlich, Basel & Stuttgart, 1976.*

A little girl launched the most serious attack on Semper's majestic account of the origins of art. She was called Maria da Sautuola; she was then just five years old and accompanied her father on a visit to the caves at Altamira. Marcellino da Sautuola was a local gentleman who had already found a number of paleolithic tools in that cave, such tools as he had also seen exhibited in the prehistoric room at the Paris Exposition of 1878. He had gone to look for more such tools, and had put down his lantern to dig in the clay deposit underfoot when his daughter, Maria, looked up and cried with astonishment: 'Papa, mira los toros pintados!' So discovering for the first time since their creation the riches of parietal cave art which had been hidden for some 15,000 years and more.[1]

It was in 1879, and in the May of that year, Semper had died in Rome.

I am over-dramatising my story a little perhaps, but not much. Painted caves had been known for some time, but the paintings had gone unnoticed. Marcellino da Sautuola had himself remarked some 'black lines' on the cave wall, although he did not attribute any importance to them. Prehistoric archeologists looked down, they never looked up: that was left to the little girl. They had, however, discovered a certain amount of paleolithic mobiliary art buried in the cave deposits, but these discoveries had made relatively little stir. Edward Taylor, in the two volumes in which he brilliantly described the progress of civilisation and which went through three editions between 1873 and 1891,[2] spends barely half a page on it.

Another famous paleontologist, who was also a student of prehistoric society, Sir Charles Lyell, though familiar enough with the latest discoveries of the tools of early man in France, treats these flint objects as 'Works of Art', but devotes very little space to the engraved bones.[3] Lord Avebury, whose *Origin of Civilization and the Primitive Condition of Man* had almost half a century's popularity and republication, does not need to give more than a couple of pages and two illustrations to the Magdalenian engraved bones.[4] It was still relatively unusual to consider them prehistoric: in the sixties, they had been attributed to lively local rustics, or at best to the Celts.[5] Later still at the end of the century, when Ernst Grosse published his *Anfänge der*

Kunst, it is largely the engraved bones he speaks of when he considers paleolithic art: the only piece which he actually reproduces is a coarse and nasty line-block of a carved reindeer which had appeared in Edward Lartet's book. And Lartet was the first to have realised the real antiquity of the paleolithic engravings.[6]

Ernst Grosse's *Anfänge der Kunst* was conceived in a new intellectual atmosphere; like many of his contemporaries, Grosse was convinced that a 'science' of art was being formulated. He writes as a social anthropologist: but his fundamental attitude to art is influenced by Gustav Fechner and his disciples. At any rate, this is true of his view of the function and the nature of the work of art. Fechner had attempted to construct a scientific as against a speculative aesthetic; even if in his system the ultimate sanction of beauty is given by divine immanence, yet he believed that he had established experimentally a relation between stimulus and its reception, which could be codified, even quantified, and elaborated to deal with complex entities such as works of art. The academic discipline which was once called physiological aesthetics arose from Fechner's experiments.[7] Grosse was aware, too, of the speculations of anthropologists, and he was particularly interested in Herbert Spencer's notion of the play origin of ornament and the expressive origin of music.[8] He was also well acquainted with field reports by the latest ethnologists. But what marks his attitude most strongly is his concentration on spectator reaction. Spectator reaction is to him the true field in which the aesthetician exercises his investigation. This is diametrically opposed to the *practical* aesthetic of Semper. The experimenter sought to examine the criteria of choice which motivated a spectator in his preference among a given number of shapes and colours. Semper, on the contrary, investigated the elementary methods of making or fabrication and their transformation into formal devices through a social and therefore through a historic adaptation.

I shall only consider here the mature view of this process which he presents in *Der Stil*.[9] A presentation which begins with the abrupt offer of the wreath as the archetypal work of art.[10] For Semper, a wreath is the prime example of a textile object. The functions which led the first man to connect pieces of material, materials whose characteristics were elasticity, ductility, toughness, were *first* the desire to order and to bind and *second*, that to cover and to shelter, to delimit. Semper describes the details of textile materials at some length before he returns to the conceptual process which the making of textiles involves: fibre leads to thread and twine, thread and twine suggest knots. The knot is

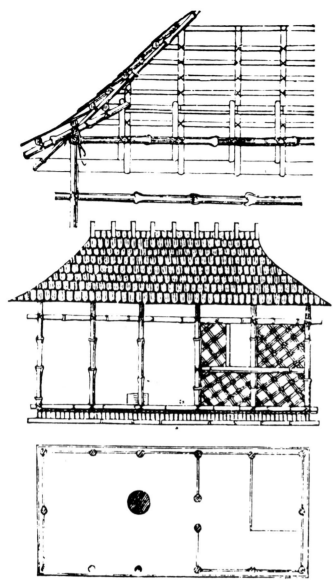

GOTTFRIED SEMPER *Der Stil* vol 2, page 263, Caraib hut.

GOTTFRIED SEMPER *Der Stil* vol 2, page 294, house from the Bavarian Tyrol.

'perhaps the oldest technical symbol and the expression of the first cosmogonic ideas which arose among the peoples'.[11] It is of the greatest regret to me that Semper did not develop the allusion to the symbolism of the knot any further.[12] He would, I imagine, have supported it by the observations of ancient writers and of eighteenth-century travellers, rather than by ethnologists' reports. His own basic anthropology was derived from Gustav Klemm's discursive *General Cultural History of Mankind*, which had appeared in Leipzig between 1843 and 1852.[13] This Cultural History was – as Klemm explains in the preface to the last volume – a justification and a description of his own Ethnographic collection, as well as of those which were housed in the Zwinger, and of the way in which both were set out.[14]

The material of these collections came from 'primitive' people in the sense in which Semper uses the word. To Semper the word most usually refers to the 'primitive' people who were his contemporaries, not those of the Stone Age. He knew such 'primitive' art through museums and descriptions; he extended his knowledge by analogy to the men of much earlier ages.

In fact, the most 'primitive' building discussed in *Der Stil* is a bamboo hut from the West Indies (British Guiana presumably, since it is called a 'Caraib' hut) which Semper had seen at the Great Exhibition of 1851, and of which he reproduces a diagrammatic sketch.[15]

It is no imaginary construction, he says of it, but a highly realistic instance of building in timber which ethnology offers and which is set before the reader as an instance, in all its essential features, of the Vitruvian primitive hut. These essential features are the raised floor, the central fireplace, the roof carried on columns and the plaited matting of the walls.[16] Semper, for all his apparent materialism, accepts the legend of the timber origins of classical architecture which Vitruvius had discussed in such detail, and embroiders on it. The true positivist, Viollet-le-Duc, writing about the same time, rejects it totally. Read his account of the Doric order in the second of his *Entretiens*: what Semper's enemies had to say against *Der Stil* applies much more fairly to the crude and overbearing assertions of Viollet-le-Duc.[17] And this Gottfried Semper saw as clearly as anyone: the notion that the cylindrical form of the Doric column was dictated by the method of transporting the column from quarry to site (as Viollet had suggested) was absurd. But Viollet was for Semper the extreme exponent of a school which wanted a Doric order originating in pure stone construction, against the traditional account supplied by Vitruvius and supported by some other ancient writers. This whole tendency Semper condemned. The Doric temple was, to use his word, a 'Gezimmer', a joinery-work, a frame, *described* or symbolised in stone. The root-forms of timber construction are much older than the art of building and had reached their full development before the monumental joinery-work received its form as a work of art. It follows therefore from the general laws of human making that the Doric temple was necessarily a modification of that which joinery had fashioned out of its resources in creating the ancient type.[18]

But even this older type is not a simple object, but a combination of three basic methods of making: of weaving, joinery, and ceramics; to be translated into the fourth one, that of stone building. The importance given to the mat raises a problem to which I referred a little earlier. This problem is the relevance of a textile art to architecture. It is a problem which Semper had already stated in his early paper on colour in classical architecture: the argument is familiar to the faithful Semper reader.[19] But it is worth noting that he reasserts it in a slightly different form. 'The process of dyeing is more natural and easier than painting and *therefore* more primitive. This thesis is a very important point for the theory of style ...'[20] The next step is to suggest the making of patterns by weaving and even by weaving different coloured stuffs; Semper argues the priority of weaving and dyeing in the conception of pattern-making.[21] If his argument holds, then you can extrapolate the laws of style, which he has formulated for the tectonic and useful arts, to the arts in general. And this is one of the most interesting things about Semper's stylistic theory: that there is no distinction in his mind between the laws which govern the work of art and those of a product of the crafts. The same laws work for *Kunst* and *Kunstgewerbe*: and moreover, that the laws which govern the conception of a work of art can be inferred from the practice of a simple craft.

Following on from this, Semper argues the close but ambivalent analogy between the covering of the body with a cloth and the covering of the building with ornament derived from woven forms. The German word *Bekleidung* for which there is no exact English equivalent, allows him to perpetuate this ambiguity throughout his long discussion of this connection.[22] And he occasionally stretches our credulity, as he does in the parallel between the lotus flowers which Egyptian ladies stick in their hair or behind their ears and the formalised lotuses which he shows us stuck into the bands imitated by those mouldings which separate the shaft of an Egyptian column from its capital.[23]

The ambiguity is resolved to some extent when Semper considers the basic notion of the wind-break or fence, woven of reeds or branches, as the first type of 'textile' which is used to divide space.[24] Unfortunately, the passage to this notion is too rapid; moreover, Semper extends the argument. There are primitive tribes who do not know the use of clothing but construct shelters of textile and fur.

By a curious use of word-play, Semper foreshadows his later reference to the knot as the essential work of art quite early in the textile chapter, when he considers the term *Naht*: the seam, the joining. It is, he says, an expedient, a *Nothbehelf* for the joining of two planes of similar or dissimilar material. But the very juxtaposition of *Noth* and *Naht* suggests a connection. The seam is an analogue and symbol which has archaic roots, for the usage of joining originally separated planes. Here he presents the reader with a primary and most important rule of art in its simplest form: to make a virtue of necessity.[25]

In a footnote, Semper confesses that the word-play might have seemed so facile as to be meaningless; though the connection between *Naht* and knot (*Knoten, nœud, nodus*) seemed to him in some way related to the Greek 'ανάγκη force, necessity. Presumably he had made himself familiar with the articles *Knoten, Naht* etc. in Jakob and Wilhelm Grimm's German dictionary.[26] However, he found the answer to his problem after he had written this passage, in the work on Linguistics by Albert Höfer – a disciple of von Humboldt.[27] Höfer justified the word-play, and pointed out the relation of such words to the Indo-European root *noc*, Latin *nec-o, nexus, necessitas, nectere*, νέω (to spin).[28] Linguistic details apart, the making a virtue of necessity is advanced by Semper at the beginning of the book.[29] It is in fact the first of the two essential rules which govern all human fabrication; which is always the result of a need,

GOTTFRIED SEMPER *Der Stil* vol 1, colour plate X. *Figs. 1–6* Egyptian ornament on walls and ceilings of graves; *Fig. 7* Scandinavian embroidery patterns.

GOTTFRIED SEMPER *Der Stil* vol 1, page 198, Egyptian head-dresses.

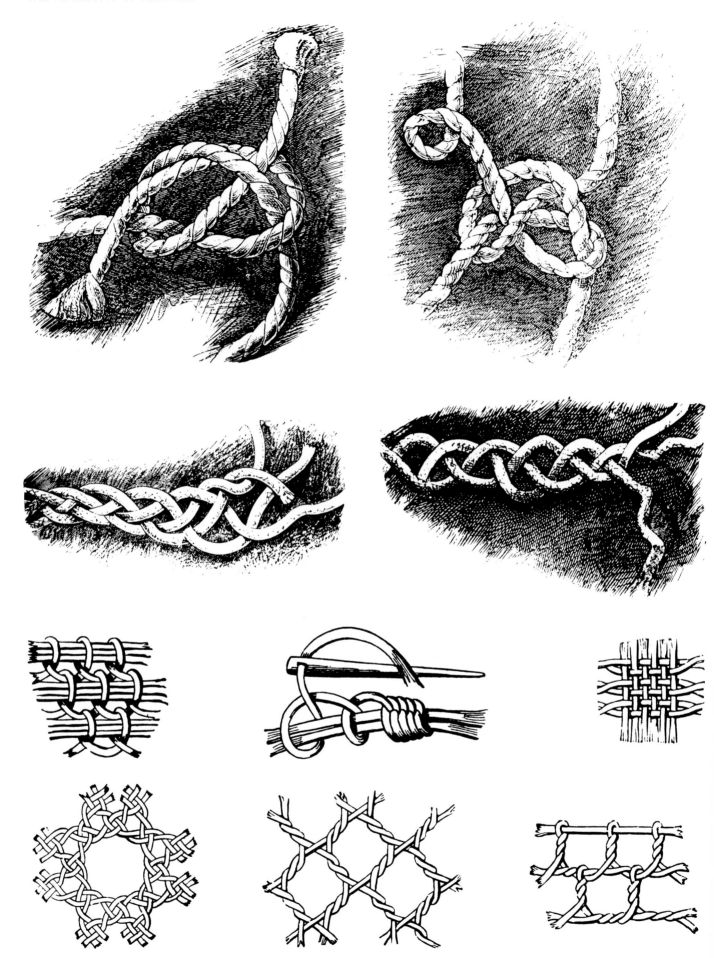

GOTTFRIED SEMPER *Der Stil* vol 1, pages 172–175, examples of knots.

whether physically experienced or raised to a symbolic plane.[30] The second rule is that it is conditioned by the material used in its fabrication, as well as the actual process by which it is made. Only the use of colour is not bound by these two fundamental rules.[31] But this materialist law is prefaced by the categoric statement that the work of art can only be understood as a whole and cannot be analysed into a series of stimuli to be considered under laboratory conditions, an attitude which Semper condemns even more severely than he does the older idealist speculations to which, after all, he owes some debt.

The work of art, he says succinctly in the Prolegomena, is man's response to the world which is full of wonder and mysterious powers, whose laws man thinks he might understand but whose riddle he never resolves, so that he remains forever in unsatisfied tension. The unattained completeness he conjures with play – and by building a miniature universe for himself. In this the cosmic law can be observed within the smallest dimensions of a self-contained object. By inference, therefore, the pleasures of art are analogous to those of nature. 'And yet', Semper observes, 'primitive man takes more pleasure in the regularities of the oarstroke and the handbeat, of the wreath and the bead-necklace, than in the less differentiated ones which nature offers him directly'.[32]

This teleological structure of the beautiful introduces the exposition of the 'three moments' through which (in Semper's notion) forms are seen as unified and beautiful. These are symmetry, proportionality, and unity of movement. He examines them in relation to natural phenomena: to snowflakes, flowers, astronomical movement, and briefly alludes to their reference to human works. But the application of this conceptual framework is never made explicit in the book.[33]

At any rate, the structure of the two volumes reflects the ideas suggested in the Prolegomena only by remote implication.[34] The four materials basic to Semper's division of his argument: textile, ceramic, tectonic and stereometric, are given twin treatment. The first is formal in the more general sense; the second technical/historical, as Semper calls it. They do therefore correspond to the two organising principles: the microcosmic/macrocosmic one (symmetry-eurythmy) and the 'vitalistic' one (direction) whose dialectic is mediated by proportion. The result is fragmented and often inconclusive; and hardly ever attains the sort of insight which odd remarks traduce. Gothic building, he says in the Prolegomena, was a lapidary translation of the scholastic philosophy of the twelfth and thirteenth centuries. It was an insight which Erwin Panofsky was to justify, however contentiously, many years later.[35]

The difficulty in reading Semper now is inherent in his method: we are used to a historic ordering of such material, and his is classificatory. Semper relegated the procession of interrelated epochs to his last volume, and his interest in the genesis of the restricted formal vocabulary was hinged to its social matrix, and to a possible analogy, an extrapolation into his own time.[36] His first interest, however, was in an interpretative taxonomy – in establishing the conditions under which style is generated. It is a problem with which von Rumohr had wrestled at some length.[37] In a strange passage, in which von Rumohr speaks of the members of a work of art with the precision of a morbid anatomist, he suggests the basic concern which had moved Semper. For the model which Semper followed was not offered by any connoisseur or philologist: his aim was to emulate the great

formal classificatory system of Georges Cuvier. Semper had come across Cuvier's work when he was in Paris for the first time and had held him, throughout his life, in the greatest reverence;[38] when he decided on the names of the great scientists and scholars who were to be commemorated on the facade of the Polytechnic in Zürich, Cuvier was the only biologist he chose – and this must have been after 1860.[39]

Within Semper's lifetime, Cuvier's system was both emulated and attacked, although it was to be overtaken by the evolutionary biology of Darwin, Wallace and Huxley.[40]

The great innovation which Cuvier had introduced was to shift the emphasis from description by the identifiable members of an organism, and classification by description, to classification by the function performed: so that resemblance was no longer the principal criterion of classification, but the *working* of the member within the organism.[41] The old taxonomies, based on resemblance, are broken by Cuvier's new principle. Function and its hierarchical disposition of the organism from within is the dominant principle of classification. This hierarchical disposition of the functions: breathing, digestion, circulation and locomotion, common to most animals (he later added that of the nervous system, to which he was in the end to attribute the determining role) was hierarchically attenuated on a descending scale, from man to the amoeba which does not have nervous, circulatory, locomotion organs, and only functions for ingestion.[42] Such a view of the planned and purposive organisation of the functions of organs implied a new kind of classification in biology based on the principle of the community of function rather than on resemblance; which further implied a discontinuous view of organic development. Species, in this view, were fixed and developed by their particular inherent formal laws, never by some transformation from one to another. This condition, this discontinuity, allowed Cuvier to construct a *history of nature*, a history which he saw in terms of cataclysmic change, as against the *natural history* of the eighteenth-century biologists, for whom natural development was always continuous. It is this fixity of the species which made Cuvier appear so old-fashioned to the post-Darwinian scientists; it is this same discontinuity which so marked Semper's thinking.[43] He had come to admire Cuvier first as the arranger, according to the idea just outlined, of the great collection of natural specimens at the Jardin des Plantes, which we know him to have visited assiduously.[44] This generative order must have seemed in sharp contrast to the incoherence of such a collection as Klemm's. And again he was struck by the confusion of the material in the Great Exhibition, and the inability of the Jury system, as it was organised there, to cope with the mass of evidence. His own reaction to it was set out in the paper *Wissenschaft, Industrie, Kunst*, in which he proposed a quadruple organisation of human artefacts, and in which the primitive hut provided a model of articulation. This hut is made up of four radical, irreducible elements: the hearth, which is the 'moral' foundation of settlement,[45] the walls, the terrace, the roof. These four radicals correspond to four ways of operating (not, as is often said, to four materials): moulding for the hearth, which produces ceramics; weaving and plaiting to the walls, which produces textile; carpentry and joinery to the terrace and the roof; to which is added stereotomy, or masonry which replaces joinery in the making of substructures and later even textile in walls; but stereotomy also displays a radical action, that of heaping up which cannot be reduced to any of the others. Metalworking was added as a fifth element to the book; even if Semper was conscious of

GOTTFRIED SEMPER *Der Stil* vol 1, pages XXV and XXXV, examples of snowflakes and astronomical movement.

the inconsistency of giving this non-radical work method a place within his scheme.[46]

The organisation of the museum, which was to be the means for educating the new artists as well as a new public,[47] was also the principle on which *Der Stil* was arranged. But the very use of the term *radical* is a reminder of another important influence on Semper's thinking: he was a contemporary of many great philologists: Franz Bopp was ten years his senior, the Grimms fifteen; as the curious *excursus* on *Noth* and *Naht* has already indicated, Semper had a very considerable interest in linguistic speculation. As was the case of many linguists concerned with speculation about Indo-European languages, he was also very interested in the primal Indo-Germanic 'thing'. Richard Wagner makes it clear that their early friendship was clouded by Semper's idea that the author of *Tannhäuser* (first performed in the theatre Semper designed in Dresden) was a representative of the Catholic-mediaevalising tendency, which he had opposed violently. In the end, however, Wagner succeeded in convincing Semper that he was primarily interested in the search for the ideal of an *Urdeutsch* myth, and recognised in him the one man in Dresden whose aims were identical with his own.[48]

This reflected their common political opinions, their conviction, however egotistic they both were, that the true work of art is the expression, if not the product of a collectivity which involves both the maker and his audience. And beyond that lay the heritage of Wilhelm von Humboldt, the notion that the essence of language is not the description of things but the vocalisation of action. In that memorable phrase of von Humboldt's: 'Language is not an act [*Ergon*], but an activity [*Energia*] — it is the ever-recurring work of the spirit to make articulated sound able to utter or express thought.'[49] The distinction between the form and the material of language, which is so important to Humboldt, is prefigured in Schlegel's interesting distinction between mechanical and organic form in language. Organic form, which develops from within, is innate to a thing. So Humboldt claims that identity and relationship in language are dependent on the identity and relation of their forms. And by *form* he does not understand grammatical form alone: it includes syntax as well as the building of words, while the matter of language is, as it were, outside language. Within a language material may only be recognised in relationships, as that between roots and declensions. But the contrast is a difficult one since with a language, there can be no unformed matter. So that on the one hand, the sound proper must be understood as the matter, and on the other the communality of sensations and independent intellectual moments which precede the formation of concepts with the aid of speech.[50]

Cuvier attributed a dynamic coherence to organisms, and demonstrated it through the purposive organisation of their functions. Analogously, the linguists of Humboldt's and Bopp's generation saw speech in all its architectural development, displaying the will of a people to maintain itself, through the power or ability to speak the language which is its own.[51] Hence the interest of these scholars for the oral traditions which provide a history of language more archaic than that of the written word: the traditions enshrined in the fairy-tale and the epic myth. It is the reverence for that fount of knowledge which united, as I have tried to show, Wagner and Semper.

The internal character of each epoch, the interdependence of the form and the material within it, was to be treated by Semper in his third volume. In the first two volumes, however, he provided a comparative morphology of the forms of art – I use the word now in its Humboldtian sense – and their dependence on the *energiae* from which they originated. This, with all its contradictions and repetitions, is the matter of the two published volumes of *Der Stil*; and set apart in the Prolegomena are, as it were, the structural rules by which the transformations of the root-actions are operated.

As it is set out in the two volumes of *Der Stil*, Semper's is decidedly an un-evolutionary, even anti-evolutionary theory. Its relationship to the diachronic system of Cuvier, with its insistence on the catastrophe of change, on the individuation of each species, set his view of natural development against the older, natural history kind of evolutionary theory. Darwin's book, which first appeared in 1859, came long after the main lines of Semper's theory were already set down. He was naturally, in his omnivorous way, fascinated by it.[52] But he rejected the possibility of applying the principles of natural selection to works of art and to all human manufacture decisively. 'It is true' – he said in one of his last writings – 'the monuments of the past are described as the fossilised shelters of extinct social organisations rightly; but these did not grow on the back of society like shells on the backs of snails, nor were they thrown up by blind natural processes, like coraline forms. They are the free creations of men, who employed understanding, observation of nature, genius, will, knowledge and power.'[53]

The works of man are therefore microcosmic and mirror the laws of nature: but they do so to satisfy both maker and user; they do not follow natural laws as if in obedience to some blind necessity. These laws are the dispensation with and on which the *energiae* operate. They are the products of the collective, of society exactly in the same way as the springs of language were collective in the new comparative linguistics. As linguistics also followed the example of Cuverian articulation and broke the eighteenth-century idea of a progressive history of language within which older and younger languages could be distinguished, Semper wanted, analogously, to break the organisation of the history of art, as it had been set up by Winckelmann in the first place, with its insistence on the priority of one people over another, with its hieratic attention to the individual artists. Semper's scheme was to concentrate on the unity of making, whether courtly or popular, and the growth of the arts and crafts from certain root processes, which were part of the universal human experience: settlement and partition.[54] There are therefore, in Semper's system, two primary archetypes: the hearth and the cloth, the *Urherd* and the *Urtuch*. They were the first mark of settlement and the first fabrication; but although they seem to have had the same reality for Semper as the *Urpflanze* had for Goethe,[55] yet they were not reducible to a single root phenomenon as Goethe would presumably have wanted them, nor do the other root-actions, that of jointing and of heaping, ever merge into each other, but they always, even when they overlap, retain their character through representation and symbolisation.

The enormous intellectual effort which the creation of Semper's great work involved has not been fully appreciated, I submit. The importance which Semper gave to the priority of textile arts is still underestimated, even though Heinz Quitzsch has devoted a chapter to this very matter in his recent monograph on Semper's theories.[56] If you take a look at the contents page of *Der Stil*, you will find that Semper gives almost as much space to textiles as he does to the other three arts put together.[57] And this was no accident. For the principle of *Bekleidung* allowed him to posit a unitary origin for all the arts; to give logical priority, paradoxical though it may seem, to ornament over structure, and so attempt to reconcile the ancient structure-ornament opposition which had dogged classical architectural theory. He did so, what is more, by appealing to the underlying laws of nature. This priority also meant another thing: that architecture, as queen of the arts – Semper, of course, like all of us architects, was afflicted by a certain justified professional chauvinism – was of its very nature *bedeckt*. And that part of its proper decking-out was painting and sculpture.

The major arts, as I have insisted, partake of the same nature and obey the same formative laws as *Kunstgewerbe* in the Semperian system. The proper mediator of these laws is architecture, and they are embodied in an exemplary and seminal manner in the first man-made objects. There is therefore no major category distinction between the major and the minor arts, between arts and crafts, between *Kunst* and *Kunstgewerbe*, to use these German terms which were to assume the character of slogans at the break of the century. Indeed in his whole conception of the link between necessity and beauty, Semper departed radically from the historians of art on whom he draws, as well as from his contemporaries.[58] Although the break between art and craft is inherent in the development of nineteenth-century 'arts and manufactures', to use a phrase familiar to Semper, yet another, and perhaps more decisive break between man the tool-maker and man the image-maker was made by social anthropologists.[59] The caves of Altamira, with which I began, were unacceptable to the social scientists as well as to the historians of art who were Semper's contemporaries and immediate juniors. The progress of man from the shaping of rough tools to the making of beautiful images seemed as natural as any part of the evolutionary process, and the continuity which this implied did not admit the abrupt and integrated view of the making process which Semper held. Which is why so many dismissed the paintings at Altamira, if they took any notice of them at all, as the work of rustics or even as forgeries. They were only described accurately and given a tentative dating at the beginning of the twentieth century.[60] When that happened, the great beauty of the prehistoric paintings and bold carvings appeared much more impressive than the clumsy and repetitive paleolithic cutting tools. The changed view of prehistoric man was contemporary with a more radical shift in the intellectual climate. Of this, Alois Riegl's attack on what he called the materialistic structure of Semper's system was symptomatic. In Riegl's view, the artist could not be thought of as conditioned by his materials and methods of manufacture. Riegl saw him as bound only by an intellectual horizon exemplified by the concepts of *Kunstwollen*, which I do not wish to discuss here. Enough to say that Riegl's rejection of what seemed to him a straightforward materialist account of the genesis of art has been the screen through which many art historians have looked at Semper.[61] It is difficult otherwise to justify such a description of *Der Stil* as you may find in Lionello Venturi's *History of Art Criticism*. 'Repulsive as it is', says Venturi, 'such a materialistic conception of art as Semper's has had its use: it has recalled the attention of the historian to the way in which the spirit is realised in matter, to the way in which material has been sensitised by art'.[62]

Such a gross caricature misses the fine ambiguity of

Semper's system. This, as I have tried to suggest, is partly his own fault. Any explicit discussion of conceptual problems such as the meaning of the word 'type' is consigned to occasional writings. The brilliant account of aesthetic 'moments' which seize the underlying laws of nature; these are held up as examples of integrity, though they are never related directly to the artist's and the craftsman's activity.[63]

Such flaws were inevitable in a system which could never be fully realised. Its great lesson, that of adapting a comparative morphology to the history of art, foundered. On the one hand, was the Scylla of the discovery of man, the first image-maker: a discovery with which even Riegl found it so difficult to come to terms.[64] On the other, was the Charybdis of the decisive division between arts and crafts. In the first decade of our century, the division had become acute and contentious. The Deutsche Werkstätte were founded just before the century turned, at the time when Alfred Lichtwark first popularised the notion of *Sachlichkeit* as an aesthetic criterion.[65] In 1907, at the foundation of the Werkbund, the division was institutionalised.[66] And in the next year, you have Loos' resounding attack on the very notion of ornament.[67] In the same year comes a definitive statement about the division, all the more definitive because it comes from outside the field of art history and art theory: it is embedded in the bulky text of Georg Simmel's *Soziologie*. The chapter concerned with secrets and secret societies as social forms has an excursus on ornament. By 'ornament', Simmel primarily means body ornament. 'Style', he says, 'is always something general. It brings the contents of social life and activity into a form shared by many and accessible to many. In the case of a work of art, we are the less interested in its style the greater the personal uniqueness and the subjective life expressed in it. For it is with these that it appeals to the spectator's personal core – of the spectator who is, so to speak, alone in the world with a work of art.'

'But, of what we call handicraft (and which because of its utilitarian purpose appeals to a diversity of men), we demand a more general and more typical articulation . . . that makes it possible for craft-products to be incorporated into the life systems of a great many different individuals. It is the greatest mistake to think that because adornment always functions as the adornment of the individual, it must also be an individual work of art. Quite the contrary is true: *because* it is to serve the individual, it must not itself be of an individual nature, as a piece of furniture on which we sit or the eating utensils which we manipulate must not be individual works of art.'

'The work of art cannot, in principle, be incorporated into more than one life: it is a self-sufficient world . . . the essence of stylisation is precisely this dilution of individual poignancy, this generalisation beyond the uniqueness of personality . . .'[68]

I thought it worth quoting almost the whole of this passage since it shows the Semperian attitude stood on its head, or perhaps more accurately, seen from the other side of the mirror. From Simmel's description of the work of art, the maker and his concerns are entirely absent. In this sociological account of style and of stylisation as a social process, the only relationship which is of interest is that between the spectator and the object. The divergence between the work of art and the craft or industrial product, between *Kunst* and *Kunstgewerbe* is as clearly, as emphatically stated, as it ever was in the great debate between Hermann Muthesius and Henry van de Velde which was to shake the Werkbund in 1914.[69]

In conclusion, let me return to Semper and the problem of Style. Familiar as he was with 'the styles' as a cant phrase of his time, his view of style as a concept was, like that of his contemporary, Viollet-le-Duc, quite free of the taint that 'styles' were ornamental vocabularies, to be applied at random, or even with some associational overtones. However slack and undistinguished his own architectural practice may have been, he was passionately involved in the construction of a theory of style, to resolve the many conflicts which the academic tradition had left in question. He did so while the horizon of historical knowledge extended immeasurably and the pressure of new functions and new materials made unprecedented demands on the designer's ingenuity. It is perhaps hardly surprising therefore that Semper adopted the primitive hut as the organisational principle of all artistic phenomena, and provided an analogue of it in his ideal fourfold museum, in which the unity that the hut represented could be reconstructed by the visitor through his re-experience of the four ways of making come together. It is easy to understand his scheme; and yet it had a powerful influence on such diverse matters in the teaching of art in Great Britain;[71] on the development of ethnology, particularly on Franz Boas and his school;[72] and most surprising of all, on the architects of the Chicago School. The notion of the curtain wall is said to have been formulated with reference to Semper's insistence on the conceptual priority of textile art.[73]

But it is the whole structure of Semper's system which now looks more interesting, yes, and more relevant than it ever did since its publication. We have lost the cheerful certainties of the Werkbund. We do not read Ruskin and Morris again simply as historical documents: their views have acquired a new urgency. In this climate, Semper's concern to trace all artistic activity to a transformational morphology, based on four root ways of the willing hand's working of inert material, acquires fascinating possibilities.

In spite of a century of speculation, we are no nearer to having formulated a theory of style adequate to the psychological and historical problems it involves.[74] Semper's intellectual preoccupations, on the other hand, have acquired a new and unexpected currency. Morphology, even in a Cuvierian sense, has had a notable revival in biology through such writings as d'Arcy Wentworth Thompson's[75]; the Gestalt school has added a whole range of morphological discussions to psychology. The interest in linguistic morphology hardly requires comment.[76]

A morphology such as Semper's seems remote from our own concerns; in so far as there is a generally accepted view of aesthetics, it is concentrated on the relationship between the spectator and the object. A theory of art (and a consequent view of aesthetics) in which the maker's view of the object of his work is the primary evidence – that runs contrary to the current commonplace. But perhaps with a shift of the focus, a shift of the kind suggested by Semper's formulation, we may revalue some of our immediate problems, or at any rate view them from a new vantage point. It is Semper's great insight into the way in which the artist and the craftsman relate what they think to what they do, an insight obscured by his own flaccid belief in the continuity of the Renaissance as a movement and a style, which seems to me invaluable and urgent. Conceived at the moment when thinking and doing were to be disastrously divorced, it may well contain a hint for their new reconciliation.

The Purpose of Ceremonies

For Lotus *17, which concerned itself with architecture and the theatre, this essay was written to link the matter of performance and display with the current problems of the city fabric.*

Of all the faculties, memory has most to do with architecture: memory, whom the Greeks personified as Mnemosyne, mother of all the muses, is her true patron. That is why, I suppose, Victor Hugo prophesied that the book shall bring about the death of architecture; not the ornate and tortuous hand-lettered books of another time, but our own machine-printed book which implied the ideal of universal literacy. Hugo put the prophecy into the mouth of Claude Frollo, the Archdeacon of Notre-Dame, who could still 'read' his cathedral and its surroundings as one might read a hieroglyphic scripture. He saw the prophecy fulfilled at the time of his writing, the beginning of the July Monarchy. Once the mysteries could be spelt out – so Hugo thought – from printed words, the desire for a built *summa*, for the cathedral and for the monument, would atrophy and so dispose of the whole notion of a man-made environment charged with meaning.

The hidden meaning of the built scripture was revealed slowly to her attentive 'reader' and was only obscurely apparent to the casual observer. In Hugo's day, the pleasures of deciphering which were also pleasures of memory were replaced by the archival accuracies of eclecticism. The buildings of total recall had a dimension of tragi-comedy which Hugo could not estimate; they marked the final stage of an architecture he saw as an obsolete accomplishment. Now that the book is dying in its turn, shall the relapse into the instability of the spoken word (however fixedly it may be recorded) have an additional benefit? Will it stimulate a demand that environment offer once more the enveloping polyvalence which we used to call architecture?

Perhaps: but only if we begin to reconsider our built world in terms of movement again. I am not thinking of the routed movement of goods and traffic. We are all too well aware of that. As our cities become increasingly and often catastrophically congested, so the power of the traffic engineer seems to become more absolute and hieratic, and as his operations become more self-defeating, the call on his services increases. In the meantime, the viscera of the city, like those of some dying animal, are clogged and smoky.

In all this, the movement of people is quite disregarded. People who move of their own power and on unscheduled paths are of no interest to the traffic planner. Old city-centres, where streets and squares have become completely impassable to vehicular traffic may be zoned as pedestrian areas: quaint islands in which the tourist may observe natives in their traditional habitat. And yet movement, not the purposive movement from one place to another but the apparently aimless *flâneur's* pace, is an essential part of our cognitive experience as citizens. It is only by pacing and touching the surfaces which articulate any space, by inhaling its good and bad smells that we can come to terms with it, come to know and possess it, make it ours. A city which does not allow for such movement in its physical structure is not really fit for human habitation. The support which it may give the individual in terms of supply: energy, water, sanitation, protection – all that cannot compensate for a failure in scale and quality which the zoning and embalming of the pedestrian precinct inevitably underlines.

The individual may come to know and appropriate his city through sensory habit; but a group may only come to possess a space through more complex stratagems; and working inevitably with coarser means than those of the individual.

Above all, such group action requires repetition. For the collective sensorium to function, the repetition must be rhythmic. And the rhythmic repetition of communal action inevitably appears to be ritual: 'Man' said Marcel Mauss, in a memorable phrase, 'is the rhythmic animal, socially and individually'. Naturally, such action can't be daily and continuous: it requires privileged points in space and time: central and high places as well as borders and thresholds; lucky (or suitable) days as well as unlucky ones. Our cities seem to have lost any such social forms irretrievably: though atrophied survivals of them sometimes assume gigantic and all-consuming dimensions. An obvious instance is the holiday season. Holidays must be taken at appointed days of the year: think of the exodus from French cities on the first of August, or from Italian ones for the Assumption week-end. On both occasions vast crowds issue from the greyness of the city to the brightly-coloured beaches or mountain slopes where they may restore themselves for the time in-between, for the dun period of everyday. On such days, the atavist instincts of holidaymakers and of stay-at-homes are propitiated by graphic accounts of the bloody human sacrifices offered to the machines of transport with which all the news channels regale them in the most highly-coloured detail.

Vacations, however ritualised, are not really a communal act of the city-dweller; individual holidays are increasingly common. More often holidays are taken by small groups: ad hoc, family, commercial, religious or merely friendly. They share their collective assertion of their detachment from the city. Look at any airline or organised holiday advertisement, think of the very concept of 'leisure clothes', and you will see that what is being ritualised in this procedure is not any kind of unifying conception, but a radical social conflict: between the role of the consumer and that of the producer, a conflict for which the travel-poster is the representative icon.

This conflict of roles – particularly the crucial one we all feel as producer/consumers in an industrial society – has an inverse representation in the take-over of the city on the part of various groups, usually of the underprivileged. It is all happening as if – to use the venerable Weberian categories – the possibility of communalisation having lapsed in the modern city, only forms of sub-association offer any hope of valid social action, the communal institutions having decayed with the community itself. The most familiar and most conspicuous of such actions are those of the vandals.

It is ironic that they go by the name of the old conquerors of Spain and of North Africa who 'Did all the matchless monuments deface' since our cities have no monuments left, not to speak of: and the defacing itself is most often the scratching or (here is a misnomer!) spraying of 'graffiti' to personalise the neutral products of technology. It is carried out by groups which might loosely be described as proletarian, but which include a socio-political variety of activists for extreme causes, assertive individualists and warring urban gangs whose principal weapons – as may be seen in the New York subway system – are the spray paint can and the felt marker. At a higher, more settled social level, the symptoms differ: new associations proliferate which call on older and more respectable forms of ritual activity. They have not been classified convincingly as yet; at the time of writing they have been popular for a decade or so but already they are appearing as the stabilisers of consumer culture. Most of them use some form of group therapy. As in many of the mystery cults of the ancient world, there is a structure of public confession, acts of repentance, closeness, sharing of some physical substance (touching, common meals), ceremonial or semi-ceremonial meetings. The adepts display a missionary fervour and a moral intolerance of outsiders which might seem to indicate the presence of a major religious movement. And yet the word *therapy* is inescapable in this context, if only because most of the groups, all of them thoroughly urban, do not offer the devotee any vision or explanation of the universe and of his place in it, but only, more humbly, a *solution* to his *problems*. Such concentration on a technique generates a quasi-scientific terminology. It should not conceal the religious nature of their observances, which often include the pilgrimage to the consecrated place of origin (Esalen, for instance) or to a venerated master.

These groups are the core of counter-culture in that their members, now adult, were the adolescents of the Zen-Krishna-Psychedelic generation. They find their only social bond in a mythless ritual, one in which they are both actors and patients – or spectators if you prefer the term. It is a ritual without any proper aetiology: since the only proper aetiology for a rite is a myth. I use that last word here in the most generalised sense of any explanation (allusive or explicit) of man's fate, of the world and of his place in it. The mythless ritual cannot have any imperative: it is a form of religiosity which has been described commonly enough.

Dead cells of religiosity in a secular world become, if we are to believe Adorno, poisonous; since religiosity drives its followers into isolation, discourages reflection and elevates unreflective isolation into a virtue. The particular religiosity of our time does not wish to establish any analogy between the order of the individual and the order of society, or between that of society and that of the world. It is constructed to offer a pragmatic solution to the individual's problems and may be 'tested' like a drug by the number of cures it performs. It therefore acts as the prop of any existing social convention; it is developed out of individual pathology and can offer a cure only into the normalcy of a social convention. Since it knows of nothing outside convention, its treatment can only remedy the transgressions of social conformity. The rites of religiosity may rescue many a disorientated ex-hippy, but they are powerful social solvents by the very harsh accent they place on the purely consumer aspect of their activities, which have more in common with secret societies than with exoteric religious groups.

There was a time when – in one sense – secret societies were quite exoteric, when the whole of community could be described as a system of overlapping secret societies – as in the mediaeval European city, or for that matter in many a contemporary Islamic one, in which the insignia, the gestures of recognition, their public ceremonies were part of the everyday spectacle of the street. But above all, such secret societies were most often attached to forms of production – many of them were simply craft-guilds – and all were part of the display of authority which could be said to culminate in the celebrations of sovereignty, from ostensory coronations to public executions.

It is all too easy, and too common to praise the mediaeval city for the comforts of its space, for the propensity of its inhabitants to make theatre out of the simplest activities: not only crafts such as cobbling and joinery but the sweeping of streets and the removal of refuse; perhaps it is not accidental that the first textbook instance of the first Renaissance building is a foundling hospital in Florence; while in Venice it was one end of the great parade of public buildings which fronted the Basin of St Mark to make up the facade of the city.

From Chester to Dubrovnik (in 'Western' Europe alone), a whole series of cities witness the representative status of my examples. In the form of the city and in that of the individual house, the imperious demands of display were accepted as a conditioning factor of the physical fabric and of its detailed articulation. It was not at all limited to the Middle Ages. The palace replaced castle and cathedral, the bulwarks the city wall, and triumphal arches its gates – so the way display did the conditioning was transformed. Most important of all, the increasing centralising of production withdrew it from display gradually, and then the first industrial revolution made labour altogether unfit for the eyes of the middle and higher social orders.

All this is a commonplace of history and I can be brief about it: but historians rarely consider it *as a function of ceremony and spectacle*. Such matters are almost always treated as symptomatic of social or economic conditions. It is nevertheless true that for the men of the time these moments of display which we treat as marginal were regarded as the culmination of many people's labour and to all of them, high and low, as – in a sense – the justification of their troubles. Our neglect is therefore unimaginative, if not unhistorical for all that: were we to acknowledge the full range of splendours and mystery in the city of display, it would neither offer us an example, nor illustrate our problems directly, since we have now achieved a city which is constructed on principles we have adopted as criteria by which to judge the cities of the past. We tend to speak of them as if the traffic movement was truly the primary determinant of form, and the productive process only secondary. Another criterion, only too often imposed on existing cities, and often projected back into history, is that of 'rationalised' zoning, the subdivision of the city according to patterns of use. Such a division of the city which may often be sanctioned historically by the grouping of certain trades round streets and squares, is, of course, the principal enemy of display and spectacle, when they are understood as a *category* of social action in the town, which planners consign to the reservations which the zoned plan provides for leisure. Inevitably therefore spectacle is only restored to the rational city through movements of protest: the picket, the demonstration, the riot.

In the sixties, futurological fantasies coolly foresaw the growth of ever greater concentrations of the world's population in megalopolies (Bos/Wash on the Atlantic seaboard of the United States, San/San on the Pacific), where they were to enjoy – even if there was some doubt about the source of their pleasures – a life of electrified leisure. Of the various prophecies which the futurologists hawked (including some which foretold various forms of catastrophe), there was one which caught the public imagination: it promised an electronic disurbanisation through the then new mass-media. However improbable that particular scenario (to use the futurologist's cliché) now seems in the less expansionist period after the energy crisis, it nevertheless has the force of recalling to all of us who use any electronic methods of sound and image reproduction that we are operating a powerful and irreversible change in human sensibility, more powerful than that which the printed book brought about, and – in all probability – quicker in its working.

Will it in fact undo some of the effects of the printed book, and in particular, the displacement of the monument by the book? I am no futurologist, and this essay has no probable scenarios to offer. What interests me are possibilities of action in our present situation. A notable factor in it has been the multiplication out of all proportion of printed books: since electronic techniques have, as a by-product, very much improved methods of printing. It has been said that the level of a culture is in inverse proportion to the availability of texts; if true, it would make us about the lowest culture in history.

If the level of culture is to rise, our hope must lie in that gradual eclipse of literacy which we are already witnessing, though it seems to have only an indirect effect on the demand for printed matter. But the situation has its inverse – that the new illiteracy will cause people to look again at their artefacts, at the whole artificial world which is made up of them, and scry it anew for meaning. For that they must be given cities in which, like Archdeacon Frollo, they can 'read' buildings at the pedestrian's pace. Not only must the architect learn to make the built scripture readable again, he must make movement the essential, even the controlling element of his plan. Not the interested movement of traffic, but the free and articulated movement of people to whom he offers a setting within which they may play the drama of their lives with dignity.

Notes

Meaning and Building

1. In a letter to Armand Meillet quoted in the *Cahiers de Ferdinand de Saussure*, Geneva (X) 1952, 6. I am grateful to my colleague, Peter J. Wexler, for pointing this quotation out to me.
2. 1932; pp. 108–9. I do not translate, because 'aveux' and 'luxe' have rather idiomatic connotations in this context, which will become clear in the course of what I say further. In any case, 'Le luxe n'est pas aisé à définir' as the old Academy dictionary says.
3. How the best were seduced by this mirage you can read in S. Giedion's *Architecture you and me* Cambridge, 1958, pp. 70 ff.
4. '... on ne sait ce qu'on veut ni ce qu'on fait, et qu'on suit sa fantaisie qu'on appelle raison, ou sa raison qui n'est souvent qu'une dangereuse fantaisie qui tourne tantôt bien, tantôt mal . . .' in *Jacques le Fataliste et son Maître*.
5. 'Wir haben noch nicht die letzte Kraft, denn uns trägt kein Volk', in *Uber die Moderne Kunst* 1945, p. 53.
6. Meyerhold: setting for 'Strife and Victory' on the Chodinskaja field, Moscow, for the third meeting of the Communist International.
7. As well as the lawns outside the Bolshoi Theatre in the early 1920s.
8. Pravda printing house, by the Brothers Vesnin, 1928.
9. In Tatlin's 'Monument of the Third International', 1920.
10. Such as Abram Erfos: *The Spirit of Classicism*, 1922.
11. I am using Coleridge's old, but still sharp distinction: 'Fancy brings together images which have no connection natural or moral, but are yoked together . . . by means of some accidental coincidence. . . The imagination modifies images, and gives unity to variety; it sees all things in one, *il più nell' uno.*' *Table Talk*, 1836, p. 306.
12. Compare, for instance, Nervi's project for the underground basilica of Pius X at Lourdes, and Freyssinet's executed structure.
13. This is discussed at length – and very intelligently – by Mr Robin Boyd in 'Counter-Revolution in Architecture', *Harper's Magazine*, September 1959.
14. I say 'lower reaches' advisedly. Clearly there is more to the work of Peter and Alison Smithson than their 'Brutalism', as there is more to John Osborne than 'Angry-young-mannery'.
15. 'Aspirations in Retrospective' in *The Listener*, May 7th 1959.
16. *Standing and Sitting Posture with special reference to the construction of chairs*, by Bengt Ackerblom, Stockholm, 1948, pp. 153–169.
17. In the same way people who still think it necessary to justify Rietveld's wonderful 'stick' chair of 1917 will say 'it really is very comfortable, you know'.
18. In the Seiryo-den of the Imperial Palace, Kyoto. It was also strewn with earth.
19. This is documented in 'Le Trône Vide dans la Tradition Indienne' by Jeanine Auboyer, *Cahiers Archéologiques* VI, Paris, 1929, pp. 1–9.
20. See 'Visual Perception and Personality', by Warren J. Wittrein in the *Scientific American*, April 1959, pp. 56–60.
21. 'Il n'y aurait pas le présent, avec son épaisseur et sa richesse inépuisable, si la perception, pour parler comme Hegel, ne gardait un passé dans sa profondeur présente, et ne la contractait en elle. . .' Maurice Merleau-Ponty: *Phénomenologie de la Perception*, Paris, 1945, p. 277.

The Sitting Position – A Question of Method

1. W. Floyd and D. Roberts: 'Anatomical, Physiological and Anthropometric Principles', in *The Design of Office Chairs and Tables*, London, 1958.
2. Nuremberg, 1525.

3. Nicholas Andry de Boisregard: *L'Orthopédie, ou l'Art de prévenir et de corriger dans les Enfants les Déformités du Corps*, Paris, 1741. Andry constructed the word *orthopedia* from the Greek *orthos*, upright and *paidos*, child.
4. Bengt Ackerblom: *Standing and Sitting Posture*, Stockholm, 1948.
5. Marcel Mauss: 'La Technique du Corps', reprinted in *Marcel Mauss: Sociologie et Anthropologie*, Paris, 1958.
6. Gordon W. Hewes: 'The Anthropology of Posture' in *Scientific American*, February 1957, pp. 122 ff.
7. Genesis XXVIII, 10–22.
8. Cf., for example, Mircea Eliade: *Traité d'Histoire des Religions*, Paris, 1953. In particular on the Throne of Stone, cf. Jeanine Auboyer: 'Le Trône Vide dans la Tradition Indienne', in *Cahiers Archéologiques*, VI, Paris, 1929.
9. Claude Lévi-Strauss: 'Introduction à la Méthode de Marcel Mauss', in Marcel Mauss: *Sociologie et Anthropologie*, Paris, 1958.

The Corinthian Order

Two recent handbooks, *The Architecture of Ancient Greece* by William Bell Dinsmoor (3rd ed., London, 1950) and *Greek Architecture* by A.W. Lawrence (Harmondsworth, 1957) provide the essential architectural information; both have excellent bibliographies. For the religious background see *Les Religions Préhelleniques* by Charles Picard (Paris, 1948) and *Geschichte der Griechischen Religion* by Martin Persson Nilsson (Munich, 1941–50).

I found particularly stimulating two essays by Théophile Homolle, both published in *Revue Archéologique* – 'L'Origine du Chapiteau Corinthien' (Series 15, vol IV, July–December 1916) and 'L'Origine des Caryatides' (Series 15, vol V, January–June 1917).

A different point of view may be found expressed in *Stilfragen* by Alois Riegl (Italian edition, Milan, 1963) and *Histoire de l'Architecture* by Auguste Choisy (Paris, 1899).

On the Delphic Monument see J. P. and G. Roux *Les Enigmes de Delphes* (Paris, 1963).

Ornament is no Crime

For Goethe's view, modified later, see 'Von Deutscher Baukunst' (1772) in *Works* (Zürich, 1965, vol XIII, pp. 16 ff), already modified in the article 'Baukunst' (1788; ibid, p. 57). The best statement of the Polytechnic view is J.N.L. Durand *Précis des Leçons d'Architecture ... à l'Ecole Royale Polytechnique* (Paris, 1819, vol 1, pp. 19 ff, 52 ff). The conventional view of ornament is well expressed in Owen Jones' *Grammar of Ornament* (London, 1856, and many later editions) or the introduction to Charles Blanc's *Grammaire des Arts Décoratifs* (Paris, 1867). For the best known writers who saw a return to a particular place in history as a condition of progress, see literature of A.W.N. Pugin (fifteenth-century England) and Gottfried Semper (sixteenth-century Italy). Adolf Loos' 'Ornament und Verbrechen' is in *Trotzdem* (Innsbruck, 1931, pp. 79 ff) and has been variously translated; 'Architektur' (ibid, pp. 93 ff) has recently been reprinted with other pieces in *Form and Function* by Tim and Charlotte Benton with Dennis Sharp (London, 1975, pp. 41 ff also p. 26, p. 40); Simmel's 'Excursus on Adornment' in *The Sociology of George Simmel* (ed. Kurt H. Wolff, New York, 1950, pp. 338 ff).

On the history of the Théâtre des Champs Elysées, see Henry van de Velde, *Théâtres 1900–14* (London, 1974); also in his *Geschichte Meines Lebens* (Munich, 1962, pp. 327 ff). Maurice Denis gave an account of his part of the affair in the first volume of his *Journal*. For Bourdelle's part see E.

François Julia, *Antoine Bourdelle* (Paris, 1930, pp. 68 ff). For Perret's side of the story, see M. Dormoy, 'Réponse d'Auguste Perret à H. van de Velde' in *L'Amour de l'Art* (July 1925), and M. Mayer, *A. & G. Perret* (Paris, 1928). Van de Velde's later opinion is quoted from *Le Style Moderne* (Paris, 1925).

Herbert Gans' *The Levittowners* is subtitled 'The Anatomy of Suburbia: The Birth of Society and Politics in a new American Town' (London, 1967). Essential publications by Robert Venturi are *Complexity and Contradiction in Architecture* (New York, 1966) and *A Significance for A & P Parking lots or Learning from Las Vegas ...* (Cambridge, Mass. and London, 1972) with Denise Scott-Brown and Steven Izenour. For Pugin's view, see his *True Principles of Pointed or Christian Architecture* (London, 1853). For Hollein's views and projects only periodicals are available. He was for some years the editor of the Austrian magazine *Bau*.

The passage by Tom Wolfe comes from *The Kandy-Kolored Tangerine-Flake Streamline Baby* (New York, 1965). The Zürich exhibition was shown in the Kunstgewerbemuseum (August 1965) and in the Prinz Carl-Palais in Munich (January 1966). The catalogue, by various hands, is edited by Mark Buchmann.

Learning from the Street

A selected bibliography for this essay includes J.-P. Beguin et al., *L'Habitat au Cameroun* (Paris, 1952); Lindsay Black, *Burial Trees* (Melbourne, 1941); *The Bora Ground* (Sydney, 1944); V. Gordon Childe, *The Danube in Prehistory* (Oxford, 1929); *Prehistoric Migrations in Europe* (Oslo, 1950); A. P. Elkin, *The Australian Aborigines: How to Understand Them* (London, 1964); James Ferguson, *Rude Stone Monuments* (London, 1872); Raymond Firth, *We, The Tikonia* (Boston, 1966); Douglas Fraser, *Village Planning in the Primitive World* (London and New York, n.d.); Siegfried Giedion, *The Eternal Present* vol 2, 'The Origins of Architecture' (London and Oxford, 1962); M. Griaule, *Dieu d'eau. Entretiens avec Ogotemmati* (Paris, 1948); Sverker Janson and Harald Hvarfner, *Ancient Hunters and Settlements in the Mountains of Sweden* (Stockholm, 1966); André Leroi-Gourhan, *Le Geste et la Parole* vol 1, 'Technique et Langage', vol 2 'La Mémoire et les Rhythmes' (Paris, 1964); James Mellaart, *Çatal Hüjük* (London, 1967); James Miln, *Excavations at Carnac* (Edinburgh, 1881); Lewis H. Morgan, *Houses and House-Life of the American Aborigines* (Chicago, 1965, reprint of an 1881 edition); Stuart Piggott, *Ancient Europe, from the beginnings of Agriculture to Classical Antiquity* (Edinburgh, 1965); G. D. Pope Jr, *Ocmulgee National Monument, Georgia* National Park Service Historical Handbook Series no. 24 (Washington DC, 1956); Arnolds Spekke, *The Ancient Amber Routes and the Geographical Discovery of the Eastern Baltic* (Stockholm, 1957); Baldwin Spencer and F. J. Gillen, *The Native Tribes of Central Australia* (London, 1899); Baldwin Spencer, *The Native Tribes of the Northern Territory of Australia* (London, 1914); Cyrus Thomas, 'Report on the Mound Explorations of the Bureau of Ethnology' in *Twelfth Annual Report of the Bureau of Ethnology to the Secretary of the Smithsonian Institution* by J.W. Powell (Washington DC, 1894); M.W. Thompson *Novgorod the Great* (London, 1967).

Lodoli on Function and Representation

1. Andrea Memmo: *Elementi d'Architettura Lodoliana ossia l'Arte del Fabbricare con Solidità scientifica e con Eleganza non Capricciosa, Libri tre*, Zara, 1833 (Tom 2, 1834) vols I and II, whose pages are numbered consecutively, were first published in Rome in 1786 by Pagliarini as *Libri due*. I have not accounted for the slight spelling differences in the two title pages. The Zara edition is quoted for preference, being more accessible (reprinted Milan, 1973) and complete; all further references to this edition will be listed as 'Memmo'. The reference to an *organic* architecture is on pp. 84 ff. What Lodoli meant here was that furniture should adhere to the form of the human body. The shoulders should shape the back, the bottom its seat. And he had a chair made with a back curved like that of the ancient Roman chair, which, however, did not come into fashion at the time, but which Giuseppe Tommaso Farsetti, the Venetian ambassador to Paris, took with him there. Memmo remarks that Lodoli's chair was also hollowed out at the seat, as 'the English are now beginning to do'. On function see below.
2. On the destruction of Lodoli's papers see Memmo, Tom I, pp. 118 ff. And more recently and accurately, Gianfranco Torcellan: *Una figura della Venezia Settecentescha, Andrea Memmo*, Venice, 1963, p. 34, based on an unpublished letter from Memmo to Giulio Perini of 15 May, 1784.
   Torcellan is primarily concerned with Lodoli's influence on Memmo: but his disciple Angelo Querini was perhaps destined to play a more momentous part in the history of Venice, pp. 55 ff; and on Querini's part in the Memmo candidature for the *Ducato*, pp. 206 ff. On Lodoli's place in eighteenth-century Italy, see Franco Venturi: *Il Settecento Riformatore*, Turin, 1969.
3. *Saggio sopra l'Architettura*, Bologna, 1756. Although this is called the second edition it seems to have been the earliest printing, though there were many subsequent ones, including a French and German one in 1769.

Most recent and accessible is the collected edition of Algarotti's *Saggi* edited by Giovanni da Pozzo, Bari, 1963, pp. 31 ff. It is of course possible, even probable that it may have circulated in manuscript before the printing. I should like to thank Dr Robin Middleton for pointing this out to me.
4. The story of Algarotti's commission to write the Essay, and Lodoli's reaction is told by Memmo pp. 24 ff, Tom I. But he returns to the attack several times in the book (Tom I, pp. 237, 243; Tom II, 11 ff, 46 etc.).
   No recent life of Algarotti has been written, though an account of his activities as a connoisseur is given by Francis Haskell in *Patrons and Painters*, London, 1963, pp. 266 ff, 330 ff, 347 ff.
5. Marc-Antoine Laugier's *Essai sur l'Architecture* was published in the same year, since it was delivered to the censor on 5 October 1752. The Laugier *Essai* was published anonymously. At the time of its publication Algarotti was making his final move from Berlin to Italy: to Venice in the first place, where the episodes described by Memmo presumably took place. What the relationship between the two essays was, is rather difficult to determine; though see W. Herrmann: *Laugier*, London, 1962, pp. 160 ff, and my *The First Moderns*. At any rate, the most likely course is that Laugier had independently formed his ideas on the basis of his reading of Cordemoy; that the essay had been published caused some irritation in Venice, and Algarotti was suborned to provide a counterblast: which, however, misfired.
6. Memmo, vol I, p. 21 & n. See also *Opere del Conte Algarotti*, Cremona, 1778, vol III.
7. Although the philosopher was easy enough to identify for his contemporaries, nor has there ever been any doubt about whom Algarotti meant. He was fully identified in a note to the dedication of the second edition of the *Saggio*, of 1756.
8. The classic statement is in Vitruvius IV, pp. 2, ff.
9. Algarotti, p. 51. Quoting Horace: *De Arte Poetica*, pp. 151 ff. This passage is explicitly attacked by Memmo in Tom II, p. 41. 'Atque ita mentitur, sic veris falsa remiscet, Primo ne medium, medio ne discrepet imum.' (And so tell your tale [invent your fiction], so mix false and true, that the opening does not conflict with the middle, the middle with the end.) Algarotti omits any reference to coherence. Quintilian expands on Horace in his passage on false statements: IV, pp. 2, 88 ff. On the relation of this statement to arguments about imitation at this time and in the following period, see W. Folkierski: *Entre le Classicisme et le Romantisme*, Kraków, 1925, pp. 99 ff, and A. Horst-Oncken: *Über das Schickliche*, Göttingen, 1967, pp. 18 ff.
10. Quoting, almost verbatim, the preface of the Diderot-D'Alembert Encyclopaedia, whose architectural expert was Jacques-François Blondel: 'L'Architecture, qui s'étant élevée par degrés des chaumières aux palais, n'est aux yeux du philosophe ... que le masque embelli d'un de nos plus grands besoins'. The preface was written by d'Alembert.
11. Memmo, Tom 2, p. 42.
12. Tom 2, pp. 42 ff.
13. On Francesco Milizia see G. Fontanesi: *Francesco Milizia*, Bologna, 1932.
14. Francesco Milizia: *Memorie degli Architetti Antichi e Moderni*, Parma, 1781, vol I, p. xv; his sixth principle of architecture; it quotes almost literally Algarotti's dictum attributed to 'the philosopher'. '"Niuna cosa", egli insiste, "metter si dee in rapresentazione, che non sia anche veramente in funzione ..."' (I, 12).
15. Horatio Greenough's ideas were popularised most widely by Henry T. Tuckerman in *A Memorial of Horatio Greenough*, New York, 1853. Most recently, see J. Marston Fitch: *Architecture and the Aesthetics of Plenty*, New York, 1961, pp. 46 ff, and a brief anthology *Form and Function* (ed. Harold A. Small), Berkeley, 1947. Greenough's statue of Washington, conceived in rivalry to Canova's, shows the influence of Giovanni Bartolini, whom Greenough knew in Florence in the thirties, and through whom he may have learnt both current natural history of the kind Bartolini had himself absorbed in Paris, and the works of Milizia, perhaps even Memmo. Countess Lucia Mocenigo, who had paid for (and perhaps helped to edit) the Zara edition of 1833–34 from papers which were available before the 1939–45 war in the Communal Library, Treviso, kept a stock of copies, which she would present to distinguished or curious visitors. Of whom the most curious, historically, was perhaps Effie Ruskin, who presumably took her copy home. She describes the incident in detail in her letter to her mother of 18–21.1.1850. (*Effie in Venice*, ed. Mary Lutyens, London, 1972, pp. 117 ff) but in spite of researches the copy has not come to light, nor does Ruskin ever mention Memmo or Lodoli. The episode was brought to my notice by Manlio Brusatin.
16. A list of the portraits of Lodoli is given by Memmo, vol I, p. 83. The engraved portrait follows the one by Alessandro Longhi, who – according to Memmo, *loc cit* – often painted him in his pictures. On the plate he is called 'Antonio', presumably by the engraver, Pietro Vitali (c.1755–1810); an engraver who worked after Mengs and earlier masters; but was, like Piranesi, associated both with Wagner, whose pupil he had been, and with Domenico Cunego: a fairly obvious choice for Memmo.

17. Jer. XXXI, 28.

18. Which is hardly surprising, as most modern writers have taken Algarotti's account on trust, as E. Kaufmann: *Architecture in the Age of Reason*, London and Cambridge, 1955.

19. Jean Bernoulli: *Opera Omnia*, Lausanne, 1742, vol II, pp. 232 ff, reprinted from the *Histoire et Mémoires* of the Académie des Sciences for MDCCXVIII, Amsterdam, 1743. See M. Cantor: *Vorlesungen über die Geschichte der Mathematik*, vol III, Leipzig, 1898, pp. 438 ff; but see ibid, pp. 233 ff for the earlier discussion, and the correspondence with Leibniz in the *Acta Eruditorum* and the *Journal des Scavans* for 1697–98.

20. On the importance of the concept of function for the mathematicians, in particular its place in the formulation of Calculus, see L. W. H. Hull: *History and Philosophy of Science*, London, 1959, pp. 226 ff, whose definition I quote.

21. 'Le meilleur moyen d'expliquer la Nature, s'il pouvoit être employé souvent, ce serait de la contrefaire, & d'en donner, pour ainsi dire, des représentations, en faisant produire les mêmes effets à des causes que l'on connoit, & que l'on aurait mises en action. Alors on ne devineroit plus, on veroit de ses yeux, & l'on seroit sûr que les Phénomènes naturels auroient les mêmes causes que les artificiels, ou du moins des causes bien approchantes.' *Histoire de l'Académie Royale des Sciences. Année MDCC*, Amsterdam, 1734 (2nd ed), p. 69. The *Histoire* comments on Nicolas Lemery's paper about *Feux souterrains, Tremblements de Terre, Ouragans etc.* in the *Mémoires* for the same year, p. 140.

22. Giovanni Poleni, *Memorie istoriche della Gran Cupola del Tempio Vaticano, e de' Danni di essa, e de' Ristoramenti loro*, Padua, 1748, pp. 76 ff, 282 ff. On the testing of the model, pp. 368 ff.

23. On the Catenaria see M. Cantor: *Vorlesungen über die Geschichte der Mathematik*, vol III, pp. 212 ff. David Gregory (1661–1708) provided the most explicit statement of the catenary curve's value in a paper to the Royal Society (xix, 637 in the *Philosophical Transactions*; reprinted in *Miscellanea Curiosa*, London, 1723, p. 219). Although Poleni (*Gran Cupola*, p. 57) attributes the notion of reversing the Catenaria to James Stirling, it had in fact been stated by Gregory in his original paper in the *Philosophical Transactions* (II Theorem, Corollary VI). Robert Hooke did hint (in cypher) that he had found the secret of the curve, which his editor Richard Waller deciphered in the posthumous edition of his papers as: 'Ut pendet continuum flexile sic stabit continuum Rigidum inversum'. This however was some time after the publication of Gregory's paper.

Nicolas Bernoulli (1667–1759), a member of the brilliant Bâle family (nephew of the brothers Jean and Jacques) was professor of mathematics at Padua 1716–19, before returning to Bâle as professor first of Logic, then of Law. At the same time James Stirling of Garden (1692–1770; 'no relation' as some periodicals would say) later known as 'Venetian' Stirling arrived in Padua, his scholarship at Balliol having been suspended because of his open Stuart sympathies. He had been encouraged by the Venetian ambassador in London, Niccola Tron, and the egregious Abbé Antonio Conti, a friend, dangerously, of both Leibniz and Newton, to believe that he would be given a university chair in Venetian territory; but he was not told that his conversion to the Roman obedience would be a pre-condition. It may well be that Stirling was a candidate for the chair which was in the event occupied by Bernoulli (cf. Charles Tweedie, *James Stirling*, Oxford, 1922, p. 10). That both Bernoulli and Stirling knew Poleni well, and had discussed scientific matters with him is shown by Bernoulli's letter to Stirling of 29 April 1719, the first of a series of scientific letters (the last surviving is dated 1733) in which he adds 'Illimus Polenus me enixe rogavit ut suis verbis tibi plurimam salutem dicerem'; it is a letter in which he also comments how pleased he is 'quod ea, de quibus ante hac Venetiis egimus, consideratione tua digna esse judices . . .'

Stirling, who remained a confirmed Newtonian, seems to have been maintained, at least in part, through an allowance given him by Newton, and arranged by J. T. Desagullières FRS, whose reputation as a Mason has long survived his scientific fame. Cf. Tweedie, pp. 11, 13, quoting Stirling's letters to Newton and to his brother. He makes several references to Poleni's published works, and his concern with hydraulics would suggest another common scientific interest. Whether, as the DNB s.v. Stirling suggests, he also acted as an early industrial spy, sending home or at any rate collecting the secrets of Venetian glassmaking, has never been cleared up. Stirling seemed to think that he was in danger of assassination.

Galileo mentions the Catenaria obliquely in his discussion of projectiles in the fragments of *Discorsi. Opere*, ed. P. Pagnini, Florence, 1964, vol V, pp. 160 ff.

24. G. Poleni *Cupola* (op cit) pp. 32 ff.

25. These were the *Histoire de l'Académie Royale des Sciences* of Paris, the *Philosophical Transactions* of the Royal Society, and the *Acta Eruditorum* of Leipzig, to which the *Journal des Scavans* could be added as a luxury.

26. See above n. 23.

27. He had been arguing for the necessity of such a theatre, and its being adequately financed for some time. 'Per mettere questo nuovo instituto in

un piede degno della grandezza degli Ecc, mi Riformatori venerati Padroni' he writes in a very politic and well-turned letter to the university authorities on 12 February 1739, 'necessitano assegnamenti annui ... Il Musschenbroeck si celebre nell'arte di esperimentare scrive ... che le suppellettili si ottengono con grandissima difficoltà per l'enorme costo, ma senza d'esse nulla è fattibile su cui fidarsi ...' Ms letter in the Poleni deposit in the Marciana, first published by A. Cavallari Murat, 'Giovanni Poleni e la Costruzione Architettonica' in *Giovanni Poleni, nel Bicentenario della Morte*, Padua, 1963, p. 57.

On the following page (also n. p. 75) A. Cavallari Murat has noted the existence of accounts for the moving of experimental machinery from Poleni's private house, where he seems to have conducted experiments since 1710 or thereabouts, to the university Theatrum; but the machines are not specified.

28. Poleni often quoted Musschenbroeck deferentially and this respect may have been connected with the Venetian publication of Musschenbroeck's *Elementa Physice* (Leyden, 1734) in Venice in 1751; it had also been republished in Naples in 1751. The *macchina divulsoria* was first suggested in the *Physicae experimentalis et Geometricae Elementa* of 1729 (Leyden): interestingly enough, Musschenbroeck's machine is a spare but elegant utilitarian construction, while Poleni's is elaborately carved in a full-bottomed rocaille manner.

29. So, most recently E. Kaufmann Jr: 'Memmo's Lodoli' in *Art Bulletin*, 1946, p. 168. The first to point out the survival of the building recently has been A. Cavallari Murat, in 'Congetture sul Trattato d'Architettura progettato dal Lodoli' in *Atti e Rassegna Tecnica della Società degli Ingegneri e degli architetti in Torino*, July 1966, pp. 3 ff. The description of the building which follows is based on Memmo's account of the building and its origins in Memmo, Tom 2, pp. 154 ff.

30. By which he means *professionals*, rather than *academics*. Lodoli's reputation was such, that after his death more buildings were attributed to him: *Venezia e le sue Lagune*, Venice, 1847, vol II, Tom II, p. 286, on the Scuola of San Pasquale, which it attributes, wrongly, to Lodoli, as well as the adjoining convent of San Francesco della Vigna. This is the Scuola now known as that of the Stigmata. The attribution to Lodoli is not known to the best modern guide, Lorenzetti, or to Paganuzzi, *Iconografia della Città di Venezia e delle 30 parocchie*, Venice n.d. (c.1820).

31. This idiosyncratic Greek term is commented on at length by Giovanni Ziborghi in his *Vignola*, 1748, p. 46. Ziborghi uses it as a synonym for *fulcrum*: but this is not the way in which Lodoli seems to use the word – or at least Memmo. The passage about the supine column occurs near the beginning of the 'Prima Giornata' of the *Discorsi e Dimostrazioni Matematiche*; *Opere* (op cit) vol IV, p. 126.

32. The cloister was built after Palladio's death, and its authorship has often been doubted. The latest state of play may be found in Lionello Puppi's *Palladio*, Milan, 1973, vol II, pp. 428 ff. It is known as the Cypress cloister. The name 'Memmia' was given to the Island of St George because of the reputed gift of it to the Benedictine monks by Doge Tribuno Memmo (an ancestor of Andrea) in 982.

33. San Jacobus Picenus, or San Giacomo delle Marche (1394–1476) holding a lamp, and setting behind himself the mitres he rejected.

34. Not the beams in our sense: the curved space between the soffit and the relieving arch, or the rising portion above the beam to make the catenary arch.

35. *L'Architettura di Jacopo Barozzi da Vignola ridotta a facile Metodo per Mezzo di Osservazioni a profitto de'Studenti aggiuntovi un Trattato di Meccanica*, Venice, 1748. The dedication ('Al rinomatissimo Padre Carlo Lodoli, Professore celeberrimo d'Arti e di Scienze) is signed N. N., who is identified as Giovanni Ziborghi by Memmo (Tom 2, pp. 159 ff) and adds that there was a second edition in 1775, which does not seem to be catalogued elsewhere.

36. Although the week-end house has not been identified, the Palace is the Venetian Embassy in Constantinople, where he did not, however, succeed in having his design executed, but had to rest content with alterations to the existing structure. Torcellan, Memmo (op cit) pp. 154 ff and fig. 5. The drawing – not particularly distinguished – has been attributed to Memmo himself and shows the Lodolian catenary curves and rustication in a rather bland, anglicised Palladian facade.

37. The scientific curve is clearly the catenary. It is exhibited in the rather heavy cills of the windows.

38. It is impossible to reconstruct this ornament: the two main members of the pediment are centre-butted on the existing building, and not overlapping, as Memmo says. It may be that Lodoli had intended to omit the centrepieces and Memmo's 'ornament' spanned between them, though as the building now stands, it does not look as if there had been any substantial change made to the abbreviated and reformed tympani.

39. This surprising conventional view of historical progression would have been wholly approved by Algarotti. Though Squarcione was presented by Vasari (ed Milanesi, vol III, pp. 383 ff) and everyone since as the great

pedagogue of Venetian art; Milanesi attributes 137 disciples to Squarcione. And he describes Squarcione's criticism of Mantegna for following Antique bas-relief too closely in his paintings.

40. (Vitruvius I, 1, i). The whole sentence runs: 'Ea [architectura] nascitur ex fabrica et ratiocinatione', which is the old Hellenistic duality, of τεχνη against επιστημη; Lodoli deliberately sets the extra syllable ratio cinatio to play on the ambiguity and imply both reason, as a general concept and comment or dialectic.

41. It is the introductory plate of the second volume. The 'scientific' curve is used for the covering arch, for the lintel – which is in fact invisible – and for the four sections of doorjamb, two on either side, interrupted in the middle by the triple wedge described in the text.

42. The text of Vignola is given a brief but helpful, and rather uncritical commentary. The little treatise on mechanics says practically nothing about complex matters, such as the catenary, but is concerned with elementary notions, such as the bending moment, elasticity, transmission.

43. In his preface Ziborghi confesses his reluctance in dedicating the book to Lodoli: 'contenendosi in esso cose, delle quali siete divenuto publico e giusto Censore . . .' This has been taken as a reference to Lodoli's activity as a censor of books: but this can hardly be the case. The book contains nothing which a state or a religious censorship would ban; but it speaks exclusively of technical matters, which as Algarotti and Memmo both agree, were the subject of Lodoli's – as we would now say – censorious teaching.

44. It was known to Moschini (*Della Letteratura Veneziana del Secolo XVIII*, Venice, 1806–08, III, pp. 120 ff); Angelo Comolli (*Bibliografia . . . dell' Architettura Civile . . .* Rome, 1792, pp. 50 ff) who also confesses to having compiled the errata and the index (p. 50) though many manuscripts were, on Memmo's own decision, allowed to circulate (Torcellan, pp. 187 ff).

45. The book, he writes to a friend, was dictated in 'less than eight days by the effort of memory alone, without consulting anyone who might speak with me of the founder of the new institutes . . .' Letter to Giulio Perini dated 22 June 1784 in Torcellan, p. 185. Though he seems to have consulted a number of people about the matter of the book, as well as the style, before its publication two years later; although his intimates, such as his brother Bernardo and Angelo Querini did not question his version of events or his interpretation of the ideas.

46. Vico quotes Lodoli's letter to himself of the 15 January 1728, which opens the campaign (which was to finish in disappointment all round) to reprint Vico's *Scienza Nuova* in a revised version in Venice (*Opere*, ed. Fausto Nicolini, Milan and Naples, 1953, p. 77) written therefore on the basis of the *Scienza Nuova Prima*, which was first published in 1725.

Lodoli's familiarity with Vico, however, was partly responsible for the genesis of the autobiography itself. It was for a series of literary self-portraits to be written by Italian men of letters, at the suggestion and on the commission of Count Gianartico de Porcia, perhaps stimulated by Leibniz (see most recently A. R. Caponigri, *Time & Idea*, Notre Dame, 1953, p. 11, after Fausto Nicolini, *Bibliographia Vichiana*, 1947–48, I, p. 61.

47. On the conception of law and history taught in Lodoli's 'school' see Memmo, pp. 51 ff, vol I, Tom 1. The school was started at the prompting of Scipione Maffei, and Montesquieu as well as Vico corresponded with him. The Neapolitan jurist and historian lived in Venice in the house of Memmo's maternal grandfather, Andrea Pisani, where he is known to have met Lodoli. 'Natural law' was the centre of his teaching, and Cicero's *De Officiis* his basic text, though he used Samuel Puffendorf's *De jure Naturae et Gentium* (1672). Puffendorf is often quoted, not always with wholehearted admiration, by Vico. Another text he was fond of using was the preface of *Chambers' Encyclopaedia*, and later that of Diderot and D'Alembert: though he clearly did not share their views on architecture.

48. The view advanced in *de antiquissima Italorum Sapientia ex Linguae Latinae Originibus eruenda libri tres*, Naples, 1710, was later modified, particularly through the two main redactions of the *Scienza Nuova* (1725, 1744) in that Vico gave fantasy an increasing part in the creation and articulation of language against that of reason. But even in his later writings, as in the appendix on the origin of the law of the XII tables added to the 1744 (with a shorter appendix on the 'Lex Regia Triboniana') and last edition of the *Scienza*, he defended the conception of the coherence of national institutions in general, and of the autochthonous origins of Roman law in particular; a matter of the greatest weight to the understanding of both law and of history, since 'la giurisprudenza principalmente fece grandi i Romani', to use his own words. Indeed primitive law, compounded of the natural law of the nations, and the particular law of a people was in the first place a kind of poem, composed of gestures and actions which were polyvalent, in the same way as the hieroglyphs of the Egyptians and of the Chinese (paragraph 1035 ff).

49. Memmo, Tom I, pp. 290 ff, pp. 325 ff; on p. 296 Lodoli's opinion that the Doric order was in fact Greek is reported.

50. Piranesi's dependence on Lodoli has already been suggested by R. Wittkower in 'Piranesi's Architectural Creed', *Studies in the Italian Baroque* (London, 1975, p. 238); so also U. Vogt-Göknill, *Giovanni Battista Piranesi*,

'Carceri', Zürich, 1958, pp. 61, 90, n. 7.

A more developed treatment, which relies on the probable influence of Vico and Gravina, in M. Calvesi's preface to the catalogue of the Piranesi exhibition, Calcografia Nazionale, Rome (1967–68), pp. 6 ff, 20 ff. Piranesi's debt to Lodoli was already emphasised by Memmo, Tom I, p. 222; in Tom II, p. 139 he records Piranesi's gift of a copy of his *Della Magnificenza ed Architettura de' Romani* (Imprimatur May, 1760) to Lodoli a few months before the latter's death (27 October, 1761) as a token of friendship; the friendship must have been of long date, since Piranesi seems to have left Venice for the last time in 1744, when he was 24; and although he may have seen Lodoli's building on that occasion, there can be little doubt that he was familiar with the argument which informed Lodoli's approach. Memmo recounts his meeting with Poleni in the house of Marco Foscarini, when he made an attempt to arrange a public or semi-public disputation between Lodoli and Poleni about Vitruvius; Poleni refused on grounds of his great friendship for Lodoli and equally great veneration for Vitruvius.

Marco Foscarini was, as Bally of the Republic to the Holy See, the first protector of Piranesi in Rome; another close connection would have been Matteo Lucchesi, Piranesi's uncle and his first teacher of architecture (H. Focillon, *Piranesi*, Paris, 1918, p. 24), who was sufficiently erudite to write his letters, when the occasion arose, in Latin verse, and who disputed with Lodoli's fiercest enemy, Tommaso Temanza (who had called Lodoli an insolent critic and a shameless impostor – 'critico insolente ed impostore sfacciato' in *Vite dei più celebri Architetti e Scultori Veneziani*, Venice, 1778, p. 87, n. a; cf Memmo, Tom I, pp. 124 ff) about the proper attitude to take to the ancients, adopting a rather Lodolian stance in a letter, only the answer to which is known (Temanza in *Raccolta d'Opuscoli Scientifici e Filologici*, vol V, pp. 175 ff).

Memmo writes as if he had known Piranesi; he was certainly in a position to discuss the matter with Piranesi's son Francesco, who dedicated several plates to him in the *Collection des Plus belles Statues de Rome* which he published in the same year as Memmo did the *Elementi*, 1786. At this time he also engraved a three-plate view of Memmo's pet 'improvement', the Pra' del Valle in Padua. Memmo's secretary published an explanatory text about the engraving: *Descrizione della general Idea concepita, ed in gran parte effetuata dall' ecc . mo Signore ANDREA MEMMO . . . quando fu per la Serenissima Repubblica di Venezia nel MDCCLXXV, e Vi Proveditor Straordinario della Città di Padova sul materiale del Prato che denominavasi della Valle onde renderlo utile anche per le potentissime Vie del diletto a quel Popolo ed a maggior decoro della stessa Città, a maggior intelligenza delle due grandi Incisioni, che stanno per uscire dalla Calcografia Piranesi . . .* Rome, 1786. Don Vincenzo Radicchio, who signed the book, may well have been acting as Memmo's ammanuensis, as Gianfranco Torcellan suggested (Memmo, p. 125, n. 1). Since he was *Segretario de' Memoriali di S.E. medesima, attuale Ambasciatore alla Santa Sede*, he may well have been the person who wrote the *Elementi* to Memmo's dictation. In the *Descrizione*, Radicchio describes Francesco Piranesi as 'familiare di S.E.' (p. 5); too little is known about this relationship, and Francesco in general (Focillon, p. 130).

Giambattista Piranesi was very much moved by the issues which Lodoli had raised, and certainly took many of the views on the priority of Egyptian and Etruscan architecture from Lodoli. But he even uses arguments which recall Vico. His passionate plea for the independence of Roman law, and of the antiquity of the XII tables (*Della Magnificenza*, pp. ix ff) smacks of Vican argument and Vican method. But he is, I suspect, more profoundly influenced by Vico's belief in the power of the heroic imagination. Piranesi believed himself, as he continuously reiterates, to be living in a time of architectonic decadence, and his apparently irrational compilations of extravagant ornament are more in the nature of a 'poetic' reinvention of built surface, which contains an essentially 'rational' internal structure.

51. Most obviously in the general repertory of ornament at Newgate, but also in certain minor works. See G. Teyssot: *Città e Utopia nell' Illuminismo Inglese*, Rome, 1974, pp. 55 ff, pp. 78 ff. But cf Dorothy Stroud, *George Dance*, pp. 98 ff.

52. Memmo, although he recognises the debt Milizia owes to Algarotti, refers to him constantly; and names (Tom I, p. 152, n.) him colonel of the regiment of architect-philosophers. Milizia's handbook is discussed in great detail in Comolli's *Bibliografia Architettonica* (vol IV, pp. 42 ff) just before Memmo's Lodoli (ibid pp. 50 ff; 34 pages make it one of the longest articles of the bibliography); and indeed Comolli declares himself a follower of Lodoli/Memmo. He claims to have been responsible for the index of the book, and the errata, but may well also have worked over the notes. Comolli also provides analytical articles about Algarotti's *Saggio* – in which he reports Frederick the Great's bitchy remark that Algarotti kept all his knowledge in small change – and about Laugier's *Essai* as well as his Observations, so that a comparison was available to all later historians. Milizia deals, incidentally, with the catenary curve (Bassano, 1823, vol III, pp. 190 ff) but perversely draws it (figs 13 ff) as a semi-circle.

53. This tag was coined by Poleni's friend and disciple Simone Stratico, who

was also a friend of Memmo ('amico mio, che pregio ed amo sommamente') who was to edit finally and have printed Poleni's great commentary on Vitruvius (Udine, 1825–30). It is the slogan which most Italian Neo-Classicists would have adopted cheerfully.

On Comolli see A. Cavallari-Murat, 'Schedula sulla Bibliografia Architettonica di Angelo Comolli' in *Boll Soc., Piedmontese di Archeologia e Belle Arti*, 1964, N.S. XVIII, pp. 173 ff.

Augusto Cavallari-Murat first encouraged me to pursue this matter. The Rev Fr Guardian and the Friars of San Francesco della Vigna were most generous of their time and information about their monastery.

Semper and the Conception of Style

1. An account of this episode is given in most handbooks to prehistoric art. See, for example, A. Leroi-Gourhan: *Préhistoire de l'Art Occidental*, Paris, 1965, p. 26; or H. G. Brandi & J. Maringer: *L'Art Préhistorique*, Bâle, 1952, p. 20.
2. *Primitive Culture, Researches into the Development of Mythology, Philosophy, Religion, Art and Custom*, (4th ed.) London, 1903, vol I, pp. 58 ff.
3. *The Antiquity of Man* by Sir Charles Lyell. The first edition, London 1863, has an account of the latest French and German paleontological discoveries, pp. 75 ff, 112 ff, 153 ff; and a mention of Magdalenian engravings, pp. 190 ff. On Flints as 'Works of Art', pp. 154 ff. This material is repeated with little variation until the fourth edition (London, 1873) in which the engraving of Elephas Primigenius from La Madeleine (now in the Museum at St Germain-en-Laye) is inserted. The engraving is much simplified.
4. Sir John Lubbock: *The Origin of Civilization and the Primitive Condition of Man*, London, 1870. Lubbock devotes two pages (pp. 29 ff) to these representations. He reproduces the same Elephas engraving as Lyell, and one of two reindeer from Laugerie-Basse. This remains unchanged until the 1902 fourth edition. (Lubbock had meanwhile been created Lord Avebury.) The first edition to discuss prehistoric art in any detail is the fifth one, of 1912.
5. A discussion of the origins of the study of prehistory and of human society in M. Boule and H. V. Vallois: *Fossil Man*, London, 1957, pp. 10 ff.
6. E. Grosse: *Les Débuts de L'Art*, Paris, 1902 has the premium of an introduction by Léon Mariller, cf pp. 124 ff. The engraving of the reindeer was done, as the caption says, from a plaster cast. The engraving came from Laugerie-Basse.
7. On Grosse's use of Fechner's *Vorschule der Ästhetik* (Leipzig, 1876), see his op. cit. pp. 38 ff, 221 ff. Though Fechner's principal theories had already been formulated in his *Elemente der Psychophysik* (Leipzig, 1860) in which the essential intuition that the immanent, spiritual nature of the universe could be demonstrated through the measurement, and therefore through the physical 'existence' of apparently subjective responses, is elaborated and codified. The intuition, which Fechner claims to have received while lying in bed on the morning of 22.10.1850 is half-seriously celebrated by psychologists as the birthday of their discipline. It is ironic that Fechner's whole endeavour was to counter what he considered an excessively materialist psychology.

On Grosse's place in the history of Ethnology, see R. H. Lowie: *The History of Ethnological Theory*, London, 1937, p. 95, p. 189.
8. For Grosse's comments on Spencer's theories, see his op. cit., pp. 211 ff.
9. *Der Stil in den technischen und tektonischen Künsten oder Praktische Ästhetik. Ein Handbuch für Techniker, Künstler und Kunstfreunde von Gottfried Semper*, vol I. 'Die Textile Kunst, für sich betrachtet und in Beziehung zur Baukunst', Munich, 1863. The second edition, which is quoted, appeared in Munich in 1878 and 1879, with a preface by the author's son, Hans Semper. The second volume included an obituary of Semper by Friederich Pecht reprinted from the *Augsburger Allgemeine Zeitung*, but had few changes in the text or even in the footnotes. The increased paragraph numbering is due to the repetition of paragraph numbers 6 and 29; the correction results in two extra paragraph numbers in the second edition. Other changes, as Hans Semper says in the preface, are minimal. Many spelling mistakes, for instance, remain uncorrected in the second edition.
10. Semper: *Der Stil*, vol I, 1878, p. 12.
11. Ibid, p. 169. 'Der Knoten ist vielleicht das älteste technische Symbol und . . . der Ausdruck für die frühesten kosmogonischen Ideen, die bei den Völkern aufkeimten.'
12. Semper: *Der Stil*, vol I, 1878, p. 73, cf. pp. 14 ff, 75 ff, 163 ff.
13. (Friederich) Gustav Klemm: *Allgemeine Cultur-Geschichte der Menschheit*, Leipzig, 1843, 1834–1852 (vol. X). Klemm's own collection was divided at his death: some went to the British Museum, but most of it was to form the nucleus of the Museum für Völkerkunde in Leipzig. For Klemm as an ethnologist, see R. H. Lowie, op. cit., pp. 11 ff, 189.
14. At the time when Semper was working on the buildings of the Art Gallery in Dresden, Klemm was director of the Royal Library to which he was appointed in 1834; the year in which Semper was given the Chair of Architecture. He was also working on the Royal collections, and assembling and ordering his own. Klemm eventually also became curator of the porcelain collection house in the Zwinger.

15. This was, in fact, not a full size, but a model. It is noted in the *Crystal Palace described and illustrated by Beautiful Engravings chiefly from Daguerrotypes* by Bernard Myall & C & C (John Tallis & Co.), London & New York, n.d. vol II, p. 130: 'The same conclusion may be drawn in favour of the capacity of the North American Indian to adopt our usage, from the model of the house of the once wild Carib, the cannibal of Columbus, with every household convenience minutely represented. The easy chair, the wax taper, the neat table, the tinder-box, the old man's modern bed, as well as the aboriginal hammock . . . and a hundred other articles are there, to show the profusion of comforts which civilization produces. This little Indian picture of civilized barbarism is a lesson that should be perpetuated by such a simple work being deposited in the British Museum.'

Semper himself discusses it in an unpublished manuscript at the Victoria and Albert Museum (MS 86 FF 64): 'Practical Art in Metals, its Technology, History & Styles', p. 13, folio unnumbered. 'Architectural Parts: Mats, hides and carpets were the original divisions of space for domestic comfort – see the models of Carribean cottages [huts] exhibited in the W. Indies allotment at the exhibition of 1851. Hence is derived the ancient custom of covering walls with carpets, leather, wood panels, stucco, stone panels or metal plates.'

The manuscript is dated 1854 but must have been written in 1832. I want to thank Robin Middleton for directing my attention to this passage. It echoes the ideas already set out in *Vier Elemente der Baukunst. Beitrag zur Vergleichenden Baukunde*, Braunschweig, 1851, pp. 56 ff. But, of course, Semper's and the commentators' in Tallis' *Crystal Palace* view of the hut use it to demonstrate opposite points. Tallis' commentator sees the model as showing the 'Caribs' rapid adaptation to Western ways, while Semper sees it as the evidence of archaic ways persisting into his own time.

Cf. also Semper, *Kleine Schriften*, pp. 292 ff.
16. '. . . kein Phantasiebild, sondern ein höchst realistisches Exemplar einer Holzkonstruktion aus der Ethnologie entlehnt und hier dem Leser als eine Vitruvianische Urhütte in allen ihren Elementen entsprechend . . . alle Elemente der antiken Baukunst [treten] in höchst ursprünglicher Weise und unvermischt hervor: der Heerd als Mittelpunkt, die durch Pfahlwerk umschränkte Erderhöhung als Terrasse, das säulengetragene Dach und die Mattenumhegung als Raumabschlüsse oder Wand.' Semper: *Der Stil*, vol II, 1879, pp. 262 ff; cf. also p. 202, ibid.
17. Ibidem, p. 200. Cf. E. Viollet-le-Duc, *Lectures on Architecture*, translated by Benjamin Bucknall, vol I, London 1877, pp. 45 ff. As the first volume of the *Entretiens* was not published until 1863, the same year as the first volume of *Der Stil*, and Semper did not quote any publication later than 1858, he presumably saw the separate issue of this *Entretien* which appeared in that year. Cf. R. Middleton, supra.
18. Ibidem, p. 200. 'Nun sind aber die Würzelformen der Tektonik viel älter als die Baukunst und bereits in der vormonumentalen Zeit an dem beweglichen Hausrath zu vollster . . . Ausbildung gelangt, ehe die heilige Hütte, das Gottesgehäuse, das monumentale Gezimmer seine Kunstform erhielt. Daraus folgt nach dem allgemeinen Gesetze des menschlichen Schaffens, dass diese . . . nothwendig eine Modifikation desjenigen war, was die Tektonik an ihrem älteren Objekte aus sich heraus gebildet hatte.'
19. It is explicit in the title of *Der Stil*: the first volume refers particularly to the relation between textile art and architecture; the second volume does so, of course, for four other materials. But the importance of the first relationship is paramount. The earlier writing is *Vorläufige Bemerkungen über bemalte Architektur und Plastik bei den Alten*, Altona, 1834.
20. '. . . das Färben ist natürlicher und leichter, daher auch ursprünglicher als das Anstreichen und Malen. Diese These enthält ein sehr wichtiges Moment der Stiltheorie.' *Der Stil*, vol I, p. 190.
21. See his colour plate XI. Semper even claimed that tattooing was also patterned with thread (*Der Stil*, vol I, pp. 92 ff). Though in this case the word *Faden* takes almost a metaphorical sense.
22. Semper, *Der Stil*, vol I, pp. 75 ff, 196.
23. Ibidem, vol I, p. 197.
24. Ibidem, vol I, p. 213.
25. '. . . – das Gesetz nähmlich aus der Noth eine Tugend zu Machen.' The proverb seems to have been coined by St Jerome, but is a fairly universal proverb, which Semper proposes as the first rule of art. *Der Stil*, vol I, p. 73 & note 1.
26. J. & W. Grimm: *Deutsches Wörterbuch*, s.v.v.
27. Semper gives the reference to Höfer's *Sprachwissenschaftliche Untersuchungen*, pp. 223 ff. In fact, it appears on p. 222 of Karl Gustav Albert Höfer's *Beiträge zur Etymologie und Vergleichenden Grammatik der Hauptsprachen des Indo-Germanischen Stammes*, vol I (all published), Berlin 1839. It was dedicated to the Manes of von Humboldt; and although criticised from the Humboldtian camp, nevertheless established Höfer's reputation. He was later to turn his attention also to his native dialect variants (*Denkmäler Niederdeutscher Sprache und Literatur nach alten Drucken und Handschriften herausgegeben*, Greifswald, 1850 f). On Höfer generally, see

Theodor Benfey: *Geschichte der Sprachwissenschaft und Orientalischen Philologie in Deutschland*, Munich, 1969, pp. 406 ff, 584 f, 673.

28. Semper's further reference is to L. Diefenbach: *Vergleichendes Wörterbuch der Gothischen Sprache*, Frankfurt A/M, 1851, s.v. Nauths, and to J. Grimm: *Deutsche Grammatik*, Berlin, 1822. Semper does not refer to, and perhaps did not know the work of another pupil of K. O. Müller, which deals with the religious symbolism of knots: 'Vorstudien zur Topologie', in *Göttinger Studien*, 1847.

29. Semper, *Der Stil*, vol I, p. 7.

30. The word symbol was very much under discussion since Kant's rethinking of the term; but it had been given very close attention by the students of language. (Georg) Friederich Creuzer's *Symbolik und Mythologie der alten Völker, besonders der Griechen* (Leipzig & Darmstadt, 1810 and 1812) was widely known. But Semper knew also Karl Otfried Müller's rather different views of the matter, since he heard his lectures when a student at Göttingen. Müller sets out his difference with Creuzer in the *Prolegomena zu einer Wissenschaftlichen Mythologie*, Göttingen, 1825, pp. 331 ff.

The earlier discussion is summarised by Bengt Algot Sørensen in *Symbol und Symbolismus in den Ästhetischen Theorien des 18. Jahrhunderts und der Deutschen Romantik*, Copenhagen, 1963; for the term after Hegel, see Johannes Volkelt: *Der Symbolbegriff*, Leipzig, 1876.

31. Semper, *Der Stil*, vol I, p. 189. 'Das Beitzen und Färben der Haut gehört zu der merkwürdigen Gruppe von Erfindungen, deren Mutter nicht die Noth, sondern die reine Lust ist und die zu den allerfrühesten gehören, weil gleichsam der Instinkt der Freude sie dem Menschen einblies.'

32. Ibidem, vol I, p. xxi. 'Umgeben von einer Welt voller Wunder und Kräfte, deren Gesetz der Mensch ahnt, das er fassen möchte, aber nimmer enträthselt . . . und sein Gemüth in stets unbefridigter Spannung erhält, zaubert er sich das fehlende Vollkommenheit im Spiel hervor, bildet er sich eine Welt im Kleinen, worin das kosmische Gesetz in engster Beschränktheit . . . hervortritt; . . . durch diese Illusion (im Einzelnen die Harmonie des Ganzen zu vernehmen) so ist dies Naturgenuss, der vom Kunstgenuss . . . prinzipiel nicht verschieden ist . . . Aber dieser künstlerische Genuss des Naturschönen ist keineswegs die naiveste . . . vielmehr ist der Sinn dafür beim . . . Naturmenschen unentwickelt, während ihn schon erfreut, das Gesetz der bildnerischen Natur, wie es in der Realität durch die Regelmässigkeit periodischer Raumes und Zeitfolgen hindurchblickt, im Kranze, in der Perlschnur, im Schnörkel, im Reigetänze, in den rythmischen Lauten, womit der Reigetanz begleitet wird, im Takte des Ruders u.s.w.'

33. See, for example, the references to proportionality in clothing, in which, unusually, Semper refers back to the treatment of proportionality in the *Prolegomena. Der Stil*, vol I, p. 83. In spite of his declared anti-mediaevalism, he seems to something in this formulation to the Schlegels, particularly to August Wilhelm. I very much doubt if he was familiar with Michelet's *Histoire de France*, Paris, 1833, which Cuvier seems to quote, without acknowledgement, in his *Histoire des Sciences Naturelles* (below, n. 41).

34. The contents of the third volume, which was presumably begun at the same time, are set out in the prospectus which may sometimes be found bound into the first edition. It was to be devoted to architecture, divided into seven sections (Ancient, Hellenistic, Roman, Christian-Roman, Mediaeval, Renaissance); and in the last section, the question was to be asked whether the new mediaevalising tendency has any future, since the Renaissance section was also to consider whether the Renaissance had only begun, or if a new era was opening. The book was to be concerned with the great field of invention in which we consider the social demands of our time analogically as the comparative material of history, and evaluate them artistically as the 'moments' of the style of our architecture. *Der Stil*, 'Prospektus', p. 7.

35. In *Gothic Architecture and Scholasticism*, New York, 1957. This passage and its context in Semper's theory is discussed in detail by Paul Frankl: *The Gothic, Literary Sources through Eight Centuries*, Princeton, 1960, pp. 589 ff.

36. 'Prospektus', p. 8.

37. C. F. von Rumohr: *Italienische Forschungen*, Berlin & Stettin, 1828, vol I, pp. 48 ff. In the same place, von Rumohr also concerns himself briefly with the notion of 'Type'. Semper was very familiar with von Rumohr and his work, indeed designed his tomb in Dresden. The passage in question is in vol I, pp. 103 ff.

38. H. Semper: *Gottfried Semper, Ein Bild seines Lebens und Wissens*, Berlin, 1880. See also Semper: *Kleine Schriften*, (ed. M. & H. Semper), Berlin and Stuttgart, 1884, pp. 7 ff.

39. These include, besides Cuvier, von Humboldt, Bernoulli and James Watt, among the moderns.

40. It was, of course, attacked earlier, and Goethe was much involved in the controversy. See J. W. Goethe: *Werke*, ed. E. Beutler, Zürich and Stuttgart, 1966, vol XVII, pp. 380 ff; these essays were first published in the *Jahrbuch für Wissenschaftliche Kritik*, Berlin 1830 and 1832.

41. The place of Cuvier in this history of biology, and the importance of his theories, as well as their relationship to economic theory and linguistics is

discussed by Michel Foucault in *Les Mots et les Choses*, Paris, 1966, pp. 229 ff. Cuvier, while not maintaining an active interest in contemporary German philosophy, knew of the earlier linguistic speculations, as is clear from the *Histoire des Sciences Naturelles, depuis leurs Origines jusqu'à nos Jours*, edited from Cuvier's lectures by M. Magdaleine de Saint-Agy, Paris, 1841, whose conception of the place of the Indians in world history and their relation to other cultures, the Egyptians in particular, owes much to Friederich von Schlegel's *Über die Sprache und Weisheit der Indier*, Heidelberg, 1808, to which he makes specific acknowledgement in vol I, p. 30.

42. M. Foucault, op. cit. p. 276 ff.

43. The catastrophic theory of biological development is set out in his *Recherches sur les Ossements Fossiles . . . par M. le Baron G. Cuvier* (2nd ed.), Paris 1821, vol I, pp. iii ff. On the recent appearance of homo as a species, ibid, pp. lxiv ff.

44. H. Semper in *Kleine Schriften*, op. cit. and G. Semper, ibid. pp. 259 ff.

45. Semper, *Der Stil*, vol II, pp. 335 ff. Cf. *Kleine Schriften*.

46. Because of its importance, and because of its essential affinity to the moulding of ceramics; Semper had anyway already met this difficulty when dealing with glass under the 'moulding' section, vol II, pp. 178 ff. He therefore abandons the normal formal/technical/historical division of the section, and justifies the inconsistency in vol II, p. 459. There is, of course, no metal section in Semper's ideal museum, based on the four radical processes. See Semper: *Wissenschaft, Industrie und Kunst*, 1966, p. 78 where the placing of the metal objects is shown.

47. 'Die Sammlungen und die öffentlichen Monumente sind die wahren Lehrer eines freien Volkes.' *Wissenschaft, Industrie und Kunst*, 1963, p. 368 ff, 378. '[Semper] hielt mich beständig für den Repräsentanten einer mittelalterisch katholizierenden Richtung, die er oft mit Wut bekämpfte. Sehr mühselig gelang es mir, ihn endlich dazu zu belehren, dass meine Studien und Neigungen eigentlich auf das deutsche Altertum und die Auffindung des Ideales der Urgermanischen Mythus ausgingen. So wie wir nun in das Heidentum gerieten . . . ward er ein ganz anderer Mensch und ein offenbares grosses und ernstes Interesse begann uns jetzt in die Weise zu vereinigen, dass es uns zugleich von der übrigen Gesellschaft gänzlich isolierte . . .' Wagner followed the composition of *Der Stil* with interest, and records visiting Semper in his Studio 'after many doubts and change of publisher' when he was carrying out the illustrations for the book 'mit grosser Sauberkeit selbst auf Stein'. As the only illustrations on stone are the twenty-two coloured lithographs at the end of the book, it may well be that Wagner also saw Semper preparing the wood blocks.

48. Richard Wagner, *Mein Leben*, Munich, 1963, pp. 368 ff, 378. '[Semper]

49. Wilhelm von Humboldt: *Über die Verschiedenheit des Menschlichen Sprachbaues und ihren Einfluss auf die geistige Entwicklung des Menschengeschlechts*, Berlin, 1836, p. lvii. 'Sie [die Sprache] ist kein Werk [Ergon], sondern eine Tätigkeit [Energia] . . . Sie ist nähmlich die sich ewig wiederholende Arbeit des Geistes, den articulierten Laut zum Ausdruck des Gedanken fähig zu machen.'

50. W. von Humboldt, op. cit., p. lxi. 'Der wirkliche Stoff der Sprache ist auf der einen Seite der Laut überhaupt auf der anderen die Gesamtheit der sinnlichen Eindrücke und selbsthätigen Geistesbewegungen, welche der Bildung des Begriffs mit Hülfe der Sprache vorausgehen.'

51. M. Foucault, op. cit., p. 303. On Humboldt and Bopp, see Pieter A. Verburg 'The Background to the Linguistic Conceptions of Franz Bopp', in Thomas E. Sebok: *Portraits of Linguists*, Bloomington, 1966, vol I, pp. 226 ff and further on from Humboldt, pp. 234 ff.

52. H. Semper, op. cit.

53. G. Semper: 'Über Baustile' in *Wissenschaft, Industrie, Kunst*, p. 106. 'Man bezeichnet richtig die alten Monumente als die fossilen Gehäuse ausgestorbener Gesellschaftsorganismen, aber diese sind letzteren, wie sie lebten, nicht wie Schnekenhäuser auf den Rücken gewachsen, noch sind sie nach einem blinden Naturprozesse wie Korallenriffe aufgeschossen, sondern freie Gebilde des Menschen, der dazu Verstand, Naturbeobachtung, Genie, Willen, Wissen und Macht in Bewegung setzte.' And in the paragraph above, explicitly: 'Uns will [diese] Anwendung des . . . axioms "Die Natur macht keine Sprünge" und der Darwinischen Artenenstehungslehre auf die besondere Welt des kleinen Nachschöpfers, des Menschen, doch einigermassen bedenklich erscheinen . . .'

54. On the human skin as the primary ornamented surface, *Der Stil*, vol I, pp. 92 ff. Though even in this connection, Semper allows the possibility that naked peoples who tattoo their skins may be imitating the crafts of some higher and forgotten culture. In any case, tattoos (writes Semper, following Klemm) were usually done in colours which suited those of the people's skin and were 'structurally' adapted to the musculature of their bodies. Riegl contests this also in *Stilfragen* (pp. 84 ff) by showing the elaborately spiral tattooing of the Maoris (out of Sir John Lubbock's *Origin of Civilization* pp. 50 ff) to have been devised without the benefit of knowing any textile technique.

The larger issue of assuming that body-painting and tattoo may have been a primary, perhaps the original art could not be raised as long as painting was considered an art 'of imitation'. Riegl is much more firmly attached to this classical notion than Semper. It recurs in much anthropological literature, from the generalised classificatory kind (A. C. Haddon, *Evolution in Art*, London, 1895 – see particularly the chart on p. 8) to specialised studies, as Adama von Scheltama's *Die Altnordische Kunst* (Berlin, 1923). The basic hypothesis was documented at the end of the nineteenth century by Hjalmar Stolpe in a number of publications, to which Riegl also appealed (p. 39, n. 1). Semper's view, that figuration always has its origin in action, was developed with great subtlety by Franz Boas, who denied *a priori* the possibility of an aesthetic reaction to natural phenomena without a 'making' experience of form (*Primitive Art*, New York, 1927, p. 11). A further development of this notion is Ernst Grosse's postulate (*Les Débuts de l'Art*, Paris, 1902, pp. 157 ff, suggested by Herbert Spencer) that dance was the *Urkunst*. Grosse also affirms the heraldic nature of body-marking. *Per contra* Claude Lévi-Strauss had already evoked lyrically in *Tristes Tropiques* (Paris, 1956, pp. 185 ff) the erotic power of Caduveo asymmetric body-painting and its subtle sado-masochistic seduction, noted more coarsely by earlier travellers (Guido Boggiani, *I Caduvei*, Rome, 1895).

Though body-painting and body-decking may be 'structural', as Semper maintained, it may also be destructive of the body-image. This was dryly set out by Marcel Mauss (*Manuel d'Ethnographie*, Paris, 1967, pp. 66 ff) and treated at greater length in his critique of Wilhelm Wundt's *Völkerpsychologie* (reprinted in his *Oeuvres*, Paris, 1968, pp. 198 ff). However, since Captain Cook brought the word *tattoo* into a European language, body-marking has been regarded and studied as an eccentricity of savages and criminals (as by Alexandre Lacassagne, *Les Tatuages*, Paris, 1881; or by Paul Cattani, *Das Tatuiren*, Basel, 1922) and in that way discussed by Cesare Lombroso about the break of the century. Adolf Loos' views on tattooing were probably influenced by Lombroso (below, n. 67) and have deformed much subsequent discussion of the subject. At any rate, a new approach to the subject of body-marking is still to come.

On the archaic, even archetypical nature of the platted screen, see vol I, pp. 27 ff, 213 ff, in which the nature of the *Urtuch* is described, while the *Heerd* is given a special section in vol II, pp. 335 ff. Semper, *Die Vier Elemente der Baukunst, ein Beitrag zur Vergleichenden Baukunde*, Braunschweig 1851, pp. 55 ff.

55. First formulated as a 'type' in the letter to Charlotte von Stein (from Naples and Rome, June 1787) and discussed at length with Schiller in Jena in 1794; Goethe, *Werke*, vol XIX, pp. 84, 752 ff. It was to become an obsessional idea: 'Ich verfiel längst auf jenen einfachen Urtypus ... das ist mein Gott, das ist der Gott den wir alle ewig suchen ...' Goethe, reported by Friederich von Müller on 7th May 1830 in *Werke*, XXIII, p. 692.

56. H. Quitzsch: *Die Ästhetischen Anschauungen Gottfried Sempers*, Berlin, 1962, pp. 65 ff.

57. Textiles, pp. 468; Ceramics, pp. 198; Carpentry pp. 134; Masonry pp. 124; Metals pp. 106.

58. e.g. Carl Schnaase: *Geschichte der Bildenden Künste*, Düsseldorf, 1843, vol I, p. 16 ff. '... Die Härte des Zweckes zerstört die Schönheit ...' or C. F. von Rumohr, op. cit., vol I, pp. 49, 90 ff.

59. See, for instance, R. Munro: *Paleolithic Man*, Edinburgh, 1912, pp. 203 ff, cf. A. Leroi-Gourhan, op. cit., pp. 28 ff.

60. E. Cartailhac and E. Breuil: *La Caverne d'Altamira à Santillane, près de Santander (Espagne)*, Monaco, 1906.

61. A. Riegl, *Stilfragen*, Berlin, 1893, pp. 17 ff. His insistence on the priority of representational art over ornament, and in particular of carving over any form of weaving or platting, ibid, pp. 26 ff.

62. Lionello Venturi: *Storia della Critica d'Arte*, Turin, 1964, p. 231: 'E anche se ripugnante, una tale concezione materialistica dell'arte ha pure avuto il suo compito: quello di richiamare l'attenzione dello storico sulla realizzazione dello spirito nella materia, sul modo con cui la materia è stata sensibilizzata dall'arte.'

63. They are perhaps formulated more explicitly in their primitive form: see G. Semper: *Über die Formelle Gesetzmässigkeit des Schneckes und dessen Bedeutung als Kunstsymbol*, Zürich, 1856 (*Akademische Vorträge I*), especially pp. 17 ff.

64. Riegl found it difficult to explain why the first artists did not model plants which are still, and therefore easier to observe, in preference to animals, pp. 51 ff.

65. Through the review *Pan*, and his books: *Makartbouquet und Blumenstrauss*, Munich 1894 and *Palastfenster und Flügeltür*, Berlin, 1899, and his patronage as director of the Hamburg Kunsthalle. C. Gurlitt: *Die Deutsche Kunst seit 1800*, Berlin, 1924, pp. 464 ff also N. Pevsner: *Pioneers of Modern Design*, Harmondsworth, 1960, pp. 33, 108.

66. In October 1907. See P. Bruckmann, 'Die Gründung des Deutschen Werkbundes 6.10.1907', in *Form X*, 1932, reprinted in *Die Form, Stimme des Deutschen Werkbundes, 1925–1934*, pp. 82 ff.

67. Adolf Loos, *Ornament und Verbrechen*, 1908, reprinted in *Trotzdem*, Innsbruck, 1931, pp. 79 ff.

68. Georg Simmel: *Soziologie, Untersuchungen über die Formen der Vergesellschaftung*, Leipzig, 1908 (revised 1922), p. 280 (in *Exkurs über den Schmuck*). 'Stil ist immer ein Allgemeines, das die Inhalte des persönlichen Lebens und Schaffens in eine mit vielen geteilte und für viele zugängliche Form bringt. An dem eigentlichen Kunstwerk interessiert uns ein Stil um so weniger, je grösser die personale Einzigkeit und das subjektive Leben ist, das sich in ihm ausdrückt; denn mit diesem appelliert es auch den Persönlichkeitspunkt im Beschauer, er ist sozusagen mit dem Kunstwerk auf der Welt allein. Für alles dagegen, was wir Kunstgewerbe nennen was sich wegen seines Gebrauchszweckes an eine Vielheit von Menschen wendet, fordern wir eine generellere, typische Gestaltung ... die seine Einordnung in die Lebenssysteme sehr vieler Einzelner ermöglicht. Es ist der allergrösste Irrtum zu meinen, dass der Schmuck ein individuelles Kunstwerk sein müsse, da er doch immer ein Individuum schmücken solle. Ganz im Gegenteil: weil er dem Individuum dienen soll, darf er nicht selbst individuellen Wesens sein, so wenig wie das Möbel, auf dem wir sitzen, oder das Essgerät, mit dem wir hantieren individuelle Kunstwerke sein dürfen ... [Das] Kunstwerk [kann] überhaupt nicht in ein anderes Leben einbezogen [werden, da es] eine selbstgenügsame Welt ist ... Dieses Auflösen der individuellen Zuspitzung, diese Verallgemeinerung, jenseits des persönlichen Einzigseins ... das ist das Wesen der Stylisierung.'

The translation is that in *The Sociology of Georg Simmel* (ed. Kurt H. Wolff), New York, 1964, pp. 342 ff.

69. On this incident, see Julius Posener: *Anfänge des Funktionalismus*, Frankfurt a/M, 1964, pp. 199 ff.

70. E. Viollet-le-Duc, *Dictionnaire Raisonné de l'Architecture Française*, Paris, 1867, s.v. Style.

71. See, R. Redgrave: *Manual of Design*, 1875, pp. 15 ff.

72. See Gene Weltfish: *The Origins of Art*, Indianapolis, 1953, pp. 25 ff.

73. Semper, *Der Stil*, vol I, pp. 8 ff. On the American translation of Semper, see N. Pevsner: *Some Architectural Writers of the Nineteenth Century*, Oxford, 1972, p. 252, n. 3. I owe the suggestion of the origin of the term, and perhaps in some part also the concept of curtain-wall in Semper's thinking, to Mrs Rosemary Bletter.

74. See Meyer Shapiro, 'Style: Form and Content', in *Aesthetics Today*, ed. by Morris Philipson, Cleveland and New York, 1961, pp. 110 ff.

75. d'Arcy Wentworth Thompson: *On Growth and Form*, Cambridge, 1959, pp. 1034 ff.

76. Morphology has become a technical term for certain linguistic procedures. But the comparative linguistics of Semper's contemporaries have had a very considerable revival. See in this connection, Roger Langham Brown: *Wilhelm von Humboldt's Conception of Linguistic Relativity*, The Hague/Paris, 1967.

Acknowledgements

Thanks go to the following individuals and institutions for making material available for publication: Accademia Patavina de Scienze, Lettere ed Arti, Padua 118; Anderson 81; Archives de l'Art Moderne, Brussels 94; Aldo Ballo 20–21 bottom; Bibliothèque Nationale de Paris 61–63; British Museum, London 38–39; René Burri Zürich 11 top; Cairo Museum 28 top left; Richard Cheatle 79; Curzon Museum of Archaeology 24 bottom left; Giancarlo de Carlo 20–21 top; Design Council, London 15, 26 bottom; French Government Tourist Office 108–109; Ezio Godoli 68 right; Michael Graves 78 centre; Eileen Gray 50, 53 top, 54–57; Allan A. Hedges Pty. Ltd. 11 bottom; John Hejduk 78 bottom; Hans Hollein 101; Charles Jencks 14 right; Leon Krier 78 top; Sam Lambert 104 bottom; Mrs Lawrence K. Marshall 102–103; Panstwowe Muzeum Archeologiczne 112; George Pohl 99; John Read 14 left; Aldo Rossi 75; Frank Russell 110; Joseph Rykwert 13, 19 bottom, 36, 37, 40, 42, 43, 80, 114–115, 120; Tate Gallery 100; Venturi and Rauch 98.

Other illustrations were taken from the following sources: Bengt Ackerblom *Standing and Sitting Posture with special reference to the construction of chairs* Stockholm 1948; *L'Architecture au XXIème Siècle* Paris n.d.; *Architektur von Olbrich* Berlin n.d.; *L'Architettura di Jacopo Barozzi da Vignola* Venice 1748; A.V. Avtishovsky, B.A. Kolchink and M.W. Thompson *Novgorod the Great* London 1967; Jean Badovici and Eileen Gray *E-1027 Maison en Bord de Mer* Paris n.d.; Lindsay Black *The Bora Ground* Sydney 1944; Lindsay Black *Burial Trees* Melbourne 1941; *Casabella 208*; Silvia Danesi and Luciano Patetta *Il Razionalismo e l'Architettura in Italia durante il Facismo* Venice 1976; R. Fréart de Chambray *Parallèle des ordres antiques et modernes* Paris 1651; J.N.L. Durand *Précis des Leçons d'Architecture données à l'école royale polytechnique* Paris 1819; Albrecht Dürer *Vier Bücher von menschlicher Proportion* Nürnberg 1528; A.P. Elkin *The Australian Aborigines How to Understand Them* London 1964; James Ferguson *Rude Stone Monuments* London 1872; D. Fraser *Village Planning in the Primitive World* London and New York n.d.; Sigfried Giedion *Mechanisation Takes Command* New York 1952 (2nd edition); G. Hallstom *Monumental Art in Northern Sweden*; *Jahrbuch des Deutschen Werkbundes* Munich 1915; Andrea di Jorio *La Mimica degli Antichi investigata nel Gestire Napoletano* Naples 1832; Yves Klein *Selected Writings* The Tate Gallery London 1974; Heinrich Kulka *Adolf Loos* Vienna 1931; Le Corbusier *Oeuvre Complète 1910–1929* Zürich 1964; G. Mamlok and S. Sax *Der Sieg* 1932; Piero Manzoni *Paintings, reliefs & objects* The Tate Gallery London 1974; Andrea Memmo *Elementi d'Architettura Lodoliana ossia l'Arte del Fabbricare con Solidità scientifica e con Eleganza non Capricciosa. Libre due.* Rome 1786; James Milne *Excavations at Carnac* Edinburgh 1881; Claude Perrault *Les dix livres d'architecture de Vitruve* Paris 1673; Giovanni Poleni *Memorie Istoriche della Gran Cupola del Tempio Vaticano* Padua 1748; M. Pozzetto *La Fiat-Lignotto*; A. Welby Pugin *The True Principles of Pointed or Christian Architecture* London 1841; Karl Friedrich Schinkel *Sammlung architektonischer Entwürfe* Berlin 1820–40; Gottfried Semper *Der Stil in den technischen und tektonischen Künsten oder Praktische Asthetik. Ein Handbuch für Techniker Künstler und Kunstfreunde von Gottfried Semper* Munich 1863; John Shute *The First and Chief Groundes of Architecture* London 1563; *Le Siège* Paris; Arnolds Spekke *The Ancient Amber Routes and the Geographical Discovery of the Eastern Baltic* Stockholm 1957; Baldwin Spence and F.J. Gillen *The Native Tribes of Central Australia* London 1899; Robert Venturi, Denise Scott Brown and Steven Izenour *Learning from Las Vegas* Cambridge, Mass. 1972; *Werk und Zeit* 1/1978; Hans M. Wingler *The Bauhaus: Weimar, Dessau, Berlin, Chicago* Cambridge, Mass. 1969; H. Zimmern *Indian Art*.

If not credited, illustrations are from the archives of Academy Editions.

Index

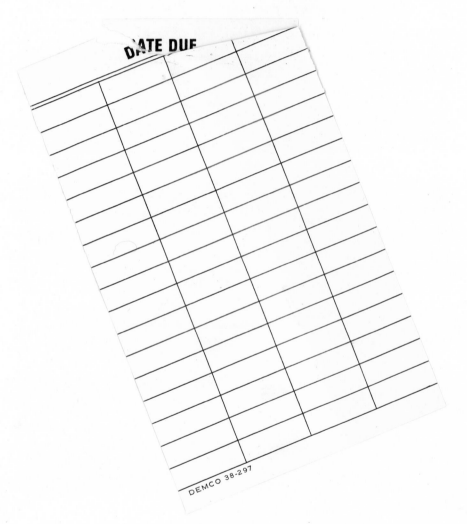

DATE DUE

DEMCO 38-297